CONSOLATION:

IN

DISCOURSES ON SELECT TOPICS, ADDRESSED
TO THE SUFFERING PEOPLE OF GOD.

BY

JAMES W. ALEXANDER, D. D

SIXTH EDITION.

WIPF & STOCK · Eugene, Oregon

Wipf and Stock Publishers
199 W 8th Ave, Suite 3
Eugene, OR 97401

Consolation
Discourses on Select Topics, Addressed to the Suffering People of God
By Alexander, James W.
ISBN 13: 978-1-55635-706-0
ISBN 10: 1-55635-706-0
Publication date 11/8/2007
Previously published by Charles Scribner, 1864

CONTENTS.

	PAGE
PREFACE	7

I.

GOD'S EVERLASTING MERCY A SOURCE OF CONSOLATION   11

II.

THE PROVIDENCE OF GOD A GROUND OF CONSOLATION   35

III.

THE SAME SUBJECT IN ITS APPLICATION TO THE WHOLE PATH OF LIFE   59

IV.

THE OMNIPOTENCE OF GOD A GROUND OF ENLARGED CHRISTIAN EXPECTATION   85

CONTENTS.

PAGE
THE GOODNESS OF GOD A REFUGE IN TIME OF TROUBLE   109

VI.

THE SOUL SUSTAINED BY HOPE RISING TO ASSURANCE . 133

VII.

REST IN GOD 157

VIII.

CHRISTIAN JOY EXPELLING THE DISTRESSES OF THE SOUL 181

IX.

CONSOLATION DERIVED FROM THE USES OF CHASTISEMENT 211

X.

THE HOLY SUBMISSION OF CHRIST'S WILL CONSIDERED AS
A SOURCE OF CONSOLATION 239

XI.

CONSOLATION FROM GOD'S PROMISE NEVER TO FORSAKE 259

XII.

THE BELIEVER SUSTAINED BY THE STRENGTH OF CHRIST 279

CONTENTS.

XIII.

THE COMPASSION OF CHRIST TO THE WEAK, THE SORROWING, AND THE SINFUL 299

XIV.

CONSOLATION UNDER THE JUDGMENTS OF MEN . . 321

XV.

CONSOLATION DERIVED FROM A REVIEW OF CHRISTIAN MARTYRDOM 343

XVI.

THE AGED BELIEVER CONSOLED BY GOD'S PROMISE . 367

XVII.

CONSOLATION IN REGARD TO THE SAINTS DEPARTED . 389

XVIII.

ALL CONSOLATION TRACED UP TO ITS DIVINE SOURCE . 423

PREFACE.

REASONS might be given, if it were seemly and important, why the mind of the writer has been strongly drawn towards this particular subject. It is, however, sufficient to say, that in the course of a ministry which now oversteps the quarter of a century, he has, like his brethren, often felt it to be his obligation and pleasure to attempt the work of comforting sufferers. One of the facilities afforded to the gospel by the press is, that it enables the preacher to extend his voice, according to his measure of ability, beyond the walls of his own church; and it is natural, and will perhaps be thought pardonable, that he should desire this increase of influence and fruitfulness. Of the discourses contained in this volume, some are for substance the same which have been pronounced from the pulpit, and others have been written expressly for publication.

The whole of Divine Truth may, in a certain aspect of it, be regarded as matter of comfort to Christian disciples. Even in a more restricted view, the range of subjects which are consolatory in their nature is very extensive. Only a selection, therefore, of these has been attempted in the present instance, and no expectation must be indulged that the volume now offered will contain either, on one hand, an exhaustive analysis of the Spirit's work as a Comforter, or, on the other, a detail of all the particular circumstances of life in which consolation may be needed.

If any should be surprised at the large amount of doctrinal discussion, he will probably acquiesce in the reasonableness of such a method, on considering that true evangelical comfort is little promoted by mere hortatory address. If the exhortation contains no solid matter of doctrinal truth, it will avail little for the end proposed. We do not reach the case of the disheartened by commanding or imploring him to be of good cheer, but by setting before his mind those great everlasting truths, the acceptation of which lays the basis for joy and peace. Such are the glorious attributes of God, his wonderful providence, his covenant of grace, his magazine of precious promises, and his rewards of heavenly bliss. In discussing the attributes and the providence of God, it is not possible to avoid some truths which are subjects of controversy among Christians; and the writer has not sought to disguise his views on these articles by omission or compromise.

Delightful as is the work of administering the cordials of grace to God's suffering people, it is to be performed with a discerning hand; and he that "speaketh unto men to edification, and exhortation, and comfort," must beware how he cries, Peace, peace, when there is no peace. This may account for the frequency with which consolation is here intermingled with warning and rebuke. If the book should find any favour with persons as yet unrenewed in the spirit of their minds, it will not be the less profitable for these occasional attempts to arouse the benumbed conscience.

But, after all, this is a book for afflicted believers, and to such it is affectionately dedicated. If it shall soothe the ruffled spirit of the careworn disciple, or assuage the grief of the bereaved, or brighten the chamber of illness, or add a drop of balm to the cup of old age, the writer will be more than repaid for the pains which he has bestowed upon it. That this may be the case, and that the humble effort may be owned of God to the refreshment and support of the afflicted, is the prayer with which it is now surrendered to the public.

New-York. Nov. 18 1852.

GOD'S EVERLASTING MERCY A SOURCE OF CONSOLATION.

I.

WHEN, amidst the sorrows of life, we look abroad in quest of consolation, we find none real and permanent till we resort to God himself; and our most complete solace is that which founds itself at once on some divine attribute. Especially is the mercy of God, in its large Old Testament acceptation, a cause of relief and hope in times of distress. Ancient Israel found it so, and hence there is no topic which more frequently awakens the praises of psalmists and prophets. It is fitted, therefore, to lead the way in a volume which seeks to furnish suffering Christians with topics of consolation.

When David had found a place for the ark, the august and fearful emblem and centre of their religion, the people accompanied with "shouting, and with sound of the cornet, and with trumpets, and with cymbals, making a noise with psalteries and harps." Perhaps we have gone too far in hushing all the more festive outbreaks of popular joy. On this great occasion, the royal poet delivered into the hand of the chief musician the lyric effusion since known as the one hundred and fifth psalm; and towards the conclusion of a sublime and glowing ascription we first meet with these words, "O give thanks unto the Lord, for he is good, for his mercy endureth for ever." And among the appointments, we read that Heman, Jeduthun, and their companions were designated to give thanks to the Lord, because his mercy endureth for ever. It seems to have been taken as the established formula of praise, especially within the courts of the Lord. When the ark of Jehovah no longer dwelt within the curtains, and Solomon had builded a house to the Lord, and assembled the people for its dedication, the record is remarkable. "And it came to pass, when the priests were come out of the holy place, as the trumpeters and singers were as one, to make one sound to be heard in praising and thanking the Lord; and when they lifted up their voice with the trumpets, and cymbals, and instruments of music, and praised the Lord, saying, For he is good, for his mercy endureth for ever; that then the house was filled with a cloud, even the house of the Lord, so that the priests could not stand to minister, by reason of the cloud; for the glory of the Lord had filled the house of the Lord."*

Nor was the usage forgotten in later times; for two hundred years after, in the reign of Jehoshaphat, when the eastern nations were threatening to come down like a whirlwind on Judah, and the sovereign had called his subjects to humiliation, and the voice of a prophet had encouraged the host,

* 2 Chron. v. 11–14, vii. 3.

and the Levites had stood up to praise the Lord God of Israel with a loud voice on high, we are particularly informed that when the king had consulted with the people, he appointed singers unto the Lord, that should praise the beauty of holiness, as they went out before the army, and to say, *Praise the Lord: for his mercy endureth for ever.* So likewise, passing over nearly three hundred years after the captivity, when the foundations of the second temple were laid, amidst the commingling shouts and weeping of the multitude, " they set the priests in their apparel with trumpets, and the Levites the sons of Asaph with cymbals, to praise the Lord, after the ordinance of David king of Israel; and they sang together by course, in praising and giving thanks unto the Lord; because he is good, for his mercy endureth for ever towards Israel." (Ezr. 3: 11.) It need not then surprise us, to find this ascription filling an important place in the book of sacred song. In the one hundred and thirty-sixth psalm, it forms the closing part of every verse, and was, doubtless, the chorus which was taken up, with the glorious reverberation of voices and instruments, by the multitude of worshippers. I see no reason why it may not now resound among the heavenly arches; why it may not be rehearsed with new glorious meanings in a future world; as reasonable surely is it to admit it in glowing characters over the arch which conducts us to the New Testament Church: HIS MERCY ENDURETH FOR EVER!

This brief sentence comprises three of the most

sublime of all the ideas of reason, viz., the idea of *God*, the idea of *Goodness*, and the idea of *Eternity*. Let us meditate a little on this wonderful conjunction of luminaries.

I. *The idea of God.*—While in regard to a multitude, God is not in all their thoughts, there are those who feel this divine idea to be the great, absorbing, ever-delightful object of their contemplation. As light irradiates all nature, so the thought of God diffuses gladness over all the moral world. The proposition which, above all others, should fill all intelligent creation with transport, is this, THERE IS A GOD. Conceive of a world without it; conceive of a planet, rolling far away in some dark aphelion, where this prime revelation has never shone, having the light of common day, but no knowledge of God; conceive of the poor, blank, cheerless dwellers on this atheistic orb, and then figure to yourself some beautiful and mighty angel, who has been thousands of years filling his lamp at the central founts of light, dispatched by infinite love, and speeding to carry these tidings to the ignorant planet; who can measure the glory of the advent? It is a change like that when God said to chaos, Let there be light! If in all human knowledge there is a truth which should transport us beyond ourselves, it is, that there is a God. The Lord reigneth, let the earth rejoice! Without it, we are a fatherless brood, and our world an orphan universe. The names of God are names of relation; and among the relations, we have found something more great, more tender, and more lovely, than parent, brother, or husband, when we have found a God. Whether, however, fallen reason would unaided have arrived at the idea of God, is made a question. That the idea, when once revealed, is more than all others consonant to the faculties; that it is more than all others congenial to the soul; that it delightfully enters, pervades, and fills capacities which were otherwise unemployed, must be acknowledged of all. " The invisible things of him, from the creation of the world, are clearly seen, being understood by the things which are made, even his eternal power and Godhead." And the God thus seen is the personal, the paternal God of the Scriptures, and not the blind, ever-changing, ever-developing impersonality of modern philosophy. To rob the universe of such a guardian and indwelling glory, is a capital offence against humanity and nature. Yet false philosophy, and poetry as false, unite to rob us of the blessed solace; and an ignorant, undiscriminating appetite for whatever is new and startling in literature, makes refined cabinets and drawing-room tables admit the blasphemous atheism of Shelley, while they would reject the scurrilous impiety of Paine or Kneeland. The green and gilded snake creeps into the closet and the boudoir, and the modern Eves are tempted to deeper sin against their native persuasions than she of Eden. Almighty God! of thine infinite compassion, preserve our people from the entrance of any speculation which shall involve the denial of Thee!

Atheism deforms all it touches. "It robs the universe," says Hall, "of all finished and consummate excellence even of idea. The admiration of perfect wisdom and goodness, for which we are formed, and which kindles such unspeakable rapture in the soul, finding in the regions of skepticism nothing to which it corresponds, droops and languishes. In a world which presents a fair spectacle of order and beauty; of a vast family, nourished and supported by an almighty Parent; in a world which leads the devout mind, step by step, to the contemplation of the first fair and the first good, the skeptic is encompassed with nothing but obscurity, meanness, and disorder."

The infant embraces the earliest suggestion of a God without repugnance, and without effort. When grown to adult strength, and trained to philosophic inquiry, he still gazes on this as the grand and only satisfying object. It should seem that our capacities crave some glorious consummation of the pyramid of truth, some crowning point, some declaration of the infinite; so that the soul without God is incomplete,—a basin of earth without its ocean.

As knowledge increases, as our capacities grow, there is no more comprehension of this vast idea than there was before: the sun seems no smaller and no less bright as we approach his central residence. Expand the faculty as we may, to the standard of the highest seraph, there is still that in God which shall fill it all. Climb as we may, from Alp to Alp, in our researches, the vaulted heaven of the Divine Idea is still above us.

Human science reaches no point where the divine wisdom has not anticipated its march. There is not a discovery in optics, though the fruit of ages of inquiry, concerning which we do not feel authorized to assert, that the long-latent principle was known before creation, and that God has adapted the lenses of the eye to light, and light to the lenses of the eye. The remark may be generalized in its application to every law of physical and moral nature. So that a knowledge of God would really be the knowledge of all things.

I need not go about to show by argument why the being of God is a cause of rejoicing to the universe. Other things are drops, but this is the fountain. Other things are transient, insulated favours; fragments and atoms of beneficence; single flowers of mercy; single draughts of bliss; single odours, wafted from fields of fragrance: but God (let me speak reverently) is the very atmosphere, all-comprehending and all-pervading, in which we live, and move, and have our being. Therefore, he that glorieth, let him glory in the Lord! He that would be joyful, let him be joyful in the Lord! The book of Psalms is a chamber of holy voices, echo answering echo, deep calling unto deep, with the enthusiasm and rapture of adoring ecstasy and fearful love. We do but rehearse here what we shall utter above, when we call upon all things, silent or vocal, to praise the name of the Lord. "My meditation of him shall be sweet. I will be glad in the Lord. Sing unto him; sing psalms unto him: talk ye of all his wondrous works. Praise ye the Lord from the heavens; praise him in the heights. Praise ye him, all his angels; praise ye him, all his hosts. Praise God in his sanctuary; praise him in the firmament of his power. Praise the Lord, O Jerusalem! Praise thy God, O Zion!

These are happy exercises, and he has never begun the course of true felicity, who is still a stranger to God. These afford the ultimate basis of all consolation.

II. *The idea of goodness*, in that particular mode of it which is entitled *mercy*. In Scripture usage, the term is not always employed with the nice discrimination of the schools, but is applied to all the modifications of divine favour to creatures. Yet the word undoubtedly carries with it some tinge of compassion; it speaks of pity; it points to tears which tremble in the eye of infinite love; it is God looking upon meanness, and wretchedness, and sin. It is a great idea, and fit to be coupled with divinity. Heathen mythology did not contain it. The Scriptures are full of it, and we see the temple praises were full of it. It is the essential property of God, whereby he regards the miserable. It is more specially the same perfection, viewed as flowing through its sole channel in the Mediator. The fall, which rendered mediation necessary, rendered Jesus Christ the sole depositary of infinite mercy. Not more truly is the sun the organ and centre of all the light of the universe, than Jesus Christ is the organ and centre of all mercy for men. He is the Saviour of all men, especially of them that believe. A merciful God is moreover their God in Jesus Christ. A world of sinners can look in only one direction to see God, to wit, in the direction of the ark and mercy-seat, which gives a propriety to the repeated use of this ascription in such temple-services as are connected with the ark of the covenant. God dwelt there, between the cherubim, that is, over the propitiatory. Hence the cry, O thou that dwellest between the cherubim! It was an inhabitation of mercy. There he received incense; there he presided over the sprinkling of blood; there he shone forth in a glory which any where else would have been consuming. The other instances of mercy contained in this psalm are favours and deliverances towards a sinful but accepted people, which are all founded on the covenant of which this ark was the symbol. It is part of his royal name and title, the Lord God, merciful and gracious—keeping mercy for thousands; long-suffering and of great mercy; he delighteth in mercy. Such are some of the phrases of the Old Testament, while in the New, this is the great topic, and every page seems to exhale the fragrance of the benediction, Grace, Mercy, and Peace.

The Goodness, the Love, the Grace, and the Mercy of God, are only so many phases of the same orb; all the outshining of one and the same benignant Jehovah; and all entitled to our praise.

The goodness of God is his infinite disposition to do good to the creature. The love of God is the same goodness in its more distinct propension toward the person of the creature, whereby God tends to bless the creature, by the communication of himself, and this in various degrees—the love of the *creature*, the love of *man*, and the love of his *people*. The GRACE of God is his infinite disposition to communicate himself to the creature, in divine gratuity, irrespective of all merit in the object. And the Mercy of God, regarding man as fallen and sinful, is God's disposition to pardon sin and succour misery. It stands related to goodness, as kindness to pity, in the human soul; it flows from the spring-head of mere goodness; it contemplates misery, and misery which might be left unrelieved, as being justly inflicted. It is, therefore, pre-eminently a *sovereign* perfection. This mercy of God may be received as *general* and *special*. God's general mercy flies to the succour of mankind in general, in their various deserved troubles; his special mercy contemplates them as united in covenant to the Lord Jesus Christ. To have any proper view of the divine mercy, we should consider who and what HE is, of whom it is predicated; how high, how great, how all-sufficient, how independent and infinite in perpetual bliss. We should consider who and what its objects are; men, fallen men, undeserving, condemned enemies of God. The whole dealing of God with men, as revealed in the Scriptures, proceeds on this basis. We mistake fatally, if we assume any other. Thus viewed, the mercy of God is amazing, in its mode of action, its means and instruments, its sublime and tender events, its stupendous sacrifices, its elaborate, complicated, yet simple arrangements, and its extraordinary and immeasurable results. There was a dawn of this benignity in the Old Testament; but it is a clear shining under the New. Its very nature is embodied in the name of Jesus. When, after long journeyings through a land of wilderness, abounding in convictions, fears, legal restraints, and unavailing endeavours, the weary pilgrim-soul first obtains a glimpse of this attribute, thus revealed, it is as when the remnant of the ten thousand Greeks, under Xenophon, after long battling and travel, caught a sight of the Euxine, and cried in a shout of rapture, *the sea! the sea!* Old Testament saints had glimpses, as when one sees the ocean from a favoured hill-top, in a distant view; New Testament believers are allowed to come and stand by the side of the mighty, interminable main.

It is our unspeakable privilege, brethren, to live under this dispensation of divine mercy. And we can rehearse displays of it far more wonderful than those which are recounted in any psalm. When we praise "him who alone doeth great wonders," we can include the wonders of redemption. When we ascribe glory "to him that made great lights," we can rejoice in that true Light which now shineth. He that "smote Egypt in their first-born" is indeed the God of mercy; but still more, he who delivered for us his only-begotten Son, " for it pleased the Lord to bruise him." The overthrow of Pharaoh, of Sihon, and of Og, was but a type of our deliverance. So that we can exclaim with even higher transport than the Hebrew, " who remembered us in our low estate; for his mercy endureth for ever; and hath redeemed us from our enemies; for his mercy endureth for ever."

If it was right for Israel to recount the memory of these national advantages, it is doubly incumbent on Christians to speak to the praise and the glory of that grace wherein we are accepted in the Beloved. Especially should we record the great transaction, the chosen display of divine goodness to mankind, in the election of Messiah—his taking human flesh—his companying with rejecting men, in circumstances of lowliness, and shame, and pain— his conflict with the hour of darkness—his bloody, mysterious death, and his godlike resurrection. Herein is love, not that we loved God, but that he loved us, and sent his Son to be the propitiation for our sins.

The main channel and torrent of mercy flows in a majestic stream in the redemption of the soul; but its flood receives and embosoms ten thousand lesser currents of temporal bounty. Divine mercy does not neglect the less while she accomplishes the greater. As she marches heavenward, with eyes fixed upon the crown and kingdom, she scatters largesses at every step. All our blessings flow from this same open hand, and are, therefore, properly denominated *mercies*. The covenant includes these, and the believer hopes for them, on the principle, that all is his. Each returning season exposes to view some new aspect of divine benignity. *Thou crownest the year with thy goodness.* Our persons, our landscapes, our neighbourhoods, our city, our state, our nation, our race, are recipients every moment of this boundless favour; magnified inconceivably when we consider that it descends upon the unworthy, and made most tender and impressive, when we consider that it descends upon us. And there is no view of the divine glory which so exalts him, as when he is beheld as the source of incessant and innumerable and immeasurable rivers of good; himself the Great Parent, on whom all the ranks of creatures hang and are nourished. It is the theme of celestial worlds:

> "And where the river of bliss through midst of heaven
> Rolls o'er Elysian flowers her amber stream;
> With these that never fade the spirits elect
> Bind their resplendent looks inwreathed with beams:
> Now in loose garlands thick thrown off; the bright
> Pavement that like a sea of jasper shone,
> Impurpled with celestial roses smiled.
> Then crowned again their golden harps they took,
> Harps ever tuned, that glittering by their side
> Like quivers hung, and with preamble sweet,
> Of charming symphony they introduce
> Their sacred song, and waken raptures high;
> No voice exempt, no voice but well could join
> Melodious part, such concord is in heaven."

III. *The Idea of Eternity.*—The strict translation of the text is, "Thy mercy ... to eternity!"

In its fulness of significancy, it is predicable of God alone, "who only hath immortality." At the grove of Beersheba (Gen. xxi. 33), Abraham invoked Jehovah under the name of THE ETERNAL GOD. "He *inhabiteth* eternity,"—a sublime phrase, teaching us, that as time and space are the limits of all things finite, so God overleaps both by his immensity; the one—space—by his omnipotence, the other—time—by his eternity. The tracts of space are vast, and confounding to our imagination. Our own day has witnessed the first exact measurement of the distance of the nearest fixed star, which is twenty-one millions of millions of miles. A learned calculator has shown, that "in the space around our solar system devoid of stars, there is room in one dimension, or one straight line, for twelve thousand solar systems; in two dimensions, or in one plane, there is room for one hundred and thirty millions of solar systems; and in actual sidereal space of three dimensions, there is room for one and a half million millions of solar systems the size of our own." Such are the *blanks* in the scheme; how fearful the thought of such physical immensity! I call your mind to it, to say that God is there—*in* all conceivable space, and *beyond* all. So in regard to time; God is from everlasting to everlasting. He is without beginning and without ending. Incomprehensible as this is, the reverse is inconceivable. Something must be without beginning: else nothing could ever have been. And what can be so reasonably assumed to be without beginning, as the infinite First Cause? There is something about the idea of eternity which oppresses the soul. Yet from under this incubus we cannot escape. There is something mysterious in the way whereby we arrive at the idea of eternity. I cannot think it is by enumeration—by adding unit to unit—even though the process were continued for a lifetime, or a lifetime of the world; for at the last of this process we should still be as far from eternity as when we began. No such summation of a series can, as I suppose, generate the conception. I rather conceive it, though not an innate, an uncompounded idea of the infinite. New and startling as the suggestion may be to some, eternity has no parts. It therefore has no succession. The Eternal One is ever the same. To his mind all the past, the present, and the future, are present at once. The life of God is enjoyed, not by a passage from the past into the present, and the present into the future, but is possessed perfectly, wholly, and interminably, all at once. No years, no centuries, no sidereal cycles, measure Him whose name is, I AM THAT I AM. Of our lives, a portion vanishes every moment; but it is not so with God. And that which most interests us now, is that his *mercy* is everlasting—his mercy endureth for ever. Wherever and whenever God is, he is in the plenitude of mercy. Divine benignity spreads those ample wings more widely than the universe itself. There are regions beyond the most distant nebulous outskirts of matter; but no regions beyond the divine goodness. We may conceive of tracts where there are no worlds, but not of any where there is no God of mercy.

Let me particularize one or two meanings of the declaration.

1. God's mercy endureth for ever, in the sense that he will never cease to be merciful. He must at the same time cease to be God. The burdened soul turns with expectation to an unchangeable Being. As this is one of the sublimest, so it is also one of the most consolatory truths. Every thing around us and within us is suffering mutation; but the changeful stream of creatures and events, flowing in perpetual broken waves, washes the base of that awful pyramid of being, whose summit is lost in the unapproachable clouds of divinity. Under the discouragements of our frailty and nothingness, we look away, almost by an instinct of our nature, to discover something solid and permanent. This we can find nowhere short of the Great Supreme; and when we have reached this centre, we repose with a serene complacency of spirit. Thus the prophetic bard sings, " Return unto thy rest, O my soul, for the Lord hath dealt bountifully with thee."

Let the troubled soul consider, that in all the diffusion of his omnipresence, God is everywhere merciful. As he hath been, so he will be. His benignity is subject to no fitful waning or caprice. The day can never come when he shall be less merciful than at this instant. This mercy has no bounds, in regard to those creatures who are its proper objects. "A God all mercy were a God unjust:" this cannot be denied or forgotten; and there are those who, rejecting the mercy of God against themselves, fall upon the sword of his eternal justice. Yet within the circle of his gracious plan, and where he has undertaken to save, we may believe, that taking a large and comprehensive view, God's communication of benefit is limited only by the capacity of the creature; and that this capacity will be continually increasing, in accordance with a love which endureth for ever. We look forward, therefore, to a display of this attribute, which shall never cease, but have new developments to all eternity! For the Most High will act as God; that is, with an infinitude of glory in all his merciful acts; and the radiance of his benevolence in this world is only the preparatory twinkle of a day without cloud or sunset. If we may so express it, Jehovah takes a holy complacency and satisfaction in acting forth his divine attributes, in creating fit objects, in moulding them for this purpose, in widening their susceptibilities, and magnifying their joys. In this is displayed the glory of his nature, in the view of all holy and intelligent worlds; and thus will it be, increasingly, for ever: so that thousands of ages hence, the adorable Lord, whom we now justly regard as infinitely merciful, will not only show himself clearly such towards a greater number of creatures, but will in each of these shine resplendent with a lustre becoming perpetually more bright. The contemplation of this will form in a high degree the bliss of heaven; and the beatific vision will include a view of the divine mercy as enduring for ever.

This aspect of the divine perfection is therefore a never-failing source of comfort to a soul disturbed by sin and sorrow. Whatever may be the cause of disquietude, immediate peace is found, when the soul reposes itself on God. It has then gravitated to its true centre. It has no longer any thing to seek. Our attempts at consolation often fail, because we stop short of this ultimate idea. Even when meditating religiously, we are apt to rest in the creature, as in some of God's gifts, instead of plunging at once, without reserve, into the boundless ocean of that divine mercy which can never suffer loss or termination.

2. God's mercy endureth for ever, in the sense that he will never cease to be merciful to his church. This is consolation indeed to those who belong to this favoured community. From the beginning to the end, as long as there shall be a church, God will be its covenant and merciful Father, through Christ Jesus. For the church may be regarded as a special organ for the exercise, transmission and display of this very benevolence. After the introduction of sin, God has no channel so remarkable for the flow of his mercy as the church of Christ. It was for the manifestation of his glorious attributes, that he chose it in Christ Jesus, before the world began; and among these attributes, for manifesting those of Goodness, Grace, and Mercy. For this purpose, the calling and gathering of individuals have been conducted through different dispensations. The mercy of the Lord is perpetually and gloriously displaying itself by means of the redeemed; and it is God's

unchangeable purpose to bring this whole plan to a consummation, when the number of the elect shall be made up, and the Bride, the Lamb's wife, shall be shown to the universe in the last days. Now as these are God's purposes towards his church, and as his mercy in regard to it is everlasting, every member of this spiritual body has a source of consolation, altogether withheld from the world without. It is not a small thing to belong to that community for which Christ died, for which he prays, and unto which he purposes to give dominion. Temporary afflictions may break over the heads of Christ's people, but the nature of the covenant is such that they cannot be unsafe. The very hairs of their heads are all numbered. To destroy them, would be to frustrate the divine plan. They are the objects of an everlasting love. This comfort, therefore, may be taken by the humblest believer, from his connection with a covenant which is well ordered in all things and sure.

When days are dark, let the soul turn itself to him who dwelleth in Zion, and who can never forget her. Christian supports are the more sure and abiding when they are taken in common with all the chosen seed, and on the grounds of covenant faithfulness. When we can place ourselves in such a position that the promises of God towards his church become promises to us individually, we are drinking waters which flow out of the sanctuary itself.

3. God's mercy endureth for ever, in the sense

that in future eternity, otherwise called *the world to come*, there will be glorious developments of this very attribute, as known to us. In that coming age, that expanse of blissful knowledge and possession, which we hope and pray for, and to which every returning day brings us so much nearer—what is it, think you, that shall make our heaven? An everlasting drowsiness and dream of listless inaction? mountains of odours, fragrant meads, crystal rivers, Elysian fruits, melody and harmony?—simple rest? simple exemption from pain? simple lamblike innocence? Is this heaven?—learning nothing, doing nothing? This is *not* heaven. I will tell you what it is: it is seeing God—it is seeing him more and more—it is going from star to star, and from system to system, in this voyage of divine discovery. There is enough in God for all eternity; for all that there is in creatures, is in him by way of eminence. There are attributes of God, we may reasonably suppose, of which we have not even a conception, and in relation to which we are now in the condition of a man born blind, in relation to colours, or a man born deaf in relation to sounds. An animal with one sense (there are such) can know but little of nature; less, far less, in comparison, do we know of God. I suppose there are faculties absolutely latent in the human mind which are to reveal themselves in that new state, in the presence of objects now beyond their reach. It will not be a lesson of a day to expatiate on the divine nature. Duration must expand. Astronomy has revealed certain binary stars, as 66 *Ceti*, one of which revolves around the other in a period of several thousands of years. Conceive the uniting line, the radius of these two suns, as the hand that moves upon the celestial dial-plate. It has proceeded a revolution. Worlds may have perished during this hour of heaven; but the soul is still learning to know more of that infinite benignity which shines in the face of Jesus Christ. Some have rendered the text, " His mercy is for the coming age :" it is true. Then shall we see face to face, and know, even as also we are known ; and this in regard to the mercy which has ransomed man. We shall better comprehend all the transaction of Gethsemane and Golgotha, and look more nearly into the heart of God, when the Man Christ Jesus, bone of our bone, and flesh of our flesh, shall be the daysman and the interpreter. Then shall we know the privilege conferred on us, in that we are made immortal beings. Then shall we discover that this world has revealed but the beginning of his kindnesses unto mankind. Then shall the overflowing goodness of the Divinity display the true bliss of Him whose power is exerted in every direction to make his people happy. With no stinted hand will he cast abroad the greatness of his benign endowments on the family of redeemed ones, while each one of the palm-bearing multitude, pointing out to its sister spirit the now exalted cause of all this favour, shall cry, " This is my Beloved, and this is my Friend."

THE PROVIDENCE OF GOD A GROUND OF CONSOLATION

II.

MEN are prone to think of God, says the excellent Melancthon, as of a shipbuilder, who, when he has completed his vessel, launches and leaves it. In opposition to this error of the Epicureans and Stoics, we are to be reminded that God never abandons his work, but is as much with it the last day as the first. This governing presence of God with all his creatures and all their actions, is called *Providence,* from a Latin word which means to see beforehand. If we look on creation as God's first revelation of himself, we may look on Providence as the continuance of that revelation. It is that general agency of God, whereby he abides with the creature, upholding and directing it for all the ends for which it was made. Hence the twofold topic of PRESERVATION and GOVERNMENT. If a volition of the Almighty was necessary to bring creatures into being, a continued volition is necessary to keep them in being. The mere will of God was creative; it brought creation out of nothing: the like will continued is the divine Providence. No more can beings continue to exist without God, than they could have begun to exist without him. This has not been sufficiently considered. The infinite and eternal God is the basis of all being. In him we live, and move, and have our being. If that incomprehensible influence, whereby each thing *is*, and is *what it is*, should be withdrawn for an instant, all things would lose their existence, and would go back into annihilation. No positive act of God would be necessary to reduce the universe to nothing. This perpetual and indispensable sustentation of all things is part of Divine Providence. Hence, the old divines were accustomed to speak of Providence as a *continued creation*. As creation is the will of God that things should exist and begin to be, so Providence is the will of God that things should continue to be. The created world continues by the very same power which caused it to begin. This preservation of all things is the first act of Providence, and that without which other acts would have been impossible. None but God, the infinite One, can be conceived of as competent to so great a work. It demands for its execution *omniscience*, to know the universe which is to be preserved, and to know how to preserve it; *omnipresence*, to apply this divine knowledge in every place; and *omnipotence*, to carry out the amazing work on the immensity of things. This preserving power extends to the twofold universe of matter and of spirit. (1.) To *the world of matter*. It is kept what it is by this never-ceasing influence. The properties of matter are maintained such, by an abiding will of God. We may talk of gravity, of motion, and of divisibility; these are only modes of existence which have no substantiality in themselves, but are kept such by God. We may talk of the laws of matter, and sometimes may ignorantly think of them as principles or powers existing in matter, even independently of the Creator, but these laws are only God's methods of producing effects by material means. Every existence, and every property and quality and act of each, is maintained simply by the everlasting power of God. Were this power to be withheld, they would not only cease to have such qualities, but would cease to be.

The dream of atheism is, that the laws of nature constitute all the power there is; and that these laws are only a tendency of material things, rendering unnecessary the supposition of a first cause distinct from matter. The equally absurd dream of PANTHEISM is, that every thing is God (hence the name), and that all the revolutions of the great mass are stages in the development and growth of divinity; for Pantheism believes that God may develop, and change, and grow. But reason suggests and revelation declares that the material world is upheld by a most powerful, wise, holy, and infinite Being, separate from itself. (2.) Again, this preserving power extends to *the world of spirit.* God, who inspired the soul of man, and created all embodied spirits, continues their being by his perpetual sustentation. Not as the Pantheists imagine, that all spirits are parts or modifications of God, but that God, while eternally distinct from all spirits, is intimately present with all, sustaining them in all their properties and acts. In this important sense, God is not far from every one of us. Surrounded and contained by him, and upheld in all the more glorious attributes of manhood by his power, we may in truth be said to be nearer to God than our bodies are to our souls. "Whither shall I go from thy Spirit, and whither shall I flee from thy presence? If I ascend up into heaven, thou art there; if I make my bed in hell, behold thou art there; if I take the wings of the morning, and dwell in the uttermost parts of the sea; even there shall thy hand lead me, and thy right hand shall hold me." Ps. 139. This upholding power is properly due to none but God; and hence we derive an irresistible argument for the divinity of our Lord Jesus; since he who thus upholds must be omniscient, omnipotent, and omnipresent, that is, must be God; and since this preservation is ascribed to Christ, Heb. 1 v 3: "Who being the brightness of his glory, and the express image of his person, and upholding all things by the word of his power;" and Col. 1:17, "All things were created by him and for him; and he is before all things, and by him all things consist."

The view which we here take of Providence, regards the universe of mind and matter, not as a machine, wound up and left to run its career of centuries, without the Maker's care, but as requiring and receiving at every moment his mighty influence, a stream of power perpetually proceeding from the Godhead. The very essence of God is, therefore, everlastingly present with every atom and every spirit. This is exactly accordant to those places in Scripture where God is spoken of as the universal cause, and is said to do those things which are done, secondarily, by creatures. Ps. 104: 8, 30. And to this is referred the supporting of life in the most insignificant birds. Matt. 10: 29. Enough has been said in regard to this primary acting of divine Providence, in preserving all things. How God does this it would be madness for us to inquire. The simplicity of the divine acts causes them to elude our faculties. He wills it, and that is enough; just as at the beginning he willed creation. What we chiefly need is to bear this in mind, with daily faith, awe, and thankfulness. Such is God's preserving of the creature, as a part of Providence.

II. But there is another equally important agency, put forth by the infinite Creator; it is the *direction of all things.* God not only PRESERVES but GOVERNS the universe of matter and spirit. He continues to " direct, dispose, and govern all creatures, actions, and things, from the greatest even to the least, by his most wise and holy providence, according to his infallible foreknowledge, and the free and immutable counsel of his own will, to the praise of the glory of his wisdom, power, justice, goodness, and mercy." C. F. c. v. 1.

What is to be proposed will have regard to a twofold objection; against God's providence concerning *trifles*, and his providence concerning *sins*.

And here, let me acknowledge, I have often wondered at the distinctions taken by some men who would hold rank as philosophers, but who nevertheless, affirm a general while they deny a particular providence, as if the general were not made up of the particulars, or as if God could attend to the whole without attending to the parts. This error is perhaps increased by our forms of expression, allowable in themselves, when, for example, we say of this or of that event, that "it is providential," when in very deed all are providential, as all are ordered from the greatest to the least. Under pretext of exalting God, and raising him above the care and trouble of earthly things, we betray really low notions of his divinity. We judge of him as of ourselves, and of God as if he were man; our language implies that what is burdensome and annoying to us must be so to him. We allow him to direct suns and stars and comets, and things in heaven, but the sparrow and the hairs of the head we deem too small for him. Yet, you remember, these are the very instances which he has chosen. That which was fit to be created, is fit to be preserved, though it be the infinitesimal muscle or nerve in the microscopic animalcule or *infusoria*. We make too much of our distinctions of greater and smaller, when we carry them into eternity: such quantities reach not Jehovah. It costs him no more thought, no more labour, no more exertion, to maintain an atom in its sunbeam, than to whirl systems of suns and planets and satellites along the shining galaxy. In this sense, we may accept as true the celebrated words of the poet, though false in another—

> "Who sees with equal eye, as God of all,
> A hero perish, or a sparrow fall,
> Atoms or systems into ruin hurled,
> And now a bubble burst, and now a world."
> *Essay on Man*, l. 88.

When God beholds his eternal plan spread out in the infinite idea of his own wisdom, his perfect knowledge reaches not only to the grand portions, but to every ramification and filament; and with perfect ease plans and directs for the insect of an hour, as for the triumph of an emperor. We, therefore, attribute to the care and guidance of God "all things without exception, whether celestial or sublunary, small or great, good or evil, necessary or free, so that there is nothing in nature which can exist or occur, without his distinct permission." If it were glorious to create, why not to govern? God is nowhere greater than in the smallest things—the plumage of the insect, and the circulation of a system, the very existence of which is revealed to us by the solar microscope. God is in such wise great in great things, that he is no less great in the very least. This ought to answer the objection drawn from the littleness of the affairs which a particular providence would refer to God.

But there is another objection to our doctrine of God's government of all things, which has still more strongly operated to make some banish the Creator from his moral universe; it is that God's providence cannot have any thing to do with sinful acts; and that to say that it has, were to destroy all freedom of the creature, and all accountability for crime. It may be well to say at once; that if we assert that evil acts may not be foreseen and provided for, we may as well deny the Bible at once. There never was a more evil act than the death of Christ; yet it was provided for, and (not only so) was indispensably necessary to the salvation of men. It was provided for during ages preceding; and Peter says of it very distinctly (Acts 2: 23): "*Him*, being delivered by the determinate counsel and foreknowledge of God, ye have taken, and with wicked hands have crucified and slain." The act is declared to be *wicked*, yet it is equally declared to be by the "determinate counsel and foreknowledge of God;" therefore, acts which are evil may be included in the plan of Providence. A lesser, but equally demonstrative case, is that of Joseph. The act of his brethren, in selling him into Egypt, was an evil act, yet it was governed by Providence. It was all arranged and foreseen. It formed a part of God's plan. It was intended to produce the most beneficial results. What says Joseph? (Gen. 45: 7, 8.) "God sent me before you. It was not you that sent me hither, but God." And again (50: 20): "As for you, ye thought evil against me, but God meant it unto good, to bring to pass, as it is this day, to save much people alive." Now, here I would ask of every objector two questions: 1. Was the sending of Joseph to Egypt providential or not? To this there can be but one answer: Scripture gives answer in God's name: "God sent me before you." 2. Was the act of selling Joseph sinful? There is no answer, but one, in the words of Joseph; "Ye thought evil, but God meant it for good." *Ye thought evil;* here is sin: *God meant it unto good;* here is providence. So likewise in the case of the Assyrian invading and punishing the Hebrews (Isa. 10: 6, 7): "I will send him against a hypocritical nation, and against the people of my wrath will I give him a charge, to take the spoil and to take the prey, and to tread them down like the mire of the streets. Howbeit he meaneth not so, neither doth his heart think so; but it is in his heart to destroy and cut off nations not a few." The Assyrian committed crime in his invasion; yet he thereby worked out the results which God intended. In the commission of his crime, he was perfectly free, and perfectly accountable; yet this crime was not only foreseen, but, as we observe, *predicted* by the Almighty. God was not the author of the sin, though the sin occurred providentially; and, foreseeing this, God recognizes his accountability, and denounces punishment (v. 12): "Wherefore it shall come to pass, that when the Lord hath performed his whole work upon Mount Zion, and on Jerusalem, I will punish the fruit of the stout heart of the king of Assyria, and the glory of his high looks." If we do not recognize this intervention of Providence in regard to the free acts of creatures, we can never interpret those judgments of God which are wrought by wicked men. "Saul took a sword, and fell upon it." (1 Chr. 10: 4.) It was his own act—his wicked act; yet what saith the Scriptures? (v. 13): "So Saul died, for his transgression which he committed against the Lord. And he inquired not of the Lord; therefore He slew him, and returned the kingdom unto David, the son of Jesse." This may serve to show how grave an error is committed by many persons in certain expressions of theirs. We hear them say, for example, "I could bear this trial better if there were any thing PROVIDENTIAL in it—if it proceeded from any direction of God; but, on the contrary, it proceeds from wicked men." Very well; so it may, and yet be providential. "The wicked," says David, are "thy sword." God can make the wicked acts of men a sword to punish others, and even themselves. The conspiracy against Christ was wicked; yet the early believers said, and said in prayer to God (Acts 4: 27); "For of a truth against thy holy child Jesus, whom thou hast anointed, both Herod and Pontius Pilate, with the Gentiles and people of Israel, were gathered together, for to do whatsoever thy hand and thy counsel determined before to be done." Here the wicked acts of men come clearly within the scope of Providence. Here is evidently joined with the permission of sins that "most wise and powerful bounding, and otherwise ordering and governing of them, in a manifold dispensation to his own holy ends, yet so as the sinfulness thereof proceedeth only from the creature, and not from God, who, being most holy and righteous, neither is nor can be the author or approver of sin." The instances above given, which were free and contingent with regard to their actors, are expressly ascribed to Divine Providence. And is there not a consolation in so believing? Suppose we assert providence of good things only, and not of bad: what follows? That which we most dread, and which alone can do us harm, namely, the wickedness of men and devils, is placed beyond the providential guidance of God. Surely, there is no comfort in believing that the worst, and most atrocious and destructive acts of men are under the dominion of blind chance! Yet such is the common opinion of worldly men on this subject. The government of God, indeed, with regard to evil acts, is different from his government in regard to holy acts. He may include both in his most wise plan, but he contemplates free acts as free acts, and in no degree puts forth any causative influence to tempt or compel to the commission of them. That there are difficulties here we do not for a moment deny; but they are such as arise from the depths of the divine nature, and the short sounding-line of human reason. In two things we all agree. We must all admit God's permission of evil. Without this permission it could never have existed. God was clearly under no necessity of having sin in the universe. He could clearly have made men without the faculty of sinning; or he could have made a system without men; or he could have forborne from making any system at all. The evil in the universe is clearly under God's permission: he suffers it to exist. In this, I say, we all agree. There is another thing in which we all agree, and between these two limits of undeniable truth our opinions have room to oscillate. We all agree that God has no participation in moral evil. Though he permits it, as the product of free creatures, he hates it. Our church has been charged with holding that God is the author of the sin of sinful acts; on the contrary, it says. "The sinfulness thereof proceedeth only from the creature, and not from God."* "Let no man say when he is tempted, I am tempted of God; for God cannot be tempted with evil, neither tempteth he any man." God could annihilate the sinful creature the moment his free nature breaks forth into sin. In his infinite wisdom he has chosen to do otherwise, and to uphold the existence of the creature even when rebelling against him, yet in such a manner that the taint and pollution belong only to the sinner.

All the creatures of God, then, and all their acts, are governed by his most wise, and holy, and omnipotent providence, to work out his own excellent glory. This is God's ultimate end in creation. No other can be conceived of. To make any thing but God his own end, were to set something above God. When as yet there was no creation, and no providence, God contained in himself all the reasons of what was afterwards to be; and these reasons still remain. To create, was in a manner to reveal himself,—the earliest revelation; not by

* Conf. F. c. v.

words, but acts, and every creature, with all that proceeds from it, is a part of this display. The addition of spiritual and intellectual agencies, men and angels, to the otherwise brute fabric of God's works, afforded indeed spectators of this glory, and judges of this skill; and the quality of choice, freedom, or voluntary action possessed by these beings, introduces a new principle into the universe; one which separates morals from nature, and one in which the Most High appears to take the greatest complacency. For we know of nothing which God so loves, or which he purchases at so high a rate, as the free love of a creature. This exalts his benevolence, and is the key to many of his dispensations. But all creature minds, however spiritual and however free, are infinitely inferior to Jehovah, and infinitely too small to afford the real motive of the universe, which must have been eternal,—which must have been God. All the boundless combinations and interchanges of matter and mind (the latter being far the more complicated and wonderful), all the play of wheel in wheel, of cause in cause, of thought in thought, of passion in passion, conspire to work out one and the same result—the glory of God. "For of him, and through him, and to him, are all things."

What a dismal view is that which epicurean fidelity takes of this universal frame! God is no. in all his works! He has left them. As if I should be introduced to a lofty, wide, and noble palace: its walls are strength; every quality of a magnificent structure is there; all is convenience and ornament. I gaze on its sublime colonnades, its sculptured friezes, its statued walls, its interior decorations. What is there left to be desired? One thing: it has no inhabitant. Such is the universe without a providence. Deny the actual and efficient presence of God in his works (and this is providence), and you leave me a world without reason. You give me no assurance that the very next moment may not produce some general and direful catastrophe, involving all in common destruction, without respect to character, swallowing up the good as well as the evil: for to provide for a difference between them would be a providence. The progress of history is a tangled web, but its developments are chaos indeed, without God. The unfolding of God's design is history. It is he who changes dynasties, and over the convulsion of revolutionary war, makes a highway for his own glorious approach. The study of human records, of daily journals, and even of legislative and diplomatic documents, throw very little light on the riddle of history. The great heroic instruments themselves know little. But the study of revelation, which is God's key to providence, reveals to the believer more than the world dreamed of. Nebuchadnezzar, Cyrus, Alexander the Great, and the Roman power, were all foreshown to Daniel in the visions of Chaldea. Compare with this the foresight of the great minds themselves, and how clearly do we perceive that it is not they, but Providence, that laid the plan. Think you that

Nebuchadnezzar dreamed, when he was consolidating his mighty empire, that it should presently be given to the Medes and Persians? As little, as that the great Euphrates should be turned out of its bed: and yet both took place. Think you the young, adventurous Macedonian, as he swept over Asia, conceived that in that same Babylon he should die of his debaucheries? Or Cæsar, just arrived at the summit of power, with the republic at his feet, that he should perish by the daggers of his friends? Or Napoleon, that he should die a lingering death in a remote isle? Or Charles the Tenth, or Louis Philippe, that they should become fugitives, and die in exile? As little as the great planners, legislators, and orators of Europe know this day what shall be the succeeding revolutions of the wheel. But God knows. And God has been pleased to disclose some glimpses of his plan. He shows us a delicate but perceptible thread, running as a golden clew through all these transactions and changes, even when most wilful and most unexpected. Governments, nations, and languages decay; but the Church remains. It is the great organ for manifesting God's glory, and for exalting his Son. For we live under a mediatorial dispensation, and the kingdoms of this world are to become the kingdoms of God, and of his Christ.

Nor let the humble Christian fear, lest amid the greatness of such events, his little individual interests should be forgotten or overlooked. Oh no! It is a blessed thing to be on the side of One, of whom, and through whom, and to whom are all things. We have seen it to be a characteristic glory of God's knowledge and acts, that he can condescend to the infinitely small, as well as stretch his creative hand to the infinitely great. Amidst the voices from the throne, which tell of the fall of empires, and the triumph of Immanuel, we hear also a whisper of love, saying to the Church, "Fear not, little flock: it is your Father's good pleasure to give you the kingdom;" and saying to the believer, "The very hairs of your head are all numbered." "Take no thought for the morrow." "Your Father knoweth that ye have need of these things." Ah! I know the sneering objection which poor, self-tormenting skepticism makes to this particular providence. In his zeal to make himself an orphan in the universe, he denies that God can take any measures for the relief of individual cases. This would be to step aside from his original plan. Hence the vulgar objections to trusting in God's help in emergencies, or to praying for it. How preposterous (such an one tells us) to think that God will vary from the line of his sublime acts, to meet the case of a poor woman, or an insignificant child. True enough: but God does not vary; he does not deviate. That emergency, that distress, that cry, that deliverance,—all are parts of the plan, links of the chain; and this is precisely what we mean by providence. The ignorance and obtuseness are all on the side of the scoffer, who does not perceive, what I have earnestly pressed before, that free acts of creatures are equally in the plan; and hence, when God turns aside the arrow from the heart of his praying child, he does what he foresaw to be done, even from eternal ages. I wonder, therefore, more than I can express, that one of the acutest wits that ever wrote, should so play into the hands of the vulgar and the superficial, as in these lines, which embrace the popular notion:

> "Shall burning Etna, if a sage require,
> Forget to thunder, and recall her fire?
> On air or sea new motions be imprest,
> O blameless Bethell, to relieve thy breast?
> When the loose mountain trembles from on high,
> Shall gravitation cease, if you go by?
> Or some old temple, nodding to its fall,
> For Chartres' head reserve the hanging wall?"

Here is more wit than reason. To each of these questions we may, in a sound sense, answer, Yes. Etna hath no fires, but for God's purpose. Gravitation has no cogency an instant longer than God stands by to act. And when the tower falls, whether in judgment or not, it falls just where and when infinite wisdom has predetermined it should fall. And if this concur with the earnest believing prayer of God's child, it is not an exception to the general rule, or a deviation from the plan, but a substantial part of what was provided for; that is, it is providence. It is therefore as philosophical as it is pious, for the child of God to trust in him, and resort to him. The Almighty is never greater than when he stoops to the wants and weaknesses of his suffering people. His words of promise, especially as they fell from the lips of the Lord Jesus Christ, are surpassingly sweet and encouraging. They occupy much of the sermon on the mount. Its latter parts are an application of the doctrine of Providence. And I solemnly charge every follower of Christ to believe, that he is never more reasonably engaged, than when he is casting himself on the Divine Providence. Instead of shuddering in chilly doubt as to particular providence, be assured you cannot conceive of a providence more particular than that which is. Superstition may take that for providence which is only its own morbid fancy. Presumption may rely on Providence, in idle, insolent neglect of means. But true faith will still cling to the belief, that the sparrow's fall is not too particular for God's plan. It is our privilege, not only to hope in Providence, with regard to the lesser affairs of life, but to recognize it—to see God's hand in our daily walk, with wonder and love. "They that observe providences, shall have providences to observe." The simple faith of the patriarchs saw God's hand in every thing that befell them; and so might we. I appeal to aged and observant Christians, whether the happiest persons they ever knew, have not been those who were most ready to eye God in all the events of life: in health and sickness, in business, and in family occurrences. Let us hope in Providence. Let us hope mightily. "But I will hope continually, and will yet praise thee more and more." Do days look dark? O remember, every cloud is governed by the God of truth and the God of power. The house in which you dwell is not without a master. He has issued his promise.

> "His very word of grace is strong,
> As that which built the skies;
> The voice that rolls the stars along,
> Speaks all the promises."

Though sorrow may endure for a night, yet joy cometh in the morning. It is all the more likely to come, for your trusting. "Blessed are all they that put their trust in him." Especially delightful is the thought, that the world of mind is under providence; that thoughts, and feelings, and frames, and free acts, are controlled by infinite wisdom; and that our spiritual condition is under the same guidance which regulates our birth and death. Cling fast to the hand which is leading you. Though it be through darkness, though it be in deep waters, you know whom you have believed. Yield not for a single moment to misgivings about future storms or shipwrecks, as though any part of your religious voyage could fall out by chance. Infinite love, joined to infinite skill, shall pilot the way through every strait, and temptation, and peril. God has ever loved to place his people where they had none to hope in but him only. Your own experience probably recalls such times. Let the recollection be for your abundant encouragement and support. Repose on the arm which has never failed you hitherto. And bring in the aid of a nobler consideration, drawn from an object higher than your own personal, temporary happiness. Love to God is love to his honour. If by your means his great name can be exalted; if, even by trying dispensations to you, Christ's praise can be diffused, you will joyfully cry, "Let him be magnified, by body and soul, whether in life or death." All things work together for the divine glory: this is a stable truth; but—blessed be his name—it is equally true, that "all things work together for good to them that love God, to them who are called according to his purpose." Such reliance is very different from the inert repose of the Mussulman on his Fate. It is reliance on a present God, who is all wisdom, foresight, love and power. He can cause the wrath of man to praise him; the remainder of that wrath he can restrain. Even you who disbelieve and rebel, shall be made to do reluctant honour to his name. You are equally swayed by his Providence. If his condign wrath (which may he forbid) should fall upon you in the other world, it will be to the praise of the glory of his justice. But how infinite will be the gain to you, if you freely accept of his salvation, and join yourselves to the number of those who glorify him, not in spite of themselves, not by rebellion and woe, but by the willing tribute of joyful service! In regard to your own happiness, holiness and perfection, Providence cannot be said to be on your side, while you remain unreconciled to God. And this is a very unequal war in which you are engaged; for who can stand before him, when once he is angry? God will educe order out of confusion, and harmony out of the temporary discord, however much you may rebel; but the part of wisdom is to make God's interest yours, and so to join yourselves to his certain triumph, as to participate in it. Wherefore, "be ye reconciled to God!" His indignation is intolerable, but his grace and love are heaven. And they are yours, on acceptance. None can stay his hand, when he hath a purpose to bless. He works out his own irresistible decrees. "FOR OF HIM, AND THROUGH HIM, AND TO HIM ARE ALL THINGS; TO WHOM BE GLORY FOR EVER. AMEN."

THE SAME SUBJECT IN ITS APPLICATION

TO THE WHOLE PATH OF LIFE.

III.

THE course of God's providence in regard to his own people is dark and inexplicable. The principles on which it is conducted are secrets of God's court: it is not wonderful that we should be ignorant of them. We are in darkness even with respect to the ends for which God is employing us. It is natural that many of the intermediate events should be contrary to our expectation. Not more devious or unexpected were the successive journeyings of Israel in the desert than are the ways of the believer in his pilgrimage. It is enough for him to know that his way is not fortuitous, but that every step is directed by a Providence which has the same residence with the Grace from which he hopes for salvation—a Providence which consults and disposes for the falling of every hair.

In looking back on life, there is, perhaps, no Christian who does not acknowledge that his way has been such as to contravene all his expectations and purposes, and many of his wishes and fears. Yet there is no well-instructed believer who does not likewise admit, that the way has been a right way, and that the most adverse events are part of a wise, sovereign, and merciful arrangement. Ignorant as we are both of our own strength and our own weakness, of the work which the Master demands, the preparation which he would effect, and the dangers which he foresees as awaiting us, it would be the height of presumption for us to choose our own path. In our best hours, it is our consolation that those things which we cannot control are governed by One who loves us better than we love ourselves. Who would give the babbling, puling infant a voice in the conduct of its little life? yet the comparison is all in our favour. The infant is wiser and mightier, when compared with the parent —need I say it?—than are we, when compared with God. The wonder is that we should ever dream of taking the direction of our own affairs. The mercy is that they are under the superintendence of Him who is infinitely able to govern and bless. The ravings of the wildest storm which threatens our vessel are regular parts of the plan, agreeably to which the Sovereign of nature and grace is conducting us towards a state of rest.

We shall now be led, *first*, to contemplate the truth, that while man, through ignorance, cannot order his life, God does order it; and *secondly*, to deduce the practical lessons which flow from this truth.

We can never see this world in its true light unless we consider it as a state of discipline—a condition through which we are passing to fit us for another. It belongs to such a state to be very different from a state of rest and accomplishment. Many things must necessarily pertain to it which are but for a season; many things which are not good in themselves, but good with relation to the end that is sought. To understand such a condition of discipline presupposes a knowledge of several particulars which are beyond the reach of human minds in their present state; for we must know, first, what the end is for which the Supreme Governor is preparing us; then, the true state and character of our own souls, with all their peculiarities and defects, which make such a discipline necessary; and lastly, the suitableness of every particular of such discipline to produce the end desired. This, it needs but a little reflection to see, is far beyond our intellectual power. Especially is this seen when we take notice that the problem is disturbed and darkened by involving some of the most difficult and inscrutable questions, such as the origin of evil, the nature of spiritual temptation, the decrees of God, and how far his providence may be said to concur in the product of those acts which, so far as we are concerned, are sinful. And the reason why these inexplicable questions are connected with the subject is, that our discipline in this world includes not merely the outward dispensations of God's providence, but the free act of creatures, ourselves and others, and these as well when they are evil as well as when they are good. It is the prerogative of God alone to deal with sin without contracting any taint. While he cannot be tempted to evil, neither tempteth any man; and while to make God the author of sin is impious, it is, nevertheless, true, that sin is within the sphere of his providential arrangements; and his providence has such a reference to sin as to carry with it, as we have seen, a "bounding, and otherwise ordering and foreseeing of them, in a manifold dispensation, to his own holy ends, yet so as the sinfulness thereof proceedeth only from the creature, and not from God."

The connection of this with our subject will be more apparent, if we consider that all our other trials are light and unimportant when compared with those which proceed from human freedom, that is, from the sins of ourselves and others. The direct visitations of God, in the storm, the pestilence, in wounds and sufferings and death, admit of more solace than those which flow from the unhallowed passions of men; and even these carry a less poignant sting than our own shameful neglects and transgressions, which wound the soul again and again, and keep us mourning as long as we are in the flesh. Yet even these are ordered in wisdom and benignity; and we take but a narrow view of Providence, and of our own way, unless we regard them as parts of a manifold dispensation, intended for our good.

When aged David lies under the rebukes of a vituperative foe, he exclaims: "So let him curse, because the Lord hath said unto him, Curse David." Not that the holy king would impute the sin to his Maker, but that he considers the wicked as God's sword, and their free transgressions as overruled to effect his chastisement. It is the province of Jehovah to bring good out of evil; but his method of doing so is among the darkest of his ways.

Still more painful is the doubt, when we are ourselves surprised by sin. Amidst the necessary and useful paroxysms of shame and grief which follow transgression, we do not find time or heart to turn our thoughts to this providential aspect of the subject. Yet it is not too much to say, that all our frailties, defects, and offences are so governed by the supreme Providence, as to work out our greater salvation, and the greater glory of divine grace. But here again, while the result is certain, we are absolutely incompetent to understand the means, and in this respect the way of man is not in himself. We can only bow, and yield ourselves with implicit submission to the awful hand of that Providence which leadeth the blind by a way that they know not.

To say that a man is incompetent to direct his own way, is only to say, that in a tangled forest, full of pitfalls, a wanderer at midnight, without light, path or compass, is unable to choose his direction. In the pilgrimage of this world, we know not whither we are going, or what God intends to do with us. The pillar of cloud which guides us is absolutely independent of our disposal; yet we are bound to be governed by its motion and its rest. The spirit of the declaration is still in force: "At the commandment of the Lord the children of Israel journeyed, and at the commandment of the Lord they pitched as long as the cloud abode upon the tabernacle, they rested in their tents. Or whether it were two days, or a month, or a year, that the cloud tarried upon the tabernacle, remaining thereon, the children of Israel abode in their tents, and journeyed not: but when it was taken up, they journeyed." We must expect God's signals; and those indications which are properly called the leadings of his providence. It is charged among the sins of Israel, that "they waited not for his counsel." At one time we find them disheartened by the report of the spies, turning back in heart unto Egypt, weeping tears of vexation all night, and crying, Would God that we had died in the land of Egypt! or would God we had died in this wilderness! At another, they are on the opposite extreme, rushing upon the Amalekites and Canaanites, without command, and driven before them for their sins with great discomfiture. Our course is similar, when we idly attempt to force a way, in spite of Providence; when we repine at our lot, or violently endeavour, for reasons other than those of plain duty, to throw off the yoke which is laid upon us, or to break into new paths which our Leader has not opened. The folly of such endeavours is as great as its rebellion. The horizon of our ken is very limited. The circle which encloses the legitimate field of our planning and management is small indeed. Our way is hedged in more closely than we are apt to imagine; and the freedom with which we flatter ourselves is checked and controlled by arrangements beyond our knowledge and above our reach.

Our deplorable ignorance as to our own way in life, is particularly manifest when we consider that whole trains of events, such as give colour to the entire life, are often dependent on a trivial, unforeseen, and apparently casual occurrence. By turning down one street of a city, instead of another, a man may meet the person by whom the whole current of his after life shall be determined. That Joseph, rather than some other messenger, should have been sent to find his brethren at Shechem; that Ishmaelites on their camels should have come up in the nick of time, and carried him a slave into Egypt; that the wife of Potiphar should have become his enemy; and that he should have been thrown into prison, were all what we call fortuitous and unfortunate events. So far as his brethren were concerned, their machinations were malignant; yet were they all threads in that wonderful web of Providence which was partially unfolded in the four hundred years' captivity, and more fully in the fortunes of the Jewish nation, and the plan of redemption. "As for you, ye thought evil against me; but God meant it for good, to bring to pass as it is this day, to save much people alive." It was no very important event, that the asses of Kish the Benjamite should have strayed; yet this fact gave Israel a king. It was as unimportant that youthful David should go to see his brothers at the camp in Elah; yet this led to the slaughter of Goliath, and a change of the dynasty. The Ahithophels, Machiavellis, Richelieus, and Metternichs think otherwise. But the great Oxenstierna was right, when he said, "See, my son, with how little wisdom the world is governed!" In another sense, it is governed with infinite wisdom; but God's. In his hand, a diamond necklace may cost a queen her head, and destroy a kingdom: a king, who has been deliberately shot at again and again, may, by forbidding one banquet, close a dynasty. And every day of our lives events are taking place, of which, at the time, we make no account, but which, in God's providence, are the pivots on which revolves our whole subsequent history. Yet the very smallness of these occurrences, as well as our ignorance of their bearings, would for ever prevent our arranging or ordering them.

Even of those things which, in a limited sense, may be said to be within our power, we are to a great degree ignorant whether they are good or evil, whether to be chosen or refused. It is true, even to a proverb, that what we consider prosperity and success, often results in lasting evil; and as true, that the highest earthly happiness results from events which at the time are considered disastrous. And this is more strikingly evinced, when we regard the moral consequences of such occurrences, and observe that prosperity injures the soul, and that the richest spiritual blessings are connected with suffering, disappointment, and defeat. How would it be possible for us to choose or to refuse such things, if the question were left to our own forecast? Suppose, for example, that any man were to sit down to map out the course of future life for himself. Is it not almost ce tain that his draught would exclude all distresses and trials? Yet we know upon divine authority, that these are absolutely necessary to the discipline of the heart, and the development of Christian character. But who could undertake to insert them in due measure, and at the proper points? What human tongue would not falter in saying, At such a time I shall be laid on a bed of wasting sickness. At such a time I shall be bereaved of a beloved child, or of an invaluable companion. Here I shall suffer contempt and calumny; and there I shall be vexed with indescribable temptations. How truly do we find it, that the way of man is not in himself!

What has been said is true, upon the just supposition, that man is incompetent to choose that course which is best for him: but even if we should grant him this competency, his case would be little altered, because he is able in but a slight degree to effect that which he may choose. Man knows not how much he can effect. Boast as we may of the power of human determination, the ordering of the events which concern us, is altogether out of ourselves. As we gaze with interest on a new-born babe, we can no more predict what shall be the tenor of its history, than we can declare, as we look into a mountain-spring, what the river shall be which is to issue from it. The stream may pursue a direct course to its termination, or it may turn and wander a thousand times. It may go noiselessly through sandy plains of ease, and stagnate in broad shallows of carnal sloth, or it may force its way through cliffs of opposition, dash over cataracts of passion, and reach the ocean after a way of perpetual turbulence. The greatest events of our lives, are those in which we have no option. It is not left to man's determination in what age of the world he shall be born; whether in Christian or in savage land; whether poor or rich, whether feeble or hardy; whether a genius or a fool; whether he shall enjoy parental care, or be an orphan; whether he shall dwell in a realm of peace, or have his whole character and actions moulded by revolution and war. And we might carry out the enumeration to a thousand particulars, each bearing directly on his happiness.

It would seem to be the intention of God, that the lives of men should differ as much as their countenances, and that each should be checkered by the most unexpected occurrences. The beautiful biographies of the Old Testament reveal to us the hand of God, leading the patriarchs and other holy men along a perpetual pilgrimage, in which they are as really without self-direction as was Israel in the wilderness. Surely the way of Abram was not in himself, when God called him out of the East, led him into Canaan, and into Egypt, and through a long life gave him no inheritance, no, not so much as to set his foot on. The wanderings of Jacob were as little under his own control. When the twin children, Esau and Jacob, were born, no aspect of the heavens could have shown that their course of life should run in streams so divergent and unlike. Moses, and Gideon, and David, are instances quite as worthy of our meditation. But we have only to look back upon our own little biography, however quiet and uneventful that history may have been, to learn, that of the great body of events, very few have been at our own disposal. A higher wisdom hath determined the times before appointed, and the bounds of our habitation; hath ordered how we should be educated; the time of our conversion; the field of our labour; the afflictions which have entered into our discipline, and the stations which we now occupy. The picture for the last year has for its chief lights and shades, events as totally independent of our will as the eclipse or the earthquake. Nor can you prognosticate the occurrences of this very day, any more certainly than the course of the winds.

But by the way of man, we mean surely more than that chain of occurrences which strikes the senses. There is an inner life, which, though unseen, is loftier, vaster, and more eventful. The history of the man is the history of his immortal part. While men look on the panorama of sensible things, the poverty, the pleasures, the journeys, the expeditions, the wars, the disasters, the triumphs of our race; eyes are gazing upon us from the spiritual world, intent upon those great realities which escape us, in the pilgrimage of the spirit; the shade and texture of the reason; the dangers, and crosses, and wounds of the moral part; the new birth of the soul; the mysterious assaults of principalities and powers, the sublime conflict with evil; the armour, the triumph, and the salvation. This, of a truth, is the way of man; and it is not in himself. The wind bloweth where it listeth, and thou hearest the sound thereof, but canst not tell whence it cometh, or whither it goeth. The whole ordering of the means of grace is by a sovereign hand. Appalling as the thought is, the greatest change of which we can be the subjects, is beyond our reach. We may deny, murmur, and even rage; the truth is eternal: I will have mercy on whom I will have mercy, and I will have compassion on whom I will have compassion. So then it is not of him that willeth, nor of him that runneth, but of God that showeth mercy. The most placid life of the most secluded Christian is so pregnant with spiritual events, as to be a little world of itself. And these events, linked in with eternal destiny, are not of the creature's choosing. Enter for a little while into the mysterious chambers of memory, and contemplate the shadows of departed things which flit across those walls. How unforeseen—how strange! Was it your wisdom or your will which ordered that for so many years, through so great temptations, you should go on offending God, and resisting his commandments; that meanwhile you should ever and anon be checked and wounded by the visitation of convincing truth; that, at a certain moment, you should be called of God, and illuminated by his Holy Spirit; that you should hear such a preacher, or alight on such a text, or receive such an admonition; that you should encounter such temptations, have such joys, fall into such sins, be called to such labours, and endure such sorrows; in a word, that you should be this very hour receiving, for good or evil, the impressions of which you are now conscious? No, my reader; no! you feel the hand of sovereignty in all this: and such has been the case with all the people of God. How much agency, think you, had any of the three thousand Pentecostal hearers, in adjusting their several plans, and journeys, and devotions, so as to be pricked in heart, at that moment, by the preaching of Peter? How much agency had Saul of Tarsus, lately an assistant in the murder of Stephen, and now hasting to Damascus to imbrue his hands in fresh martyrdoms, in causing himself to be smitten to the earth, a repentant soul? How much agency had the jailer of Philippi, in the events which accompanied the midnight earthquake, and the divine call which snatched him from the yawning damnation of the suicide? From whom, then, proceeded these events, if not "from the Father of lights, with whom is no variableness, neither shadow of turning? Of his own will begat he us with the word of truth."

The future, with which we so vainly perplex ourselves, is perfect darkness. We know not even where our next footsteps shall be planted. Whether death or life, whether joys or temptations await us, no wisdom can disclose to us. "How can a man, then, understand his own way?"

Are we then to fold our arms, and believ...

ourselves to have no freedom, to lie still in the arms of an inexorable fate? By no means. Between Fate and Providence, there is just the difference which subsists between darkness and light, between chance and foresight, between an unreasoning destiny and a disposing goodness, between nonentity and God. In the truth we urge, and in all our exposition of it, while it is asserted that man does not know and cannot direct himself, it is implied that God does. A man's heart deviseth his way, but the Lord directeth his steps. We are in a labyrinth indeed, but the clew is in the hand of infinite wisdom and infinite love. When we least know whither we are going, he knoweth the way that we take. When we are unable to conceive what good can result from our present distressing condition, God is using us for the very purpose for which he sent us into the world. The expert artisan, surrounded by a thousand implements, knows precisely the use of each; he takes up one, and lays it aside; he employs each in its due time and measure, and for its right end. Just in this way does the sovereign wisdom deal with men. And it is no more reasonable for the human soul, than for the material implement, to quarrel with the hand that wields it. Assyria thought herself wise and prudent and successful. But God saith: "Shall the axe boast itself against him that heweth therewith, or shall the saw magnify itself against him that shaketh it? as if the rod should shake itself against them that lift it up, or as if the staff should lift up itself, as if it were no wood." Thus even the free actions of the most wicked man are so governed, that his way is not in himself, but in God. "For the Scripture saith unto Pharaoh, Even for this same purpose have I raised thee up, that I might show my power in thee, and that my name might be declared throughout all the earth." And in regard to the crowning sin of our world, the death of Jesus Christ, when Herod and Pontius Pilate, with the Gentiles, and the people of Israel, were gathered together, it was "for to do whatsoever God's hand and counsel determined before to be done."

But if this is true even with regard to the ungodly, how much more may we expect it to be true in regard to God's peculiar people, whom he has called and sanctified, to show forth his glory. Feeling that their way is not in themselves, they delight in believing that they are led from above. It is the very law of God's dispensations, that when his people are going they know not whither, they are in the very path which the Master has appointed. "I will bring the blind by a way that they knew not; I will lead them in paths that they have not known; I will make darkness light before them, and crooked things straight. These things will I do unto them, and not forsake them." The knowledge of this should work in us both submission and hope; submission, because God is sovereign, because he is wise, because he is just, because he is omnipotent, and because all resistance and all repining are fruitless and wicked; hope, because we are assured that all things work together for good to them that love God, being disposed according to a most gracious plan for accomplishing their perfection. What though he hath not confided to us his secrets of state? The Lord reigneth, let the earth rejoice! However perplexing may be the particular case, here is a rule which covers all. "Clouds and darkness are round about him; righteousness and judgment are the habitation of his throne." Even in times as dark as those of Habakkuk, we may say with the prophet: "Although the fig-tree shall not blossom, neither shall fruit be in the vines; the labour of the olive shall fail, and the fields shall yield no meat; the flock shall be cut off from the fold, and there shall be no herd in the stalls; yet will I rejoice in the Lord, I will joy in the God of my salvation." The promise is good to every faithful soul: "The Lord shall guide thee continually, and satisfy thy soul in drought, and make fat thy bones: and thou shalt be like a watered garden, and like a spring of water, whose waters fail not."

We are more ready, perhaps, to recognize this guidance of Providence under the greater than under the lighter afflictions of life. Yet the misery as well as the happiness of man is mainly the aggregate of little things. When fortune is suddenly swept away; when disease breaks the constitution; when death by a single stroke makes the widow and the orphan, the sufferer is prompt to acknowledge that it is the visitation of God. But we live as if we would exempt from the general rule the petty annoyances of our common days; the languor which unfits for duty; the cloud that passes over the spirits; the domestic cross, the chafing of temper in trade; the slight, the unkindness, the forgetfulness which we endure from thoughtless or selfish fellow-creatures. Yet the law is universal. Not merely the journey, but every step of the journey, is ordered. No part of our way is left to ourselves. Resignation and faith behold God in the smallest hair that falls; and the happiest life is that of him who has bound together all the affairs of life, great and small, and intrusted them to God. Commit thy way unto the Lord, trust also in him, and he will bring it to pass.

The consideration of the truth, that we cannot direct our own ways, may well serve to chastise our sanguine expectations, with regard to the course of our life. It is the characteristic illusion of youth, and it varies with the temperament of the individual, but no season of life is entirely free from it. We are prone to look at the future, as if it all were within our power. We plan for earthly happiness, as if our own purpose were omnipotent. And even sore experience does not teach us that our arm reaches but a little distance; and that we are subject to a governing power, which employs us as the potter does the clay. Of the majority of the schemes and enterprises which engage the solicitude of the busy world, it may be said, they include no thought of Providence. The worldly mind, and even the

Christian mind under wrong influences, continues its way as if self-sufficient. "To-morrow shall be as this day, and much more abundant." It is to rebuke such unfounded hopes that the Apostle James says, " Go to now, ye that say, To-day or to-morrow we will go into such a city, and continue there a year, and buy and sell, and get gain : whereas ye know not what shall be on the morrow. For what is your life ? It is even a vapour, that appeareth for a little time, and then vanisheth away. For that ye ought to say, If the Lord will, we shall live, and do this or that. But now ye rejoice in your boastings: all such rejoicing is evil." Such was the joy and such the boasting of the rich man in the parable, as he surveyed the extent of his crops : " I will say to my soul, Soul, thou hast much goods laid up for many years, take thine ease, eat, drink, and be merry." But God said unto him, " Thou fool ! this night shall thy soul be required of thee." To hope, indeed, is our privilege and our duty, but our hope must be in God. Men are fond of talking about being the architects of their own fortune, and our ears are wearied with hearing of " self-made men ;" but unless the Lord build the house, they labour in vain that build it. Hope itself becomes more secure, and energy is more constant, when they are founded on the belief that all is under the Almighty guidance. Our happiness in duty is greatest, when we feel that we are conducted through all our changes by an overruling power, which uses us for ends far above our comprehension.

But such is the tendency of erring man to go from one extreme to another, that while at one moment we are inflated with idle hopes, at the next we are cast down by as idle fears. The doctrine now under consideration serves to repress our needless apprehension of coming evil. Ever attempting to pry into the future, we make to ourselves a thousand troubles which never exist but in these sickly imaginations. The foreknowledge of such as are really to befall us, would be enough to crush us; and God has wisely and mercifully concealed from us that which is to come. It is a fine conception of our great poet, when Michael sets before Adam the future history of the world, to represent our progenitor as exclaiming in anguish:

> "O visions ill foreseen! better had I
> Lived ignorant of future, so had borne
> My part of evil only, each day's lot
> Enough to bear.
>   Let no man seek
> Henceforth to be foretold what shall befall
> Him or his children; evil he may be sure,
> Which neither his foreknowing can prevent,
> And he the future evil shall no less
> In apprehension than in substance feel,
> Grievous to bear"

But not content with forecasting those ills which shall occur, we imagine a thousand which never arrive. By such perverse musings men may press into a few days all those evils which God has mercifully parcelled out through a lifetime. And as there are innumerable trials which cause more distress in the fear than in the endurance, we lade ourselves, not only with those which shall be, but with a hundred-fold more which are the mere creatures of our apprehension. Such a temper is to be corrected, by considering that the way of man is not in himself. All such cares are needless. They do not avail in the slightest degree to avert or lessen the ills which come, or to strengthen us for the burden. They fill up time, and absorb thoughts and energies which should be bestowed upon the duties of the day. In this connection, how pure, heavenly, and reviving are the directions of our blessed Saviour; how infinitely above the reach of worldly philosophy; how consistent with the highest wisdom! Sending us for our lesson to the fowls of the air and the lilies of the field, he says: "Take therefore no thought for the morrow: for the morrow shall take thought for the things of itself. Sufficient unto the day is the evil thereof." We shall be wiser, holier, and happier, if we resign ourselves and all our affairs to the disposition of divine Providence; assured that he who loves us better than we love ourselves, will lay nothing upon us which is not for our good. Let not a thought of chance intrude, even in respect to the smallest concerns. "Are not two sparrows sold for a farthing? and one of them shall not fall on the ground without your Father. But the very hairs of your head are all numbered."

If then we may use this doctrine to correct, at once our unreasonable hopes and our unreason able fears, we may also derive from it the habit of conducting our whole life with a reference to the leadings of Providence. Since it is not in man to direct his steps, let him seek the direction of God. And this direction is twofold; that of providential indications, and that of revealed duty. We are not left without signs in the course of events concerning us, which serve to show where our path lies. The traveller may not be able to see very far before him; but when he has made one cautious step, he is generally permitted to see where the next should be placed. Even in the night of storm, this direction is sometimes afforded by the very lightning which alarms him. We must not mistake our own wishes and fears, our likes and dislikes, our worldly ease and interest for the leadings of Providence; but we may with justice examine every proposed step, with reference to our character, talents, age, station, and circumstances.

But still more important is it to regard the path of duty as the path of Providence. The revelation of God's will in the Scriptures is our pillar of cloud and of fire. When we go where this directs, we cannot but go aright. "This is the way, walk ye in it." "The testimony of the Lord is sure, making wise the simple." "Thy word is a lamp unto my feet, and a light unto my path."

If instead of so often asking what is agreeable, or tending to worldly happiness, we were constantly to ask what is duty, we should attain greater holiness, greater usefulness, and greater peace of mind. Our greatest glory is conformity to the will of God. As our ways are not our own, we must eventually bow to that will, whether willingly or unwillingly However, therefore, a temporary departure from duty may seem to promise good, we may rest upon it, as the immutable truth of God, that "wisdom's ways are ways of pleasantness."

Let me now inquire, is it not in the highest degree encouraging to be thus assured, that dark as the future is, in regard to our apprehensions, it is not in the minutest particular uncertain in the mind of God? His eye discerns our whole path, even to the end; nay, his hand has marked it out. After our greatest efforts, and in spite of our greatest resistance, we do but float upon the mighty stream of his Providence. All that is past, and all that is to come, including every action, suffering, sentiment, and thought, all is carried forward by him to a consummation as beatific for us as it is glorious for our Maker.

Let me say, in recapitulation; we have found it involved in our doctrine, that our present life is a state of discipline, in which we know not the end for which God is fitting us, nor our own need of such and such particular trials; that being ignorant of the end, we must needs be ignorant of the way; that we know not what to choose or what to refuse, if events were left to our option; that even in cases where we have such knowledge, we have little power to accomplish what we may choose; that the events on which our whole life, especially our spiritual life, turns, are beyond our control; and that the future, with all its contingencies, is entirely hidden from us. But we have seen, on the other hand, that if man cannot direct his own ways, they are directed by God; from which we have derived these practical lessons: to be submissive under trials, to moderate our hopes, to repress our fears, and to follow the leadings of Providence.

It seems a proper conclusion to this essay to add, that in a future state, we have reason to believe, the children of God will be admitted to see the wisdom and the mercy of all the way by which God has led them. What our Saviour said to Peter may, perhaps, in a certain sense, be said to every believer: "What I do thou knowest not now, but thou shalt know hereafter." It is not too much to think, that when God shall have made up all his jewels, and the number of the elect shall be complete, he will make it a part of their happiness to look back from the height of heaven upon all their winding track, and to see that every step has been ordered in infinite love; that their sorest trials have been merciful; that their freest choices have been links in God's chain of purpose; that their very sins have been overruled for good. And if this shall appear amazing in the history of an individual, how shall it shine resplendent in the nations of them that are saved, when ten thousand times ten thousand intermingling and entangled lives shall visibly accord with one infinite plan, and centre in one sovereign purpose! The great end of Creation and Providence and Grace is God's own glory. This will be made manifest at the grand consummation. But in nothing will this more shine than when it shall appear that the voluntary, and even the wicked acts of innumerable creatures, all concur in the accomplishment of God's purposes; and that in proportion as man's way has not been in himself, in the same proportion has the magnificent plan been carried to completion.

There is a wonderful display of wisdom and power in material nature; and if we regard each star, even in the milky way, as the centre of a system, we are overwhelmed with the consideration of so many orbs, all moving agreeably to a uniform law, and circling their respective courses for ages without confusion. Yet still more astonishing, and still more glorious will it be, when at the last it shall appear, that of the millions of redeemed souls, each has been the free originator of thoughts and volitions; that these have flowed from each in a perpetual stream; that they have conflicted with one another, and conflicted with the preceptive will of God; that, nevertheless, all have contributed to the happiness of the saved world, and the glory of the Almighty. Then shall be heard the song of Moses, the servant of God, and the song of the Lamb: "Great and marvellous are thy works, Lord God Almighty; just and true are thy ways, thou King of saints."

THE OMNIPOTENCE OF GOD A GROUND OF ENLARGED CHRISTIAN EXPECTATION

IV.

IF any are dissatisfied with the Christian religion, it is because of their own ignorance or perverseness. It is impossible to conceive of any higher good, than that which the Gospel offers to every human being who hears it. Nothing has so revealed the capacities of the soul, as Christianity; all the speculations of antiquity are trifling in comparison; and these capacities seem to be revealed for the very purpose of exalting our delightful expectations, as to their being filled. When Christianity would lay a foundation for our hopes, it does not build on any doubtful analogies, but digs deep, and shows us the solid rock of God's infinite perfections; saying, as it were, If you would know what you shall receive, think what God is—how great and how good. "All is yours, and ye are Christ's, and Christ is God's." And we have endeavoured to set this forth, from the beginning, as the true ground of all rational comfort in religion. For if our distresses and trials do not drive us to seek support in the attributes of God, they do not afford us any benefit. The ground of all our hopes is God's love, manifested to the world in the gift of his only begotten Son. From this source we cannot expect too much. Hence you will uniformly observe, that those who dwell most on the person and work of Christ, have the brightest prospects of future blessedness. And the apostle Paul uses a fervent prayer, that those to whom he wrote, might attain to the knowledge of this love of Christ, by means of which they would learn the riches of their destined inheritance.

The apostle Paul breaks forth in a mingled doxology and prayer, when writing to the Ephesians: "Now unto Him that is able to do exceeding abundantly above all that we ask or think." God is thus able; and thus his omnipotence is a ground of consolation.

I. God's omnipotence and grace, authorize us to expect from him blessings beyond our comprehension. The little child takes a pleasure in learning its father's riches, because it knows that this is all for its own advantage, and it never dreams of the parent's being restrained from giving by any thing but want of means. In like manner the Christian who has any right views of God as a Father, and of his relation to God, only needs to be informed that God is Almighty to be assured that he will bestow all good. Hence meditation on the omnipotence of God is greatly edifying, not only as it raises us to high thoughts of the adorable divine character, but as it assures us of the infinite sufficiency there is in him. To say that God is able, is to say that he is willing. This method of proceeding from his disposition to his nature, from his goodness to his greatness, of presuming on his love and then comforting ourselves with his power, is more pleasing than the reverse. For it is dreadful to have a full view of God's power, and at the same time to be in doubt whether it is not all arrayed against us. The impression of this is what gives triple horrors to hours of conviction, when some poor dismayed soul is brought into the presence of infinite sovereignty, might, and wrath, but as yet has no ray of hope. Very different is the view which prompted the words of Paul: "Unto him that is *able* to do,"—as if he had said, Once convince me that God is *able* to make me happy, and I am content: of his disposition to bless, I can have no doubt. The apostle does not say God is *willing:* this was unnecessary.

You will possibly have a reply ready, to wit, that nobody doubts God's power: all who believe in a God, believe he is almighty. But it is important to observe, that there are many great truths which we do not deny, and which, nevertheless, we do not believe; and again, that there are degrees of faith, from the faintest assent, of which we are scarcely conscious, up to the full assurance of certainty. If nothing were necessary but to know and admit the general propositions of religious truth, much of our preaching, hearing, reading, and meditation would be superfluous; but we must keep the mind's eye fixed on these truths until our knowledge becomes more intimate, extensive, and spiritual, and our faith grows with contemplation. Thus, while we sit and look eastward, like those that watch for the morning, we behold, first the dawn, then the sunrise, then the bright morning, and then the blazing noon. This is especially true of God's attributes. We know them. The terms which express them are simple enough. Our first catechisms give us almost all we need to have expressed in the way of definition. Nevertheless, what a world of knowledge is yet to be compassed on any one of those points! And how does he who meditates on a divine perfection seem to go forth on a voyage from which there is no return! In this way the power of God, however familiar and admitted, requires to be mused upon and traversed in our thoughts; as the astronomer by nightly observations, repeated for years, tries to penetrate the wonders of the heavens; though the object which tasks his powers and arouses his curiosity is some nebula familiar to his eye from early youth. It is wise to ponder upon known truth, and he who never practises it will make slender attainments in new discovery. It was well for Paul to turn the gaze of the Ephesians upon the wonders of God's power—God "is able to do;" and to connect it with that love of Christ and fulness of God, of which he had just been speaking (Ephes. 3 : 20). There is a little cleft of heaven opened to us by these words, and some light breaks in.

Hope is a pleasant thing, even when it concerns itself about temporals; but when it overleaps the fences of time and space, and begins to expatiate in eternity; when it forecasts the condition of a soul let loose from the body; when it presses towards the lapse of ages, all blissful and ever growing in the capacity for holy delights; when it pictures heaven, and successive births of soul into new lives of joy and love, cycle after cycle, then it becomes the angelic harbinger of God's presence. The true foundation for such hope is in God. There can be none other. To this the apostle directs the view: "To him that is able to do exceeding abundantly." It is because God the Lord is God, and our God and Redeemer, that we have such largeness of expectatation. The measure of our hopes is the degree of God's ability. This is startling, but undeniable, and full of matter for thought. "If I (a believer) am not happy, it will be because God is not able to make me so." Here, indeed, is consolation. Nothing so enlarges the horizon of our expectations, as to place our hopes on divine perfections. He "that is able to do exceeding abundantly above all that we ask or think," places us on an eminence of observation, from which we may look out on the wide sea of future good, and find no shore or limitation. This, if any thing, will lift a man above the world, and inspire a heroism into his Christianity.

The people of the world go through their pilgrimage in a poor ignoble manner, analogous to the beasts which do not lift their heads above the pasture in which they browse. Men whose portion is in this life very commonly put off thinking about any portion in the life to come, till they feel their hold on present things loosening. During middle life and activity, it is really wonderful how our successful and busy citizens contrive to keep out thoughts of God and religion. Every few days there is a funeral of some old friend; these come faster and faster, as we go down the hill; neighbours attend these with proper solemnity, and look into the open vault, as if their thoughts were full of eternity. No such thing! they have acquired the art of locking God out of his creation; their minds are busy about the obsequies, or the estate of the deceased, or whether his will shall be contested, or their own loss of time, or the next piece of sordid business. They do not like to retain God in their knowledge; they know they have nothing to expect from him. A high impenetrable wall blocks up the further side of their worldly prospects. What is beyond is to them as if it were not. What though God has plainly set on record certain things about that coming state; what though hundreds whom they knew have lifted that curtain and left the stage; what though they are certain, that after a few days, they must make the plunge into the awful unseen world; all these things fail to arouse them. No sweet hope gilds the western horizon towards which their sun is sinking. No refreshing prelibations of those heavenly pleasures cheer them in their present journey. They have resolved to make the most of this life; to live as if this were all; to keep God out of their thoughts; if not (as the great infidel said of death) " to make a leap in the dark." I have gone aside to this allusion, because it throws the strong lights of contrast on the prevalent expectations of God's children. There is a low, cowardly disposition in certain Christians to seek the world's patronage, and almost ask the world's pardon, for their religion. Are they invited to some questionable amusement? they stammer out their apology of being Christ's, as a mean-spirited spendthrift would own the slenderness of his purse. Are they censured for not loving this world enough? they plead religious custom or church-rule, or the opinion of friends, instead of glorying in their birthright in the world to come. That which they should bind to them as a garland and a diadem, and should hold forth as an irresistible inducement for sinners to come over to their side, they sometimes hide in a corner, and blush to have suspected.

True, healthy, living religion takes a different view of these matters: would God we had more of it! The believer walks by faith: have you considered what this means? It is faith which realizes the unseen, and presents the future. The believer walks about this world as a foreigner walks among the sounding colonnades of some marble palace; it is fair; it awakens his momentary curiosity, but what is it to him! To-morrow he is going away towards his beloved home. The Christian goes through this life under the overhanging influence of a spiritual state, and the incomparable attraction of a glory yet to be revealed. The very indistinctness of his vision, in respect to that fair country, increases his desires. "It doth not yet appear what we shall be." But though the details of the future inheritance are not communicated to us, the principle and source of it is. A child who knows that he is an heir, and that his father has boundless stores, knows enough for his happiness, though ignorant of the precise locality of his estates. *God is able to do*—on that he rests. In this is abiding consolation. Here the soul can be firm. Were this constantly in our thoughts, we should be buoyed up amidst the waves of trouble.

We sometimes (if sincere seekers) busy ourselves in thinking of what may be in reserve for us, in that long, long existence which awaits us, and muse on the changes, the unfoldings, the ascendings, the enlargements, of which we shall be subjects, as those ages roll on. We sometimes try to imagine what these souls may become, and to speculate upon what infinite goodness, expressed in the gift of the Son and his death on the cross, may have in reserve for us. But all these thoughts of ours fall far below the measure of what God is able to do. Sometimes, again, in more devotional moments, our meditations take the form of request, and we undertake to ask of God to do this and that for us, in this life and in the life to come. But what poor, broken ignorant petitions, for the most part; if we could only compare them with the glory that is to be revealed in us. As if an infant should be craving a feather or a flower, when the parent is preparing for it a kingdom. "We know not how to pray, nor what to pray for as we ought." Thoughts and prayers are both together swallowed up and drowned in the depths of God's power and goodness; for "he is able to do exceeding abundantly above all that we ask or think." The word used in that passage is peculiar, "out of measure—surpassingly, or transcendently," breaking over all bounds of our comprehension. You will feel its force more when you take along with you the whole of the preceding glowing context, wherein the language labours and is forced into seeming solecisms, in order to indicate the great ideas. We have to comprehend the incomprehensible, and to measure the immense, and to sound the unfathomable; "to know the love of Christ, which passeth knowledge;" to comprehend with all saints the dimensions of that which stretches beyond all human lines—the "love of Christ." As in the place in Ephesians, the measure of what God will give is his power; so in the preceding verse, the measure is the love of Christ; and both are summed up in that amazing expression (v. 19): "all the fulness of God!"

It is with no niggardly hand that our Redeeming Lord scatters these flowers of Hope along our path. We are not straitened in him. We cannot hope too much, provided we hope for right things. And while the promise of the New Testament is reserved in the extreme, as to the gift of earthly things, except so far as they minister to godliness, the gates of heaven are high and wide, and opening into boundless vistas of eternal heavenly things. "Eye hath not seen, nor ear heard, neither have entered into the heart of man, the things which God hath prepared for them that love him: but God hath revealed them unto us by his Spirit; for the Spirit searcheth all things, yea, the *deep things of God.*" 1 Cor. 2 : 9. These "deeps of God" are the profound of his nature and perfections, on which our hopes are dependent. The *whole of the future* is concerned in these anticipations. For while we need not wait till after death for them to begin, but may from the present moment have some earnest, so neither need we look on them as ending with this life, but as breaking into new, vast, and inconceivable expansions in the life which is to come. For God "is able to do exceeding abundantly above all that we ask or think."

II. Of the greatness of these hopes, perhaps, enough has been said. It is proper that we should consider their *quality*. The object of the expectation is vast, but of what nature? Are they Epicurean, Elysian, Mohammedan, sensual, carnal, philosophic, infidel enjoyments, which we look for? By no means! Such images and desires would argue a mind utterly void of true spiritual illumination and taste. No Christian can begin too soon to ascertain his standard of good; and it must be moral, spiritual, eternal, and divine. He looks for that which resides in the soul, that which flows from God, that which is wrought by the Spirit. Let it be deeply graven on our minds, that all God's dealings with us, from regeneration onwards, through all eternity, is a discipline, a moulding, a training, an education.

This is sought by all convictions, all applications of truth, all mercies, all chastisements, all that sanctifies us, by our very death, and yet more fully and gloriously by the unexplained communications of heaven. His purpose is to render us holy, to raise us to the perfection of our being, and to make us partakers of a divine nature. The work has commenced, and will never cease. "He that hath begun a good work in you, will perform it until the day of redemption." He is *able* to perform it, beyond all our thoughts and prayers, yea, *exceedingly* beyond them all; and to search how, or to what extent, would be to search "the deep things of God." We are lost in a labyrinth of thoughts, yet not without a clew. This we do know, that the great thing is the spiritual work of the Holy Ghost upon the mind and heart, begun here, and completed, or rather carried ever onward hereafter. All things are subsidiary to this. Whatever relates to our bodies, our friends, our circumstances, our temporal weal or woe, our gladness or our tears, whatever is passing and external, is subordinate to this great end; and we miss the true point of our expectations from God when we anxiously look to him for any thing short of being made "partakers of his holiness."

The more sound our experience, the more pure our piety, the more shall we understand that "this is the will of God, even our sanctification." This is the heaven we desire. We shall love it, and exult in it, in proportion as we love God, and exult in

God. Herein "the children of God are manifest and the children of the devil." The children of God have a supreme taste for likeness to God: this is their chosen blessedness. The children of the devil have no such taste. They desire the incidental benefits of religion; such as escape from hell, and from the dread of it; also supports and consolations under sorrows of life; but they must own that renovation of nature, and the restored image of God, awaken none of their sensibilities. The soul that is born again is filled with expectations, which, however undefined, are at once spiritual and glorious. "Beloved, now are we the sons of God, and it doth not yet appear what we shall be; but we know that when He shall appear we shall be like him; for we shall see him as he is." The nature of the object, then, which fixes our hopes is conformed to the nature of the God who inspires it.

III. *This glory is already begun in true Christians*, and these beginnings are the pledge, earnest, and foretaste of what God will bestow hereafter. That exceeding abundant blessing which he is able to confer is set forth to us by what he is now conferring. For that which he will do is "according to the power that worketh in us." We do not sufficiently consider this. We are already under a divine influence, the same mighty power which regenerates and which will save. We are already born into this new life, and are under the daily operations of a grace which performs miracles of love, and works transformations altogether beyond the power of nature. We are prone to undervalue changes which do not fall under the observation of sense. But creation itself is not more marvellous than new-creation. That this is really an object of power, and not left merely to human volition, is proved by our Lord's words to the disciples, when they asked, "Who then can be saved?" Jesus answered, "That which is impossible with men is possible with God." In every true believer there is a work of God's power perpetually going on, compared with which conquests and revolutions are small and unimportant. The consciousness of this work within him, and the perception of its results, give him some intimation of what God will hereafter do. In the primitive age, the contrast was striking between the unconverted and the converted state; hence the marks of this divine power were more apparent, and disciples felt that they were subjected to a power which was manifestly divine. Their hopes and triumphs seem to have been in proportion. Such will generally be the case: the more we feel the renewing energy at work within us, the brighter will be our hope of what that energy will accomplish hereafter. Hence the happiness derived from a marked and advancing Christianity, such as leaves us in no doubt whether Christ be in us or not. There is nothing that can so cheer us as this inward witness; and there will be no limit to our hopes of the favour which God will bestow, "according to the power that worketh in us." These are no blind presumptuous expectations, which we are permitted to cherish with regard to the things which God intends for us hereafter. " God hath revealed them unto us by his Spirit." He has given us some beginnings of them in the work of grace within. He has told us that he is able, and so told us as to make us sure that we shall never want until his fulness is exhausted. " Open thy mouth wide," saith he, " and I will fill it." Look forward and contemplate the continuity of the work of grace. It is not a shower at noontide, which refreshes and is gone, but a well of water that springeth up to everlasting life. Would you derive some useful lessons from what has been said? Among many, accept the following:

1. Here is great inducement for impenitent persons to repent. Do you desire to have God on your side? then repent. All his power and all his goodness will be yours, and will be pledged to do you good. *God is able*, that is, God is omnipotent, signifies a different thing to the believer and to you. What can you read in it, but that he is able to destroy? and to destroy with an intensity of destruction beyond all your possibility of comprehension. God is armed against you, and each of his perfections is a tower from which irresistible assaults are made on your happiness. The infinite and eternal opposition between God's holiness and your sin must make you miserable and keep you so. There is no way to escape this, but by coming over to God's side, through the mediation of his Son. But let this once take place — and how extraordinary is the

result! What ensues? not simple amnesty, safety, or even forgiveness: these were great, unspeakable gifts; but more than these, God descends, and picks up the poor sunken creature from his footstool, and presses him to his bosom. Is this enough? No. He wipes his tears, clothes him in white apparel, enriches him with glory, and sets him upon a throne. The redeemed sinner finds that all the expensive and amazing plan of redemption, which has been opening out for ages, has had for its object the holiness and blessedness of himself, and such as he; and that the height which he has reached in the joy of his-Lord, at the day of judgment, is only the starting-point, in a career of endless improvement in all that is pure, lovely, and spiritual. I have, throughout these remarks, taken pains to represent the expected blessing as consisting in holiness, likeness to God, and communion with him. Now make sure that this is really your aim, and you cannot by possibility desire too much, or desire too ardently. Nor can you form any vision of what God is ready to communicate in these respects, which will not be ten thousand times surpassed by the reality.

2. Here is an aid in living above the world. The argument is easy: Is God preparing for me such an exaltation of holiness? which is already begun: then away with all knitting of the heart to what is terrestrial and temporary! Ungodly people think that Christianity draws off from their pleasures and idols, from a certain sourness and misanthropy, or from want of capacity for such delights. On

the contrary, the soul of the believer flies far away above and beyond these surrounding trifles, and fixes itself on the spiritual glories of the kingdom. It is believing "things hoped for," "things unseen," that cast a shade on the toys of the present. "This is the victory that overcometh the world — even our faith." Think you that is a poor, naked, barren country, on which faith's telescope fixes itself? Astonishing blunder! It may be called for largeness and beauty, and attraction — a world. "Whatsoever things are true, whatsoever things are honest, whatsoever things are just, whatsoever things are pure, whatsoever things are lovely, whatsoever things are of good report," are included in it; and included in perpetual development and increase. God will go on to bless; Christ will be more and more the fountain of light and holiness. "Of his fulness have we all received, and grace for grace." Think of this, when the world tempts you. Think what God is able to do, and will do. Think of the work as already begun within you, if you are of his people; and examine carefully whether you experience the divine efficacy of "the power that worketh in us."

3. This subject suggests matter for our desires and prayers. The doctrine is addressed to praying people; "above all that we ask or think." Unconverted persons never pray heartily and understandingly for genuine holiness; but those who are converted, if they ever pray for any thing, pray for this. The apprehension of these spiritual realities

in their beauty and glory, does not come all at once, and we must be satisfied if one whose eyes are only just opened sees "men as trees walking;" but it infallibly comes, in the course of Christian experience. And not more truly and earnestly does the blind man express the topmost wish of his heart, "Lord, that I might receive my sight!" than the believer his longing, "O that my ways were directed to keep thy statutes! In an earlier stage of experience he may have been too anxious about temporal things; but now his sober conviction is, that nothing is worth caring for, or asking of God with any importunity, but spiritual and eternal good. In the revolution of ages, the day will come, when earthly or carnal gifts will no longer be a blessing; but the day will never come when truth, holiness, love, and God's image shall be less valuable; nay they will be growing in value to all eternity. Our prayers then are most sure to be right, and to be answered, when they are for imperishable things, and for what God himself regards as real good. Praying for the future glory is the way to be fitted for it; and while we so pray to be conformed to God, we are subjected to the mighty power, mentioned by Paul, whereby he is able to subdue all things unto himself. The encouragement to such prayers need not be here rehearsed, seeing it has been our principal topic: "God is able to do exceeding abundantly, above all that we ask or think." Nothing is more pleasing to him, than our desires that this spiritual work should go on in us nightily. He inspires such prayers, meaning to answer them: I may say they are partly answered in the very asking. These are moments when the soul feels that it would rather suffer affliction than not be sanctified, and rejoices and glories in tribulation, because the experience which it derives from them is heaven begun. There is a peculiar excellency in the holy pleasures of the afflicted: it is on the face of the wilderness that this manna falls. And there cannot be named a pursuit or enterprise of human beings, in which there is so little possibility of failure as praying for sanctification. God is able to do above your asking.

4. Such expectations from God's greatness and goodness may well sustain us amidst the trials of life. If these are sharp, so as to put our utmost patience to the proof, we may look forward towards the immensity of the promise. We may have losses; but till they avail to take away our God, they cannot effectually cloud the glorious prospect. Though we have seen the blessings promised to belong chiefly to the spiritual and eternal world, yet we are not to suppose that our heavenly Father is indifferent to the condition of his children during the course of their present pilgrimage. The hairs of their head are all numbered, and the bounds of their habitation are chosen. Even in regard to this life, he is able to do more than they ask or think. He can draw off the heavy clouds which obscure their skies; nay, he will certainly do so at the very first moment when it shall consist with his infinite plan of mercy

Thus he caused the dark day of Jacob's affliction under his supposed bereavement, to brighten into an evening of peace and joy. Thus the unexampled losses of Job were followed by equally unexampled indemnity. Yet after all that we may concede, as to the profit of godliness in the present life, its chief expectations fix themselves on that which is to come; and these exceeding great and precious promises are the headspring of every believer's comfort. To these he can come, when all cisterns are dry. This is blessedness in days of poverty, pain, and bereavement. Like the ancient prophet, he still says, "Yet will I rejoice in the Lord: I will joy in the God of my salvation." The more enlarged his views of the Divine power and faithfulness, the more will he expect; and the brighter his expectations are, the less will he feel the weight of present burdens. If our afflictions are heavy, and sometimes intolerable, it is because we dwell too little in thoughts of the glory which is to be revealed. What but this enabled the Christian martyrs, in the primitive age, to endure excruciating penalties, and death in its most hideous forms, but the confidence they had in God's ability and readiness to admit them into his exceeding joy? If for a moment their belief of the truth we are considering could have wavered, they would have fainted, and given way under the vehemence of their torments. That which can support a man under the assaults of the chief and last enemy, even death, can surely hold him up under foregoing and lesser trials. But we know by edifying observation at the bedsides of the dying, that large expectation from God's power and love can thus sustain; at a juncture when it were madness to look for any thing from earthly sources. All which should encourage us to study the riches of God's omnipotent mercy, as a resource when heart and flesh fail.

In grief and pain, when frail nature is ready to succumb, this doctrine of God's ability to relieve and save comes like a cordial to the soul. It cannot deceive, because its foundation reaches down to the rocky and eternal base of all excellency and all being. Till divinity itself shall change, this must remain the firm consolation of the believer. And his peace will be in proportion to his faith: whence it is to be inferred, that we should have more ample provision for the seasons of sorrow, if in our times of prosperity we were more engaged in profound meditation on the attributes of God. The sovereign Author of Grace, who observes a holy order in his dispensations to the church, is not wont to pour his richest solace over the souls of those who have sought him negligently, or who have been driven to seek him only on the access of calamity. Even to these he shows himself to be a God of mercy; but his largest gifts of consolation are to those who have learned to make him their refuge before the tempest began to howl. True believers, educated by a long discipline to expect from God, turn to him in the hour of sorrow, as naturally as the infant to the mother's bosom. They know whom they have believed. Their confidence in this new emergency is only the exercise of a trust which has been the habit of their sunnier days. Long ago they have settled their hearts in the firm persuasion, that God is able to do exceeding abundantly above their prayers or conceptions. The Holy Spirit, the Comforter, takes of these familiar truths, and makes them effectual in the hour of tribulation. Though there be no more sign of deliverance than for Abraham, when his hand was raised to sacrifice his son, they are strong in faith, giving glory to God. Though Divine Wisdom cast an impenetrable curtain over all the ways and means of escape, they flee with confidence to the infinite attributes of him in whom they have trusted. And when every hope on this side of heaven has failed, they can still rejoice in the marvels of loving mercy which their Lord stands ready to display in the coming eternity.

5. Here is ground for high praise to God for this infinite love. The text is brought in as a doxology; see verse 21. The apostle strikes a note of thanksgiving, that is to be endless in the church, militant and triumphant. All ages shall be full of the "praise of the glory of his grace." In our present state we are most ready to express gratitude for temporal deliverances and mercies; but in the future state, we shall find these all swallowed up in the blessing of salvation, and shall understand salvation better, as being the life of God; the subduing of the will unto his; the growing like our Maker and Redeemer; and the higher and higher reaches of

knowledge and love. The longer we live the life of heaven, the better shall we know what we have to give thanks for; because we shall know better what God is, and be nearer to him, and more fully acquainted with the wonders of his universe, and the richness of his wisdom. Here, we do but babble like infants about these things; "we know in part, and we prophesy in part;" "but when that which is perfect is come, then that which is in part shall be done away." Here we form low conceptions of what our Heavenly Father is able to do; and we can give thanks only according to our knowledge: but as our comprehension of divine grace and glory increases, we shall fall down on the golden pavement in speechless rapture of gratitude. But ah! how difficult is it to speak prudently of things beyond our experience. Let us be modest, in regard to what is not revealed. Of particulars we know nothing; of the general truth we are certain. God will never let drop that work in the soul, which he has taken in hand. "Now unto him that is able to do exceeding abundantly above all that we ask or think, according to the power that worketh in us, unto him be glory in the church, by Christ Jesus, throughout all ages, world without end. Amen."

THE GOODNESS OF GOD A REFUGE IN TIME OF TROUBLE.

V

IN every age, perhaps we might even say in every Christian experience, there are junctures in which it is difficult to reconcile the dispensations of providence with the goodness of God. The controversy began in the patriarchal days, and is the grand argument of the book of Job. "Wherefore do the wicked live, become old, yea, are mighty in power?" Job 21: 7. The seventy-third psalm is occupied with the clearing of the same paradox. Jeremiah, pre-eminently a sorrowful man, breaks forth thus: "Righteous art thou, O Lord, when I plead with thee, yet let me reason the case with thee of thy judgments: Wherefore doth the way of the wicked prosper?" Jer. 12 : 1, marg. The worst men are sometimes apparently happy, and the consequence is, that the believer is envious at the foolish. Enemies of God appear to him to succeed in every undertaking. Wealth flows in on them; they arrogate to themselves an exemption from all reverses, and feel insured even against providence; they fill the public eye, they build and decorate, they gather about them the gay and the revelling, they leave wealth to their children.

In the very same view, pious men are thought to be unhappy, and beyond a doubt are afflicted. Nothing is more true of them, as a class, than that they suffer. If we look at all the retinue of believers, following Christ up the steep ascent, we behold them bearing the cross, while the rugged path is marked by the blood of their feet, and their eyes are wet with weeping. They come out of great tribulation.

Under the perplexities of this contemplation, what is left for the believer in his anguish, but to seek the resort which we have been pointing out, and to search among God's awful attributes for some one which may be a solace? The name of the Lord is a strong tower. But no gate of that fortress is unbarred for our entrance, until we approach under the banner of Christ. We compass the lofty, forbidding wall, but find no crevice open for sin. Yet these characters of God are all we have. For look heavenward, and consider :—If He were ignorant or unwise, we might suffer without his knowledge, or sink in waters which he could not explore: we might be lost in mazes where his eye could not follow us, or be carried away in whirlwinds which he knew not how to quell. If he were limited in power, we might groan under the very burden which he could not lift off. If he were afar, in some pavilion beyond our system, he could not be reached by our cry of anguish when the deep waters went over our soul; and were he not here this moment, it would be mockery to pray. If he were not good, our happiness would be nothing to him, and we might have hellish pain for ever and ever. If he were not merciful, he could not care how wretched we are; and if he were not gracious, we should sink in despair, being sinners. But because he is Almighty, All-wise, All-seeing, Every-where-present, boundless, everlasting, and unchangeable, in goodness, mercy, and compassion—we have in him a refuge and stronghold, to which we may continually resort. The perfections of God afford a refuge: and in time of trouble, faith resorts to this refuge.

The perfections of God afford a refuge. Raise your eyes towards the loftiness of our stronghold. But take off the shoes from off your feet, for the place is holy ground. As sinners, you will first be arrested by a trait of Divinity. God is just. The Judge of all the earth will do right. The reverse is inconceivable. When we think of a being who can do wrong, we no longer think of God. Nothing which he does can be unjust, arbitrary, or hard. He smites down the venerable and beloved shepherd, in the very moment when his dearest earthly stays have been purposely removed. Or he overwhelms in the tide of sudden death, a mingled throng of youth and age, loveliness and crime. Shall not the Judge of all the earth do right? Hush thy insane murmurs, O worm! "Be silent, O all flesh, before Jehovah; for he is raised up out of the habitation of his holiness!" Zech. 2: 13.

We cannot imagine a motive which an Infinite Being could have to do an act of injustice. All the earth and all heaven unite in praising Jehovah as righteous. But O reader, can we climb up to our refuge by this frowning battlement! Nay, it is impregnable. If indeed we were so far freed from personal regards as to be governed in our thoughts and judgments by a sense of general equity, and respect to the honour of God, it is conceivable that we might acquiesce fully in decisions of the Most High, which should contravene our own happiness. We should then submit to naked Justice. Some urge this as the first step in a sinner's return; but the Bible knows no such refinement of abstract submission: it would, if possible, be the last and not the first step of sanctification: the mighty effort of the giant, not the infant motion of the new-born soul. Let me not for a moment be misunderstood. Submission to God's will, and that in the most absolute sense, is the duty of every intelligent creature, and is a state of mind to which the influences of the regenerating and sanctifying Spirit infallibly lead. But there is an order in the dispensation of gracious affections; and agreeably to that order it is not the first demand on an unreconciled heart that it should yield a legal submission to infinite justice, so as to be willing to endure everlasting condemnation, however righteous. Such a submission to naked justice is not to be looked for in our present state, and this for two reasons. First, because God made man a being desirous of happiness. It is a radical principle. It is God's own work. It is not one of those desires which came from the poison of the forbidden tree, but a propensity wrought into the first Adam, throbbing in the heart of the first Eve, actuating the holy pair among the trees of the garden, and appealed to, by Jehovah, in the first threat and the first promise. Let the metaphysical divine confront his God in Paradise, and say whether the propensity which is there recognized is necessarily sinful. We are unable to think of any one as a reasonable human being, who does not, in all possible circumstances, desire his own welfare. One may choose a present evil, or relinquish a present good: but it is in every case with the hope of avoiding some greater evil, or obtaining some greater good. Speculation has added to the words that are written in this book, by enjoining a chimerical duty,—that of being willing to be eternally miserable—as impossible as it is uncommanded. Suppose it proved that my individual misery for ever shall be for the greatest good of the universe, does this make me content to suffer misery, except under a hope of indemnification or relief? No: the Gospel takes away all that is earthly, but pours back all heaven into the bosom. Indeed, when we closely examine this vaunted metaphysic, it is a contradiction in terms to say that a man desires unhappiness: inasmuch as the accomplishment of our desires is happiness itself. Therefore, a total disregard of private interest or individual enjoyment is not commanded in all this volume. We are to love our neighbour as ourselves. We may then love ourselves: may? we must love ourselves: and self-love becomes sin only when it becomes selfishness. The other reason why so stoical a submission to abstract justice is not demanded in our present state is, that it presupposes an extent of knowledge more than human. Our views are so limited, that we cannot take in all worlds and systems and ages: yet we must take these in, to determine what is best, wisest and most just in the government of God. Our ignorance, therefore, joins with our self-love, with that self-love which God's finger engraved on the decalogue, and infused into the heart, to prevent our finding a refuge in the mere justice of God. We submit to it as righteous; we do not enjoy it as happiness, till we join other views of God, and catch a glimpse of full-orbed Deity in the Sun of Righteousness.

Let us descend into our experience. A sudden or a lingering anguish comes and kills my peace. I break the seal of heart-wasting tidings, or I stand by the coffin of my first-born. The Judge of all the earth will do right. This comes home to the understanding as a glorious and undeniable truth. But then it may be right that I should be wretched. God will act as a righteous King; but it may be righteous for him to make me miserable. Justice, so far from comforting, is my terror. I look up to the precipitous side of the fortress, and see the bristling weapons of vindictive law barring my ascent. It was right for the flaming sword to keep the gate of Eden. It was right for the Salt Sea to surge over Sodom, Gomorrah and Zeboim. It was right that Judas should go to his own place. It was right that the sword should smite the Shepherd when he stood for the sheep. It is right that in yonder lake the smoke of their torments goeth up for ever and ever. It may be right that this great pang should enter my heart from the right hand of Infinite Justice. Nay more, not only it may be right—but O conscience, conscience, relentless conscience, thou ceasest not day nor night to tell me, it is right—it cannot but be right! I feel it to be right. All within me rises to confirm the verdict with horrid acclamation: I am a sinner; "the soul that sinneth, it shall die." In the mere justice of God, then, I find no solace in affliction. My unconverted friend, you deny yourself all other resource. That justice I plainly see to be against me. I cannot scale that eternal wall. Justice exacts the punishment of sin; but I am a sinner. Justice exacts obedience, full, unbroken and implicit; but I have long since broken the covenant. The stripes which I endure are but the earnest of my penalty. Yet they are just stripes: they are such as it befits Infinite Justice to inflict. Wonder it is, that I have not long since been given over to the executioner. Where can I look?—in what cleft of burning Sinai can I find a refuge?

Thus it is that the attribute of Justice, viewed alone, gives no comfort, and opens no stronghold to man, considered as a sinner. And it is for this very reason, that the eye of the sufferer is directed to another quarter of the heavens. I hasten to the point indicated in the outset. When we begin to learn from the Scriptures, that God is a God of love and tender compassion; that his very stripes are awakening us to fly; that he doth not willingly afflict and grieve; that whom the Lord loveth he chasteneth; when behind the lifted rod we discern a Father's tears; and when, as being in covenant, we consider that the same afflictions are accomplished in our brethren that are in the world; that they are not by chance, but appointed with the full consent of Him who stands by the throne, and who loved us so that he died for us, and is now our Guardian, Trustee, Surety, Advocate, and Husband— when we find that he has brought us into this wilderness with an intention, and hedges up our way with preventive tenderness—the desert begins to smile; the thirsty waste seems moist with springs of water; the sandy plain appears newly clad with trees of pleasure; the "land is as the garden of Eden;" the voice of the Lord is heard among the trees of the garden; after sultry heats, the cool of the evening reveals the form of the Shepherd; he leadeth us beside the still waters. "Yea, though I walk through the valley of the shadow of death, I will fear no evil; for thou art with me; thy rod and thy staff they comfort me."

And O how suddenly can this change be wrought in the soul! Think not even a sudden death is denied these revelations. It is not sudden to him who sends it. Whether he gently unwind the silver cord or dash the golden bowl to pieces at a blow; whether the aged servant in his bed ebbs away into eternity by long decay, or welcomes his Master in some spasm of the heart; or loses his earth¹⁻ con sciousness amidst the shrieks and strangulation of shipwreck—what are these incidents? God was there; Christ was there. On this side we see corpses and desolation; on that side they see a delivered spirit, embosomed in love, entered into the stronghold and refuge.

Justice no longer appals us, when it is satisfied in Christ. It is the love, the mercy, the grace, the long-suffering, the fatherly compassion of our God, which is our citadel. "The name of the Lord is a strong tower; the righteous runneth into it and are safe." What name is this? "The Lord, the Lord God, merciful and gracious, long-suffering, and abundant in goodness and truth; keeping mercy for thousands, forgiving iniquity, transgression and sin, and that will by no means spare the guilty." This name is our strong tower; this God is our stronghold. We may take refuge in every name and attribute as in a separate chamber of our fortress. And the consolation is not confined to any specific case, but has a generality wide enough to embrace all who find the true entrance. The promise is exceeding wide, and opens its doors to all the throng of the wearied and heavy-laden.

The teaching of the Scripture is, therefore, plain: we have a refuge. The love of God, under the various names of goodness, bounty, long-suffering, compassion, mercy, and grace, is that which opens to us in our flight. Only convince a man, on gospel grounds, that God loves him, and in proportion to his faith, you make him a happy man. Let him only know the things that are freely given him of God, and he is comforted. "When, by the Spirit of God," says Luther, speaking of his conversion, "I learnt how the justification of the sinner proceeds from God's mere mercy, by the way of faith, then I felt myself born again, as a new man; and I entered by an open door into the paradise of God. From that hour I saw the precious and holy Scriptures with new eyes." He had entered the stronghold. Let a man comprehend the import of the declaration that God is good; let him think who and how great God is; what and how copious his all-sufficiency; how boundless his ability to bless; how exquisite the pleasures at his right hand for evermore; and then let him stand and wonder at the greatness of affection affirmed of such a Being, who sits at the fount of all conceivable good, creates all susceptibilities of enjoyment, and floods them with holy fulness. Let him muse on this till he has begun to conceive what God is, what God's love is, and how it must gush from this spring-head, and stream into swelling rivers of deep and spreading beneficence, of vast and awful bliss, from its sources in the heart of infinite favour; and then let him turn inwards, and shudder to behold that the object of all this is— himself. I say, let a man thus be told, and thus understand, and thus believe that God loves him— and he is a happy man: he now knows that God is a refuge.

You do not bless the afflicted sinner, I repeat it, by saying to him that God is just. Sinners also believe and tremble. The never-failing replication of his conscience is, and "because He is just, I am wretched." But when you would revive the spirit of the contrite, say to him, *God is love.* It will be a dead letter to him, unless he looks at the cross; but let him so look, and he beholds a door. Thus the solitary young monk was led in by Staupitz: "Look at the wounds of Christ," he said to Luther, "and you will there see shining clearly the purpose of God towards men. *We cannot understand God out of Christ.*" Hence the maxim of the Reformer's after years: "I cannot come near the absolute God." *Nolo Deum absolutum!* Love is the attribute which shows us most of God. Here we gaze on most of the divine effulgence. Power might be malevolent; knowledge might be distant; immensity might overwhelm; but love, essentially, in itself, is blissful, and to all around it communicates bliss. It is only as believers that we can reconcile the seeming opposites—"God is a consuming fire," and "God is Love."

The different ways in which Jehovah shows his love may have different names; but it is only the same adorable, undivided Perfection, shining in love. The rainbow that is about the throne may have its distinguishable colours, but the ray is one, and its name is Love. "For thou, Lord, art good, and ready to forgive, and plenteous in mercy unto all them that call upon thee; a God full of compassion and gracious: long-suffering and plenteous in mercy and truth." This is not tautology: it is human mind and language sinking under repeated efforts to express the inexpressible, to go around the tower of glory, and survey first one side and then another of that structure which is the centre and glory of the Church. Let men of the world consider this. Their rock is not as our Rock, even themselves being judges. Here is our city of strength, O worldlings! "Walk about Zion, and go round about her; tell ye the towers thereof; mark ye well her bulwarks; consider her palaces. For this God is our God for ever and ever: he will be our guide even unto death, Ps. 48. Or in the words of another Scripture, Jehovah is good.

In time of trouble, faith actually resorts to this refuge. The lofty gates have been open for ages, and the fugitives of all nations have been pressing in; but yet there is room. Times of trouble have not ceased from our world. In such times, we need some refuge, stronghold and solace. Every man seeks some refuge of this kind. Let a sudden blast ruffle our bay, and the squadron of small craft are instantly dispersed, each making for its little haven. The hiding-places of men are discovered by affliction. As one has aptly said, " Our refuges are like the nests of birds; in summer they are hidden among the green leaves, but in winter they are seen among the naked branches." Ungodly men being afraid of God, and feeling that they are at enmity with him, go any where else for solace in affliction. Some turn to worldly business, and buy and sell with redoubled activity; some count up the idols that remain, and plan new enterprises; some go into light company, read light books, or flutter through the dance of light amusements; some have been known to enter the sty of drunkenness. Troubles drive each one to his refuge, and each has his little retreat, his shrine and his idol, which he seeks at such times. And the child of God has his refuge, and goes into it. Above the raging of the water-floods, when all around is consternation, he hears the voice, as of a trumpet, saying from the bulwarks: " Come, my people, enter thou into thy chambers, and shut the doors about thee; hide thyself, as it were, for a little moment, until the indignation be overpast." Is. 26 : 20. And emerging from the waves, he responds: " In the shadow of thy wings will I make my refuge, until these calamities be overpast." Ps. 57 : 1. ".When my heart is overwhelmed within me, lead me to the Rock that is higher than I." "God is our refuge and strength, a very present help in trouble; therefore will we not fear, though the earth be removed, and though the mountains be carried into the midst of the sea, though the waters thereof roar and be troubled, though the mountains shake with the swelling thereof." Such cries of exultation have often risen from the ocean-waste, when God's children have been swallowed in the deep. Can I doubt that when the long-remembered steamer *President* was mysteriously crushed by the Atlantic surge, the lofty voice of Cookman, which I have so often heard with a thrill of delight calling sinners to Christ, as with the clear penetrating notes of a clarion, can I doubt that that voice was lifted above the noise of the waves, in some such strain as this: "The Lord on high is mightier than the voice of many waters, yea than the mighty waves of the sea!" And need we doubt, that in a late catastrophe, more than one sanctified spirit, even in that little moment on the deck, or struggling in the current, or locked up in those lower chambers of death, was enabled to gather itself and say, Lord Jesus, receive my spirit! The moment of death requires simple exercises, thanks be to God; the way into that refuge is direct, especially to one who has been coming to it day by day for years. The word stronghold in the text, means in Hebrew a dwelling-place, abode, or mansion. It is the same used it the ninetieth Psalm: "Thou hast been our dwelling-place in all generations." To the believer, God is not merely a retreat, but an abode; not a refuge just found out when trouble surprises, but a habitation to which he has learned continually to resort; not a temporary shelter, but a stronghold, where he dwelleth, and where he loves to dwell. "For this," says the Psalmist, "shall every one pray unto thee, in a time when thou mayest be found; surely in the floods of great waters they shall not come nigh unto him: thou art my hiding-place."

Here is a refuge to which faith actually resorts in every trouble. The heart knoweth its own bitterness; and sometimes the keenest arrow is rankling just where the stranger intermeddleth not.

Many are the afflictions of the righteous: some of the sorest are not catalogued in books, or rehearsed in sermons. Sometimes single darts wound here and there: and then again, whole communities suffer. One disaster in war, or on the ocean, directs the river of sorrow into a thousand homes. The falling of a hoary head,—that crown of glory, if it is the head of a believer, a friend, an example, a father, a pastor,—carries down with it the sorrowing hearts of a church, or indeed, as we have felt this week, of a whole Christian population. When it was whispered from one to another in our city, that a beloved father in the gospel had been translated in the night, who was there that did not feel that it was a bereavement, and that the loss was a loss of the Christian society?*

Such will be the case with all of us, in our several afflictions, if our faith resorts to God as a refuge. It is this, far more than exemption from trials, which makes life blessed. Perhaps you have been tempted to say, Blessed are the prosperous, the rich, the unhumbled! No. Asaph had some such thoughts; but when he went into the sanctuary, and took a heavenly view, he descried the end of the wicked. It was one who knew, that said, Blessed are they that mourn, for they shall be comforted. Happy are they only, who have sorrow sweetened by the divine promise. They glory in tribulation. They have storms, but they have both an anchor and a haven. Goodness cannot be manifested more clear-

* This was penned just after the death of an eminent clergyman.

ly than in a sanctifying process, however severe. Let me thus reason with such as are in trials. We have asked to be made holy. Again and again we have besought the Lord to withdraw us from evil ways, to divorce us from the rivals which seduce us; and now we hear him saying, "I will hedge up thy way with thorns, and make a wall, that she shall not find her paths: and she shall follow after lovers, but shall not overtake them; and she shall seek them, but shall not find them: then shall she say, I will go and return to my first husband, for then was it better with me than now." And, so saying, the soul recognizes the goodness of God, and faith enters the stronghold. There are thoughts in the darkened chamber of sorrow which visit us nowhere else;— important, salutary thoughts, to instruct, confirm, purify, arm, and comfort; thoughts of our sin, our selfishness, our idolatry, our worldliness, our unbelief; thoughts of the abiding joy laid up in heaven, where sickness, alarm, despair, and sin never come. And I speak the mind of all sanctified affliction, when I add, that among them all, no thought is more constant than that of God's goodness as an eternal refuge. "Thou wilt keep him in perfect peace, whose mind is stayed on thee, because he trusteth in thee. Trust ye in the Lord for ever, for in the Lord Jehovah is everlasting strength."

1. How admirable and lovely is that religion which makes such provision for times of trial! And the provision is God. We are told, not that a refuge or fortress is found in this or that consideration, but

that the name of the Lord is a strong tower. Religion derives all its graces and all its glories from its principal object. If the believer is to rejoice, it is in God. The course of our experience shows us, that every reliance sinks away from under us, and nothing sublunary can be our support. Youth, and prime, and strength soon decay. Health is one of the most precarious and perishable of our brief possessions. Wealth—I will not condescend to name it, as a solace in heart-trouble. Friends—they are blessed gifts; let us ever thank God for them, discharge our duty to them, and dwell in love amongst them: but their arm reaches but a little way; often the most that they can do is to weep with us; and ah! how soon, how rapidly do they depart! Till at length the aged disciple looks around to wonder at his own solitude; and if he sees near him so much as one of the companions of his youth, is ready to tremble at the prospect of speedy separation. Experience, I say, shows us, sooner or later, that there is no resting short of God. Tread on any ground but this, and it proves a quicksand. But oh, how rich is the possession of God's saints! The mighty God of Jacob is their refuge, and underneath them are the everlasting arms! I will never, I will never, I will never, never, never, never—such is the reduplication of the text—leave thee, nor forsake thee. Here is a heavenly tower of vast dimensions, every chamber filled with bounty, and every gate standing wide open. As the magistracy of Israel was commanded to see that the highways to the cities of refuge were kept in good repair, so that the fleeing culprits might meet with no obstruction, so it is a chief duty of the gospel ministry to facilitate the flight of all afflicted persons to the tower of strength and-consolation. O that I were able to recount and to describe the numerous instances in which I have seen the heart-broken child of God taking courage amidst redoubled calamities, in the attributes of a reconciled God! This were enough—if there were nothing else—to recommend the Christian religion to all who suffer pain, fear, or bereavement. And hence, indeed, we observe, that the followers of the Lord Jesus consist in a great degree of those who have been drawn to him by the necessities of deep affliction.

2. How serious is the question, Am I acquainted with God as a strong tower in the time of danger? It is not every one who possesses this resort—or who knows the way to it. As has been intimated, the flying of the soul to God, in times of trouble, presupposes some knowledge of him, reconciliation with him, and trust in him. The calamities of life are such indeed, and come with poignant sting to those who have no God. The bolt falls with almost crushing violence, on the man who is at ease in his possessions, and who cries in vain to his god of silver and of gold. Beloved reader, be persuaded to remember your Creator, before the evil days come. Hearken to the voice of all experience, and believe

that you will bitterly regret your impenitence and procrastination, when sudden affliction comes upon you. You cannot possibly make a better use of these halcyon days of youth, of-health and of ease, than by providing for the dark and cloudy season. God is graciously ready to welcome him who turns to him, even in the hour of his desolation, and, like the prodigal, cries, "I will arise and go to my father:" but more pleasing is it to God, and more profitable to the soul, when one amidst the sunshine of hope and prosperity, looks up and says, "Father, thou art the Guide of my youth!" Nothing is more certain, than that the days are hastening on, in which you will find these to be true sayings. Therefore, be exhorted, without delay, to flee into this everlasting tower, that you may be safe;—safe not merely from the clouds of worldly sorrow, but from the insufferable tempest of God's wrath and curse!

3. It only remains that I should beseech those who are sufferers at this time, actually and immediately to betake themselves to this refuge. Behold the Rock of your Defence! Behold in every several attribute a chamber of protection! Call to mind the lessons of your whole Christian life, with regard to the Truth, the Justice, and the Goodness of God. Even under the Old Testament, amidst many imperfections of knowledge, God's people learned to confide in him, under the heaviest strokes. Abram, Jacob, Eli, Job, David, Ezekiel, Habakkuk, have

left us their testimonial. So clear was this, that even the modern Jew, in his wanderings has lessons of resignation, which are unknown to the pagan philosopher. "During the absence of the Rabbi Meir, his two sons died — both of them of uncommon beauty, and enlightened in the divine law. His wife bore them to her chamber, and laid them upon her bed. When Rabbi Meir returned, his first inquiry was for his sons. His wife reached to him a goblet; he praised the Lord at the going out of the Sabbath, drank, and again asked, 'Where are my sons?' 'They are not far off,' she said, placing food before him that he might eat. He was in a genial mood, and when he had said grace after meat, she thus addressed him: 'Rabbi, with thy permission, I would fain propose to thee one question.' 'Ask it then, my love,' replied he. 'A few days ago a person intrusted some jewels to my custody, and now he demands them. Should I give them back to him?' 'This is a question,' said the Rabbi, 'which my wife should not have thought it necessary to ask. What! wouldest thou hesitate or be reluctant to restore to every one his own?' 'No,' she replied, 'but yet I thought it best not to restore them without acquainting thee therewith.' She then led him to the chamber, and stepping to the bed, took the white covering from the dead bodies. 'Ah! my sons, my sons,' loudly lamented their father; 'my sons! the light of my eyes and the light of my understanding: I was your father--but you were my teachers in the law.' The mother turned away and wept bitterly. At length she took her husband by the hand and said, 'Rabbi, didst thou not teach me that we must not be reluctant to restore that which was intrusted to our keeping? See, 'the Lord gave, and the Lord hath taken away, and blessed be the name of the Lord.' 'Blessed be the name of the Lord,' echoed the Rabbi, ' and blessed be his holy name for ever.'" But all Old Testament resignations and hopes are but a morning twilight, compared with the meridian faith of the Gospel. Now, we behold in Jesus, not only a Master and a Comforter, but a fellow-sufferer, a forerunner, a sympathizing High Priest. By him, as a medium, we approach our fortress; for he is the way, the truth, and the life. Not even sin can keep us away; for he has borne our sins in his own body on the tree. Come then, and drown your griefs in the sea of everlasting love! A little longer, and you shall be admitted to a nearer view of those divine excellences, which, even in distant prospect, have sustained your head amidst the billows. And, then, when fully entered into your eternal fortress, how speedily shall you forget all the trials of the pilgrimage! My beloved brethren, what we need, in order to support our fainting souls, is only a larger measure of that faith, which is the substance of things hoped for, and the evidence of things not seen; which shall make the coming eternity as real to us, as the events of the passing life;

which shall turn our doctrines and tenets respecting God and heaven, into heart-experience, and actuating motive. Then shall we abide in God, as in our tower; then shall we be encircled in his pavilion. Then shall we dwell in the house of the Lord for ever.

THE SOUL SUSTAINED BY HOPE RISING
TO ASSURANCE.

VI

IT is a very serious and interesting question, whether a believer may in this life attain to an infallible certainty of his ultimate salvation. Nor is the problem a new one. The times of the Reformation, three hundred years ago, were much occupied with this very inquiry. The finding of the genuine gospel among the old ruins of superstitious ceremonial and semipelagian dogmas, shed such a sunshine over the Christian world, that there were multitudes whose hope was so exalted as to expel all doubt. This was consolation indeed; for such a certainty of bliss was peculiarly suitable in a day when it was needful to suffer for Christ, and when martyrdoms began to reappear in the church. The reformers, one and all, testified that a man might be assured of his eventual salvation.

But this doctrine found many adversaries. It comported well with the denial of final perseverance, to deny this. The same persons were the opponents of both. In the first place, the Papists admitted no certainty concerning one's being in a state of grace, beyond what was conjectural. They even maintained that such a certainty was not desirable,

and that it tended to relaxation of morals. It would
have been more candid, if they had maintained that
it tended to relaxation of the priestly tie, and diminution of the papal majesty. For he who is assured
of God's love, and hears his remission from his judge,
will feel little concern about human absolution.
Here is a death-blow to masses for the soul's health,
supererogatory merits of saints laid up in store for
the behoof of sinners, vows, pilgrimages, humiliations, indulgences, and universal monkery. There
is no need of these to one who has the peace of God
shed abroad in the heart.

There were other adversaries of triumphant
grace, and they set themselves to deny assurance.
The old Arminians (in this differing very much from
the modern Wesleyans) united in holding that it
was neither laudable nor useful to be placed above
doubt. They admitted a conjectural certainty, or a
conditional certainty, but none that was real. For
how can they who admit the danger of falling from
a state of grace have any assurance for eternity?
They may fall away to-morrow. They may fall
away under the next temptation. They may make
shipwreck in the very haven, and lose Christ after
they have become speechless in death.

It suited well with a slavish and legal system to
deny the possibility of assurance. Having no knowledge of a method of grace, and the ingenuous, grateful, willing service which is rendered by a renewed
soul, they dreaded ever to let the convinced come
from under this yoke of bondage. They were sure

that the moment he was sure of escape from hell, he would disobey; that there could be no Christianity, save under the lash. The effect of such a scheme is apparent, to a melancholy degree, in the character of many estimable, and of some great men. A remarkable instance is that of the celebrated Dr. Johnson. It would be difficult to point out a more gloomy record of experience, than that which is contained in his religious meditations and diary. These extend through a period of forty-six years. They are solemn, affecting, and undoubtedly sincere. But they lack one thing, and that all-important, namely the idea of free salvation by Jesus Christ. Dr. Johnson had learned that all assurance was enthusiasm. He knew no motive but fear. He is perpetually lamenting over sin, but never cherishing a sense of pardon. Almost until his latest hours, he was in bondage through fear of death. He never willingly allowed conversation in his presence to turn on this painful subject, and sometimes repressed it with his characteristic and boisterous indignation. Now how far did this absence of that assurance (which he so strenuously denied to be possible) tend to the development of Christian character? Let us read, amidst his lamentations over lost time, and his petty fasts and austerities, the record on his fifty-sixth birth-day, Sept. 18, 1764. "I have now spent fifty-five years in resolving, having from the earliest time almost that I can remember, been forming schemes of a better life. I have done nothing." It is pleasing to find reason for believing, that in the close of life, Dr

Johnson opened his mind to some more gracious views of the plan of salvation. His error with regard to the certainty of final glory, is the error of thousands, who maintain the same scheme of partial grace.

In opposition to all this, the doctrine of the Reformed Theologians has uniformly been, that there is an assurance of God's love, which may be attained in the present life: and it is the nature of this assurance which we shall now in the first place consider.

The word rendered *full-assurance*, is one of striking import. It carries with it the idea of fulness, such as of a tree laden with fruit, or of a vessel's sails when stretched by a favouring gale. It is unwavering conviction, persuasion which defies all doubt, and expectation rising to certainty. And it stands distinguished from a conviction and persuasion of any or all the propositions of revealed truth, as involving an application of that truth to our own proper case. The former is called the *assurance of faith;* the latter (of which we are treating), *the assurance of hope*, and sometimes the full assurance of hope. Heb. 6: 11. As faith unfolds into hope, so the assurance or highest measure of faith into the assurance or highest measure of hope. They therefore often coexist; yet they are distinguishable. The assurance of faith is the acme of unwavering and undoubting confidence that the revealed propositions are the very truth of God;—a persuasion so firm, as to be the basis and resting-place of all Christian reliance. It is saving faith carried to its height.

It sees Christ, and believes in him. The Assurance of Hope is a settled, unshaken, well-grounded, immovable persuasion and certainty, that I, as an individual, have thus believed; that I am in Christ; that God is my reconciled Father; that I shall never come into condemnation; and that my heaven is secure. The former is a universal duty; the latter is a gracious privilege. One is possessed by every believer; the other is a sovereign gift to a part of the flock. By one, I believe that God is true; by the other, that he is my God. By the one, I see Christ to be an almighty and a willing Saviour; by the other I am assured that he will save me in particular. By one, I lean on Christ as my only and all-sufficient supporter; by the other, I am made certain that I have actually done so, and hope without wavering that I shall eternally rejoice in him. One is opposed to unbelief, the other to despondency. One connects with Christ; the other reveals the connection. They stand to one another as the blossom to the fruit; or as the deed to the possession; or as the sentence of acquittal, to enlargement from restraint. One may coexist with many fears; the other casteth out all fear. "The work of righteousness shall be peace, and the effect of righteousness, quietness, and assurance for ever." Whether saving faith, by its essential quality, would not necessarily result in assured hope, provided such faith were only great enough in degree, is a question which would lead us into niceties of disquisition, which at the present time we may profitably wave. That the two have a perceptible difference, must appear from what has been said; and we are thus far enabled to gain some glimpse of the nature of full assurance. But we may look still more nearly at the subject, in a series of particulars.

1. This state of mind is peculiar to true believers. It is possessed by no others. There are, indeed, powerful persuasions in the minds of some;—presumptions which may outlive the pang of dying, and knock at the very gate of heaven, and be repulsed only by the Master's word, *I never knew you.* There are counterfeits of all that is precious; and Satan is the grand artificer of simulated good; and herein is one of his chief devices; and enthusiasm may show elations and raptures more heady, vociferous and boastful than humble faith. But the hollowness and falsity of such impressions must not be allowed to accomplish Satan's purpose, of cheating us into the opinion that there is no genuine assurance. God is able, not only to renew a soul, but to give an infallible persuasion that it is renewed.

2. The assurance which we are inquiring for, is not a supernatural revelation of new truth. Inspiration can unquestionably thus communicate; but in the wise and wonderful economy of grace, inspiration has ceased. Here it is that enthusiasts and fanatics have gone astray. They have shut out all exercise of reason in this matter, all examination of evidences, and sometimes all grounds of Scripture; and have relied on visions, trances, dreams, voices, and bare impressions. Nothing is more immovable than their convictions. Argument is vain: that

which came in without reason, cannot be driven out by reason. They are a Scripture unto themselves In vain do you ask their evidences. They know because they know. And it is important to say thus much upon this delusion, lest any should mistake the path to real gospel comfort, and seek it as a direct, special, immediate, heavenly manifestation, unconnected with the general exaltation of the life of God in the soul. True assurance is after all founded on the recorded Word.

3. The Assurance of Hope rests on the promises of God. It is allied to faith; nay, it grows out of faith. Where there is no faith, it cannot exist; and it increases with the increase of faith. It results from a firm, unshaken trust in God's gracious declarations. To see ourselves accepted, we must previously "see the things that are freely given us of God." As it is the open view of gospel promises of free salvation through Jesus Christ, which first brings us into vital union with our Redeemer, so it is the further application of the same promises to our own case, the seeing of ourselves as included in them, which gives us the joy of assurance.

4. The assurance that we are in the favour of God, is connected with the existence of Christian evidences in our hearts. It is to a certain extent founded on these. There are some who, in their zeal for grace, and for the efficacy of faith, go so far as to discard all examination of evidences, as legal. They declare, that all true gospel-comfort is to be obtained by a simple looking at the word of prom-

ise, and a bare, undoubting faith, without any reflex consideration of what Christ has wrought in us. Now I trust that the tenor of this whole volume is such as makes it superfluous to say, that I attribute all faith to the word of promise, and all justification to faith; yea, that it is.this simple, direct, instant faith, to which I would vehemently exhort every unconverted sinner. This is what a sinner must do, to be saved; and what a saint must do, to abide in Christ. But it is a very distinct matter, when the question is, "By what means shall a soul know that it is born of God?" It is a new case, when the anxious inquiry is suggested, "How shall I ascertain that this experience, of which I am conscious, and which I call faith, is the very faith of God's elect?" And it is no derogation from the justifying and saving power of naked faith, to agitate the inquiry, "May I employ the fruits of holiness within me, to confirm my persuasion that I am born of God?" It is agreed on all hands, that faith is the beginning of a transformation in the soul; a series of new principles, habits, and actions; that this work is wrought only in God's people; only by a divine influence; and that certain virtues, graces, or states and acts of the soul, are denominated the fruit of the Spirit. These things, I say, we are agreed in. It is as undeniable, that results of this kind are patent and palpable, within human cognizance, subject to our consciousness, and susceptible of comparison with the Word of God. No one will refuse to admit, that the presence of these graces is demonstrative of regeneration. He who has these fruits, has the Spirit, is born of God, is a new creature. Now is any one hardy enough to declare, that while the presence of such exercises is conclusive evidence of a gracious state, the believer is not suffered to look at them? Must his eyes be bandaged in regard to that which affords conviction of his being saved; that, moreover, which is always with him, in his own bosom, a part of himself? Yet this extreme position must be maintained by those—and such there are—who deny the value of gracious evidences, in regard to our estimate of our own relation to the covenant. That this is not the ground of justification, we all admit. That this is not the sole ground of assurance, will appear in the sequel. That the search among experiences may be carried too far, so as to produce despondency, and so as to supplant direct acts of faith by those which are reflex, is freely acknowledged. Nevertheless, we must maintain, that the Holy Spirit may and does employ those graces of which he is the author, as the marks of his own work, and thus as means of assurance.

This appears to be expressly stated in not a few passages of Scripture. Thus the presence of the spiritual influence is a mark of being in Christ. 1 John 4 : 13, "Hereby we know that we dwell in him, because he hath given us of his Spirit." The effectual leading of the same Spirit is a mark of grace. "As many as are led by the Spirit of God, they are the sons of God." The existence of brotherly love and obedience is a like testimonial: "We know that we have passed from death unto life, because we love the brethren. Let us not love in word, neither in tongue, but in deed and in truth. And hereby we know that we are of the truth, and shall assure our hearts before him. Beloved, if our hearts condemn us not, then have we confidence towards God. And he that keepeth his commandments dwelleth in him and he in him."

We must despair of establishing any point by Scripture citation, if these passages do not prove that the examination of the heart and life is a legitimate method of arriving at serene and satisfactory views of our own state. And I should not have spent a word on the opposite opinion, if it were not a morbid growth from a genuine branch of Christian doctrine—an abuse of the precious truth, that in seeking justification, the eye of the soul should be directly fixed on the Lord Jesus Christ.

5. It might be naturally inferred, from what has been said, that the full assurance of hope is the accompaniment of elevated piety. If graces are evidences of a renewed state, then where there is little grace, there can be little evidence. Where the divine work in the soul is faint, the evidences must be obscure. It would contradict the whole economy of holiness, if high joys and triumphs of assured love were granted to lukewarm and grovelling religion. The exaltation of divine exercises in

the soul is, therefore, the brightening of evidence. And we have little cause to wonder that we have so little assurance, when we look within, and discover that we have little faith, little love, and little self-denial. We are prepared, therefore, to expect that in producing assurance of God's love, it will be a part of the Holy Spirit's work to exalt the piety of the heart; to lift up the graces so as to bring them into view; to kindle the affections to a visible and palpable glow; and so to multiply the fruits of holiness, that old things may pass away, all things become new, and every habit and act afford a testimony of the new creature. This is in truth a part of sanctification. By making us more holy, God makes us more assured. Our religion becomes more profound, more vital, more energetic, and so more undeniable. The doubts we now have would be speedily dispersed, if we were rapt in the transport of heavenly emotions. A stronger faith would carry us away, as on the wings of the wind, towards the object of our soul. A coal from the altar, brought to our lips by seraphic hands, would purge our iniquity, and enkindle our hopes. The work of the Holy Ghost, therefore, in awakening, and multiplying, and deepening Christian exercises, tends directly to create just so many evidences of the new nature, and to give assurance of God's love. Increase of grace brings increase of security; and thus the danger of licentious presumption is avoided.

C. But is there not, over and above this, a distinct and direct influence from on high, promoting the assurance that we belong to Christ? We rejoice to think there is. It is possible to conceive of a high state of gracious affections, without any reflex acts, that is, without these affections being used by the individual as tokens of his acceptance. In his character as Paraclete or Comforter, the adorable Spirit has been pleased to pour joys directly into the soul: not independently of experience, but over and above it, giving hope; "for patience worketh experience, and experience hope, that maketh not ashamed, because the love of God is shed abroad in the heart by the Holy Ghost given unto us." The witness of our own consciousness of change is something; but here is a greater and a better witness. "The Spirit beareth witness with our spirits, that we are the children of God." It is a heavenly seal until the day of redemption. It is a heavenly earnest of the future possession. It may sometimes operate upon the mind to quicken its faculties, so as to discern the correspondence between the experience and the word. But inasmuch as all grace is from a divine agency, I see no reason why we may not admit an immediate operation on the soul itself, producing this persuasion as its immediate result, and overflowing the heart with a sense of heavenly love. In whatever way this result is attained, it is to be firmly held that it proceeds from the Author of all good, and is accompanied with the higher exercises of piety.

7. This consideration, that the assurance of God's love stands among a cluster of holy gifts, and that it

bears some proportion to the degree of holiness in the soul, effectually shuts the door against one great objection. If assurance is the fruit of holiness, then licentious, carnal ease is something spurious. Some may urge that a great motive to exertion is removed, when we take away the fear of eventual shipwreck. God may use fear, even servile fear, as a means of stimulating his people; but this is not his usual manner. There is a keener stimulus than the fear of falling: it is the mingled agency of faith, and hope, and gratitude, and love. He who is surest of the crown, will not be the first to trample on it. He who is certain of meeting Christ, will not be most ready to insult and grieve him. Paul was never more prepared for labour and endurance, than when he said: "I know in whom I have believed;" and when he exulted, "I am persuaded that nothing shall separate me from the love of God which is in Christ Jesus."

In what has thus far been said, we have answered the question, as to the nature of full assurance, and have discovered that it is attainable. There is a second inquiry, which will now be made easy, so as not to detain us long. It is this. Is assurance of personal salvation essential to saving faith? Some have maintained the affirmative, and have taught that no man can be a regenerate person without knowing himself to be such. But the negative is clearly the doctrine of Scripture. Bearing in mind the distinction already suggested, between the assurance of faith and the assurance of hope, you will readily perceive that one may have a justifying faith without any necessary reference to the question, whether he is himself regenerate or not. And inasmuch as any the least degree of faith is justifying, as uniting the soul to Christ, you will as readily perceive that faith may apprehend Christ, when as yet it falls far short of that which produces assured hope.

Some truly good men, making their own lively experience too much the rule and criterion for others, have taught that saving faith is a belief that Christ died for me in particular. But the grave defect of this hypothesis is, that there is nothing like it in the Bible. Indeed the highest and most seraphic faith may be so absorbed in the great object, Jesus Christ, as to lose all regard to self, or even its own salvation. Saving faith is not a belief that I have saving faith, but a belief in Christ the Saviour, and a receiving of him as offered in the Word; a holding of the recorded offer to be credible; and a setting-to the seal that God is true. The delightful inference, that I am a saved soul, may be true—may follow logically from the truths believed, and my act of believing—may, therefore, in some sort, be involved in the proposition, I believe; and yet it is no part of that faith which is saving. The Bible nowhere enjoins it as such. It is a happy fruit of faith. But some will ask, Can so great a change take place without the subject being conscious of it? We answer, no. The subject is conscious; but something more than his consciousness is needful to assure him. He knows there is a change, but is it *the* change? We are asked, Can it be possible for a prisoner to be loosed from such a bond without knowing it? We answer, Peter was released by an angel from prison, "and went out and followed him, and wist not that it was true which was done by the angel, but he thought he saw a vision." So it may be with the emancipated soul.

The Scripture seems to teach that this certainty of renewal may follow the renewal itself. Eph. 1: 13, "In whom ye also trusted, after that ye heard the word of truth, the gospel of your salvation; in whom also, after that ye believed, ye were sealed with that Holy Spirit of promise, which is the earnest of our inheritance until the redemption of the purchased possession." Here, you will observe, the sealing is separated from the believing, by an interval of time. If, as we have seen, this assurance is connected with active growing graces, as evidence, it is natural to believe, that those may be faint and dim, in their earliest stage. God has nowhere given this as an indispensable criterion. Let us not offend against weak or desponding brethren, by making that weakness and despondency a token of wrath. Let us not break the bruised reed, by decreeing, beyond our authority, that every one who doubts of his salvation is the enemy of God. How many of Christ's faithful servants would be cut off, by such a rule? The safer opinion is, that a man may be truly regenerate, and yet have doubts in regard to his personal acceptance.

But while this is true, it is not less true, that such a state of doubt is a most undesirable state. It is not the healthful condition of the soul; nor the condition in which pious affections are most in exercise. It is a valley through which the Christian may journey, but where he cannot willingly dwell. He may wait long for this dayspring from on high to visit him: yet there is provision made for his enjoying it; and he should never rest without it. Surely it is not a matter of indifference, whether I am an enemy or a child; whether, if I die to-day, I drop to hell, or rise to glory! If it be possible to escape from such a region of clouds and darkness, it should be attempted; and we should use all diligence to the full assurance of hope: it is the desire of the apostle and the precept of the Word. Heb. 6: 11.

It is so signal a prize, that it claims the intense and concentrated effort of every power, through every moment—" all diligence." By what means it should be sought, might be inferred from what we just now learned, as to the way in which this assurance rises in the heart. It is the fruit of faith. Would you have assurance? Be sure that you have faith. Is it as yet too weak? Let your prayer be, "Lord, increase our faith!" How is faith to be cultivated? Plainly by converse with the object of faith; by looking unto Jesus; by dwelling more on him than on ourselves; by going out of ourselves, to fall into his arms. More definitely, as the promises of Scripture are the vehicles by which Christ is offered to us, it is the contemplation of these promises which brings him into our believing hearts. These are called "exceeding great and precious promises, that by these ye might be partakers of a divine nature." Those who have had most abiding assurance of God's love, are those who have been most in meditation on the written assurances of that love. It is in the study of authentic and valid title deeds, that we are most certain of our rights. The great propitiatory work, above all, is the object which should be held before our eyes, for the removal of doubts and fears.

It is further to be considered, that a low condition of piety is not the soil for this amaranthine flower. Sorrow and tribulation cannot blight it: but it withers under the sunshine of worldliness. Professors who take their pleasure in this life do not seek it, and do not find it. In chambers of disease and mourning, on death-beds, at the stake, or amidst the wild beasts, it has risen to exultation. In the days of primitive piety, it seems to have been enjoyed by all the martyrs. God was pleased to vouchsafe it, as an indemnity for all they surrendered. In our day of half-way Christianity, when the children of this world are mingled with the children of light, it is less prized, and less freely bestowed. If we had higher graces, we should have more assurance. In a better day, when the universal Christianity shall shoot up to a loftier stature, it will reappear. And wherever among the throng, any shall rise to superior eminence in holiness, his melting heart, fused into a flow of tenderness and love by the heavenly ray, will experience the pressure of this pledge and seal. I will venture the suggestion, that cold and formal churches will produce, among their members, a rank crop of weeds, in the shape of manifold distrusts and fears and doubts; and that the graces of individual saints will be most joyful, when the collective body shall be warmed through and through. Let a whole church be lifted up, in renewed faith, and love, and zeal, and cross-bearing, and earnest labour, and these doubts will give way to assurance. Such a church is in a state of revival. Such churches ours might be, and ought to be. Let Him who dwelleth between the cherubim shine forth; and in his light we shall see light.

It is scarcely reasonable to expect this blessing amidst prevalent sin. If we would know what hinders it, in our own particular case, we should inquire into our unmortified sins. There may be some latent root of bitterness; there may be some temper indulged within us repugnant to forgiveness, meekness, and brotherly love; there may be some cross which we refuse to bear; some indulgence which we will not crucify; some duty which we shudder to attempt. In the attempt after universal holiness, the unspeakable favour is to be expected.

But since assurance is, after all, the gift of God, to whom shall we go but unto Him? It is the operation of the Comforter. And if we, being evil, know how to give good things to our children, how much more shall our heavenly Father give his Holy Spirit to them that ask him? "Ye have not because ye ask not. Ask, and ye shall receive." Make this great attainment a separate object of deliberate choice and fervent effort. Till you are no longer able to live without it, you will not use that diligence, that instant zeal, that importunity, which takes no denial, that agonizing struggle that wins the prize.

It may come to your window, like a hovering dove, with the "olive-leaf plucked off," at some moment when weakness and confinement shall make you prize it more than you do now. This angel of peace may draw your curtains, at dead of night, amidst tossing and weeping, and bring to you that white stone, in which is written the mysterious new name. You may, peradventure, remember these things, in some time of unexpected anguish. Our voyage is not exempt from tempestuous weather. You may see no tokens of it at present. Your seas are in the glassy calm of summer. You are listless in regard to these assurances of God's love. But I seem to behold a change of scene in the future. Years have gone by; comforts have become fewer; clouds have gathered; fears are in the way. You are embarked upon troubled waters. The ship is now in the midst of the sea, tossed with the waves, and the wind is contrary. You have been long in this turbulent state, for it is the fourth watch of the night. But one approaches in the moment of extremity, walking on the sea. O, troubled soul! cry not out for fear; hearken to the well-known voice: "It is I; be not afraid!" In such an hour of sorrow, bereavement, temptation or doubt, the visits of assuring love are beyond all price.

Defer not the attainment of some reasonable confidence until your day of peril. In a world so frail and precarious, it is well to live fore-armed. The sudden blow of the messenger of death may so stagger and benumb your powers, that amidst the languor or the consternation, you may find no good time to put these precepts into practice. And yet, at what moment can full assurance be so valuable as at the moment of death? Thanks be unto God, he sometimes grants it in that moment! When flesh and heart fail, his strength is near. Yes, we have seen the dying visage lighted up with the angelic smile of triumph, and have heard the song of rejoicing from lips already cold. A preternatural glimpse of worlds beyond has been granted even here. Hear the eminent theologian, Andrew Rivet, just before his departure: "I shall shortly no more know the difference between day and night. I am come to the eve of that great and eternal day, and am going to that place where the sun shall no more give light. The sense of Divine favour increaseth in me every moment. My pains are tolerable, and my joys inestimable!" Hear the dying Halyburton: "For those fourteen or fifteen years I have been studying the promises; but I have seen more of the book of God this night than in all that time." Hear good President Finley: "I am full of triumph—I triumph through Christ. Nothing clips my wings but the thought of my dissolution being prolonged. O that it were to-night! My very soul thirsts for eternal rest!" "Have you any doubts, my dear friend?" asked a pious woman of a mother in Israel,* well known in this city, who had been speaking of her sins. "O no," she replied, "I have no more doubt of going to my Saviour than if I were already in his arms. My guilt is all transferred: he has cancelled all my debt; yet I could weep for sins against so good a God." How beautiful an illustration of what was said, that the highest assurance does not relax the moral sensibilities or promote connivance at sin.

There is something inexpressibly beautiful in the Christian old age of one who, having long since committed all to Christ, has set down to wait till his change come. It is, indeed, a land of Beulah. And when such a one, by gentle degrees, approaches the term of life, how fair the spreading prospect beyond. Let me represent his exercises, in the words of a gifted believer: "This river has been a terror to many; yea, the thoughts of it have often frighted me; but now, methinks, I stand easy. my foot is fixed upon that on which the feet of the priests that bare the ark of the covenant stood, while Israel went over this Jordan. The waters, indeed, are to the palate bitter, and to the stomach cold; yet the thoughts of what I am going to, and of the conduct that waits for me on the other side, doth lie as a glowing coal at my heart. I see myself now at the end of my journey; my toilsome days

---
* Mrs. Graham.

are ended. I am going to see that head that was crowned with thorns, and that face that was spit upon for me. I have formerly lived by hearsay and faith, but now I go where I shall live by sight, and shall be with Him in whose company I delight my self. His voice to me has been most sweet, and his countenance I have more desired than they that have most desired the light of the sun."

The reader may justly be exhorted to "use all diligence," for the prize is great. To seek it is to seek eminent holiness. Look for it in the employment of those means which cause one to "grow in grace and in the knowledge of our Lord and Saviour Jesus Christ." "And the very God of peace sanctify you wholly; and I pray God your whole spirit, and soul and body, be preserved blameless unto the coming of our Lord Jesus Christ!"

REST IN GOD

VII.

THE true rest of the soul is God, and towards this it is perpetually tending, even when it knows it not, which gives us the reason why so many, indeed the people of the world at large, are constantly wandering from pleasure to pleasure, unsatisfied with any. They have not yet found their true centre, even though they may be gravitating towards it. Any thing which deserves the name of rest they have not yet attained. And yet, by an instinct of nature, men seek for rest, and include it in every idea which they ever entertain of consummate happiness. The philosophers who, without revelation, tried to discover truth, avowed it as their object to arrive at the supreme good; and this always comprised tranquillity and ease. But they knew not how to reach it; their end was right, but they had no means. They stood gazing at a prize upon the summit of an inaccessible mountain. They knew that what they wanted was repose, but how to attain this they knew not. It was reserved for revelation to make known the great mystery.

Deeply impressed with belief that many of those who will read these pages are wandering from the true rest, I would here call on them to return, by setting before them a genuine repose, which the world cannot prevent or effectually interrupt. Christianity affords true consolation. It is to find this, to catch its lineaments, and to present its portrait, that I now ask attention. Many there are who feel that the world has disquieted them, who long for something better, but know not whither to look. "Come unto me," says Christ, "*I* will give you rest." Not the rest of stupidity, or apathy, or inaction; but that which arises from the absence of all disturbing causes. It belongs to true Christians; no others can lay claim to it. There is no way to attain it but by the Cross. It is altogether different from the world's peace, yet it is real and unspeakably delightful, and thousands in earth and heaven have possessed it. No treasure of gold suddenly discovered could so enrich you as to come to the possession of this secret of happiness. I therefore claim your attention when I endeavour to set forth that rest or Christian repose in God to which you are invited to return. May God enable us, while we meditate, to understand and to attain it! I propose, first, to show what Christian tranquillity or spiritual rest is, in several particulars; and, secondly, to distinguish it from some counterfeits which bear its name. If, in conclusion, the reader shall be urged to seek it, let me bespeak his earnest attention. Spiritual Quiet of soul is founded on knowledge of God, faith in Christ, a tranquillized conscience, a weakening of the sinful principle, submission to God, trust in his promises, and holy contemplation of the supreme excellence, as offered for the communion of our spirits. It is the more important to say this, because the perversion of a great truth has led some into error on this very point, and a *Quietism* has been proposed, in various ages of the church, which is as inconsistent with man's mental constitution as with the provisions of grace.

1. *Spiritual Quiet is founded on knowledge of God.* It is a quality of sublime objects to bring the soul into repose. Deep waters are still. It is little things which agitate and excite us. There is something soothing in what is grand and soul-absorbing. In the presence of the ocean, the cataract, the volcano, or the starry heavens, we feel subdued and are silent. Thus also the thought of GOD, the sublimest of all ideas, instead of driving us to frenzy, calms the mind. Even on the sick-bed, when the irritable and too sensitive texture can scarcely bear any thing that is awakening, the thought of God rises upon the soul, as dewy morning rises on the earth, after a night of clouds. It brings refreshment and repose. We never reach any place wherein to lie down in safety, till we come to God. This is the continent and terra-firma: all other resorts are but as shifting sands. If men did but know it, they would give heed to that inward tendency which perpetually leans towards the abiding, the infinite, the absolute; that is God. Every day worldly men live, they find the ground slipping from under their feet; every day their hold

on this world becomes less; as the sands in their glass are fewer, they learn that their pleasures are so likewise; they are as far as ever from that resting-place on the summit of the mountain to which they looked forward. The truth is, the habit of seeking pleasure in excitement has become too strong for them: they cannot live in any other element. Hence we daily see men of business disappointed: they retire from the active concerns of life; they go into the country; they seek repose among friends and books. Ah! they have not discovered that the rest which they seek must be within. Nothing earthly can give them rest. Happy are they, who, at this stage of their experience, are led to think of GOD. This is the grand idea which fills and satisfies the soul. This reaches cravings, which every thing else does but tantalize. To learn to know God, in his true scriptural character, is to gain a secret of mental repose, which transforms the whole character. But here an obstacle arises in the way: I am a sinner. How can a sinner approach to God? Which leads me to observe:

2. *Spiritual Quiet is founded on Faith in the Lord Jesus Christ.* The more our knowledge of God in his absolute glory, the greater must be our dread, and the wider the gulf of separation, until we are made acquainted with the mediatorial door of access. Though God is, in his nature, the true rest of the rational creature, there is no returning to him as our rest, but by the Lord Jesus Christ. By faith we come to him, and by faith we abide. The

first actings of faith are more like resting, than any thing else: the word well expresses the recumbency of the soul on God. A sinner who has long been wearying himself with every kind of self-righteous labour, at length gives up in despair, ceases from his own works, abandons his own righteousness, and receives and rests upon Jesus Christ, as he is offered in the gospel. He throws himself into those open arms. Immediately there ensues a tranquillity never known before. Being justified by faith, he has peace with God. Some would judge of the reality of conversion, by the amount of bustling activity, and disposition to stir and labour. I would rather, at this stage, look for repose of soul, and quiet acquiescence in the plan of salvation, as one which renders every effort at self-justification superfluous. The first believing tends to calmness of spirit, and in every subsequent period of the Christian life, it is believing that must restore this calm, after interruptions. Relying on God's pardoning mercy must tend, if any thing can, to bring the heart into a state of rest. It removes at once the grand source of perturbation, namely, dread of God as an avenging Lawgiver. To say that a man believes in the Lord Jesus Christ, is to say, that he consents to be saved freely by the Saviour's righteousness: and he who does so, needs look no further, but dwells secure as in a citadel: "He that believeth shall not make haste." He has found his home: he rests.

3. *Spiritual Quiet proceeds from Peace of Con-*

science. If you have not been seared as with a red hot iron, you know the agitation produced by remorse; and if you have had much conviction of sin, you know that there can be no settled quiet, while this internal enemy rages. Only carry these agitations to their highest degree, and you produce the anguish of the damned. How can a man be at peace, with an evil conscience? Even amidst his pleasures, it utters its penetrating cry: and all within him asserts his guilt and condemnation. There is but one cure for this malady, and that is the blood of the Lord Jesus Christ sprinkled upon the conscience. The figure is derived from the Levitical ordinance; where the offender, after offering sacrifice was sprinkled with the blood, and went home satisfied that his guilt was taken away. "Purge me with hyssop, and I shall be clean: wash me, and I shall be whiter than snow." When faith has approached the altar, and laid its hand on the head of the expiatory lamb, the Holy Spirit of God performs a work on the soul, which in sacrificial language is called the sprinkling of Christ's blood. It is such an inward application of the work of Christ, as convinces and persuades the soul, that its justification is complete, that guilt is removed, and that God's anger is taken away. And this persuasion tends to gentle repose. As when on a bed of sickness, the patient is suddenly relieved from parching fever, with its heat, its thirst, its watchings, its indescribable restlessness (apt image of a sinful state), and finds himself bedewed with the bland tokens of convalescence: even though feeble, he delights in the change, and lies still in the consciousness of peace, willing like an infant to yield himself to the almost voluptuous calm: so the sinner, when first he feels the security of being reconciled, leans on the bosom of his Lord, and returns to his rest.

4. *Spiritual Quiet is promoted by the Mortification of Sin.* Sin is the sole cause of all the discord, perturbation, and misery that there is in the universe. The Holy Spirit begins at regeneration a work which is to end in extirpation of all sin: but it is not accomplished in a moment. Regeneration is the beginning of sanctification; and sanctification consists in some good measure, in the gradual destruction of evil principles, which in Scripture is compared to the putting to death (mortification) of a human body, by a violent and painful process, like that of crucifixion. In carrying on this process, the sanctifying Spirit is by the same means promoting purity and promoting peace. It was sin that produced the disorderly commotion; it was sin that tore the heart; it was sin that let loose all the fierce winds of passion to howl tempestuously over the unregenerate mind. If you catalogue the causes of your discontent, your restlessness, your excitement, your feverish fretfulness, you will find the names to be such as these: Pride, Hate, Envy, Revenge, Anger, Lust, Covetousness, Fear, Inordinate Affection. Till these caged wild beasts are driven out of the soul, there can be no quietness: sanctification drives them out. Therefore, the more a man advances in piety, the

more his inward tranquillity ought to increase. The day grows calmer, as the sun draws near its setting; hence the sweet radiance which we sometimes behold playing about the cottage of Christian old age; where the gentle breezes that open a way for themselves among the autumn-clusters, in the cool of the day, betoken the peace that is within.

5. *Spiritual Quiet is favoured by Submission.* The first law of religion is submission: "Thy will be done;" and where it does not exist there is no piety, and just as truly there is no tranquillity. What a hideous sight to see a human creature in full rebellion against God's providence; repining at his allotments; fighting against his dispensations, and cursing his judgments! But it is not more sinful than it is wretched; and hell is not only wickedness, but woe: the wickedness makes the woe, or rather is the woe. The true recipe for miserable existence is this: Quarrel with Providence. Even in the smaller measures of this temper there is enough to prevent tranquillity. And hence, when God means to make us happy, he teaches us submission—a resignation of every thing into his hands, and an acknowledgment that whatsoever He does is wisest and best. O how sweetly even afflictions fall when there is such a temper to receive them! "Shall we receive good at the hands of the Lord, and shall we not receive evil?" "Why should a living man complain, a man for the punishment of his sins?" Such dispositions tend to stillness of soul; and even amidst chastisement there is internal quiet.

6. *Spiritual Quiet is furthered by Trust in God.* How large a portion of our anxious perturbations arise from forebodings of future evils! Could we expel sinful fear from our souls, we should be happy. But who can destroy this monster? God only; and he graciously accomplishes it by shedding trustfulness over the mind, like oil over the waves. This is altogether different from the blind, unfounded, presumptuous assurance of the future which characterizes many persons of sanguine temperament. It is a covenant blessing. Trust is belief of God's promises. Those who wander about in the world, without any reliance on divine promise, are orphans, and call for our commiseration. The believer has assurances for a great while yet to come. His filial relation to God makes him look on the future with new eyes. Whatever may befall him, one thing is certain, nothing can come but what God ordains. " All things work together for good to them that love God." His life is insured. In proportion to his strength of trust is he raised above all those vexatious apprehensions which men of the world experience. In his happier hours he is enabled to put in practice his Lord's direction, and to cease taking thought for the morrow. We should all be more composed if we could do so. The opposite temper is destructive of all peace, and of much usefulness; and if we would reach the higher attainments in piety, we must make up our minds to banish for ever the habit of musing on future and possible ills How serene and balanced is the soul which has so

fixed itself on God as to feel satisfied that all his dispensations are part of a matchless plan for its good!

7. *Spiritual Quietness consists, in a great degree, in Holy Contemplation and Communion with God.* I know how strange a dialect this must seem to the children of this world; but we stand not before their tribunal. As we believe the delights of paradise consisted not so much in tilling the garden, which was the vocation and outward business of man, as in the viewing the Creator in all his works, and in gazing up into his face of love: and as, in the renewed Eden of heaven we know that the blessedness of saints will be much in the beatific vision of Divinity, so here, also, in our journey to Canaan, we are persuaded that a leading part of our Christianity consists in the contemplation of God's excellencies, and in fellowship with the Father and with the Son, through the influences of the Holy Spirit. We were made for this intercourse, and there is no higher exercise of human faculties. Moses knew this, when he made it his great request: "Show me thy glory!" But what it chiefly behooves me to observe is, that this exercise of soul, so high, so hallowed, so acceptable to God, is far from being stormy and impetuous, but is transacted in the profoundest depths of the soul's silence. It is when the hum of life has ceased, is shut out, or is forsaken; at midnight—beside the ocean, on the mountain top; on our knees, or prostrate on our faces; that we yield to those sublime and unutterable thoughts. In the lives of Augustine, Edwards, and Brainerd, you will

learn more than I can teach of this wisdom. It doth not strive, nor cry, nor lift up its voice in the streets. It is bent not so much on public works, however useful, as on the hidden work of the heart, which none can see but God. It seeks retirement, and even solitude, though not to the neglect of incumbent duties. By such means as these God may be served worthily, and even gloriously, by the infirm man and the shrinking woman, who cannot so much as stir out of their chamber, or who, peradventure, never leave their beds. For it is a work of silence and tranquillity. It shuns the glare of day, and the observation of men; and even this very feeble account of it suffers from being made amidst a world to which it stands so much in contrast. For nothing can be more uncongenial with the peace of God than the busy, hurrying, loquacious, self-seeking spirit of earthly employment. I fear not to say this, as believing that there can be no danger, in any infusion of contemplative religion which we can possibly make, into the habits of our age and country. Between the slavish toil of business, the ardent fever of covetousness, the madness of ambition, and the foolery of fashionable amusements, which has at length descended to the toys of harlequin, and the provocatives of the licentious dance; among all these causes of excitement there is not much danger of an over-attention to inward and spiritual work. A few there will still be who, in remote spots, will commune with God, and antedate the enjoyments of heaven.

Having dwelt thus far on some of the sources of spiritual quiet, I would now, in order to rescue it from misapprehension, point out some notes of discrimination, with a passing view to certain counterfeits: for, like all that is precious, it has not failed to have its imitations.

1. *The calmness of the Christian is not stupid ignorance.* Men may be quiet for want of knowledge; as we frequently see exemplified in the case of the vulgar and illiterate, and more particularly in the savage, who, after the gratification of his appetites, subsides into a state like that of the cattle reposing in the pasture. Phlegmatic temperaments readily give way to such tranquillity, which is slumber rather than calm. But we must not mistake. The blessing of Christian peace which Christ confers on nis disciples, is not a negative condition; still less is it to be ascribed to dulness or emptiness. It increases with knowledge: the more truth, the more quietness. Knowledge of the truth is its very foundation.

2. *It is compatible with high mental activity.* This is the more important to be said, because there have been some, chiefly in the Church of Rome, but with imitators among Protestants, who have placed the highest spiritual exercises in such a rest of soul, as excludes all intellectual exertion. The soul so rests in God, as no longer to think. It forgets all things, and turning inwards is absorbed in one pervading idea of rest in God. This is what has been called *Quietism*. But this is delusion, against which

one can hardly protest with too much earnestness. God has never meant the glory of man, his reason, to be excluded from the noblest exercises of religion. The quietude pretended, in which all mental activities are swallowed up, would be less like the sublime condition of an intellectual being, than the vacancy of childhood or the imbecility of age. It might be accepted as relief from pain, but could not be chosen as the means of happiness. That state in which the soul neither thinks nor wills, is not a heavenly state. In true spiritual quiet the mind chooses to be at rest. It is not the calm of stupor, as when one lies in a lethargic sleep, but the rest of the wearied labourer in his beloved home. The rest of a soul in God, though infinitely removed from the agitations of the world, and its conflicting and distressing reasonings, is, nevertheless, a state in which the thoughts are active: seeking after God, apprehending him, appropriating and enjoying him. The seraphs that adore and burn, are intellectual creatures; and we conceive of the saints in heaven as knowing, learning, and putting forth those mental exertions, which tend to the perpetual advancement and expansion of their powers. A heaven in which there is no intellectual activity would be no heaven for a rational creature; and it is a gross, though common abuse of the term rest, to apply it to a drowsy, listless, unimproving eternity: though heaven is a rest, it is neither a dream nor a sleep.

3. *The rest of a pious soul in God is not inconsistent with active service.* Even in heaven, as we

read, "his servants shall serve him." They shall have fit employments there, labour without weariness; and the best we can do in this world is to imitate their activity. The controversy between the contemplative and the active life has been very earnestly waged; and able arguments have been urged on both sides. One party has been for spending the whole life in angelic meditation: the other has made all piety consist in going about and doing good. The tendency of the middle ages was to the contemplative, of this our nineteenth century to the active life; and each in extremes. The days of hermits and anchorets, like those of the Thebaid; of monks, and nuns, pretending or endeavouring to mortify the flesh, and live in continual silence, grief and vision of God, have passed away. We have fallen on days in which there is such a bounty on haste, energy, and fruitful toil, that avarice robs God of his sabbath, drives its gainful wheels seven days in the week, and busy mortals can scarcely find time to read and pray, or to bless their families. But the active and the contemplative coincide in the religion of the gospel. Its divine founder spent whole nights in prayer to God, in deserts and mountains; but his days were active—"he went about doing good." The rest, to which you are invited, is not the mere absence of bodily motion. It is a more refined idea. It is even consistent with active labour, of any virtuous kind. The pious soul is never more at rest, than when most busily engaged in appropriate external duties. True Christianity does not cut off such duties: this was the error of times when thousands of thriftless persons forsook the plough and the loom, and thronged in pilgrimages and into cloisters. Spiritual quiet of soul coexists with lawful activity, and sanctifies it. No man has therefore any right to make his religion a cloak for idleness, whether in church or state.

4. What is still more surprising, *Christian rest may be maintained amidst trials and suffering.* Here it distinguishes itself from any thing which the world calls by its name. Worldly persons have their enjoyments; but they are dependent on worldly things, and when these are broken or removed, the tranquillity ceases. It is the glory of true religion, that it can be firm and serene amidst storms of change. In days of prosperity, when all things smile, it is easy to maintain quiet of soul: but when skies grow dark, when friends are few, when health fails, when losses and bereavements and old age come on, and misfortunes thicken every hour—to be tranquil then—to feel that all is safe—that the real portion has not been touched—that God is still the same, and that he is ours; this is what cannot be comprehended by the man of the world, or by the formal professor. And yet it is true, and is exemplified in a thousand cases of distress and consolation. Were it not so, such songs as the forty-sixth psalm had long since been blotted out of the psalter, as containing idle falsehood: whereas, generation after generation in the church for nearly three thousand years has been singing with experience and triumph: "Therefore will not we fear, though the earth be re-

moved, and though the mountains be carried into the midst of the sea: though the waters thereof roar and be troubled, though the mountains shake with the swelling thereof." If you would see the true victory over the world, visit the experienced Christian amidst his trials. At the first he may indeed be shaken for a little season in order that he may the better feel the solid foundation under his feet: but at length he finds his footing on the Rock of Ages, and can cry, "Lo! this is our God; we have waited for him, and he will save us: this is the Lord; we have waited for him, we will be glad and rejoice in his salvation." Seeing, therefore, that such causes of agitation will and must come, it will be the part of wisdom to prepare ourselves with the means of inward quiet: and what means are these, but that which our subject points out? The lesson is not to be learnt at once, nor without some severe discipline · our trials are intended to teach it. The moment is a joyful one, when it is acquired. The Psalmist seems to have been thus led to the utterances of the hundred and sixteenth psalm. It was the performing of his vow and the expression of his thankfulness. He had been in no common adversities; he had felt the need of rest: "The sorrows of death compassed me, the pains of hell gat hold upon me, I found trouble and sorrow." But in his affliction he cried to God, and with success. "The Lord preserveth the simple; I was brought low and he helped me: Return unto thy rest, O my soul, for the Lord hath dealt bountifully with thee!" It was the sense of God's mercy to him in affliction, which led him to return to God as his rest. That is blessed affliction which has this result. It is the property of trials, to show men where their refuge is. If, in hours of sadness, we lean on an arm of flesh, or seek comfort from earthly gains, diversions and excitements, it proves us to be carnal; if, on the contrary, every cloud of trouble only makes us more determinately seek our heaven in God's nature and promises; and if we never love and prize his covenant of redemption, more than when we are smarting under his rod, it affords us good reason to think that we have been renewed in the spirit of our minds. But even true believers have much yet to learn, and often need to be exhorted to return to God. In proportion as they wander, they lose their tranquillity of mind; though for a time they may not know the reason; they only know that they are disquieted. At length, some heavy, sudden blow awakens them from their worldly dream, and they look around in wild alarm for the God and Father whom they have neglected. Then they begin to discover that the soul has no rest but in God, and feel their need of returning to this.

Many persons are sufficiently persuaded of the world's unsatisfactoriness, but have taken no steps towards the supply of their great want. You, let me say, are the very persons to whom religion ought to be welcome. It is the very repose you need. In vain do you weary yourselves, to procure rest by any other means. It is not in the creature

You were made to repose in God. You deny your souls their chief blessing, while you remain alienated from him. And how strange is the illusion which prompts your delay! Your procrastination is a putting off of the happiness which you might be beginning to enjoy, and which would be always the greater during your whole existence, for your having begun now. Are there not moments when you are almost disgusted with life? when your pleasures have no longer any zest? when compunction more than neutralizes your joys? when, in a word, you feel your need of God? Though there is nothing necessarily holy in these sentiments, they bring you nearer the borders of a religious life; they should be seized on, as so many promptings to fulfil your grand obligation. Do you ask me what I would have you to do? The answer is easy, and it is momentous. Return to your rest. Return, return! O wanderer, you are in the wrong path. Every step takes you further away. Never can you supply these cravings, or quell these perturbations, but by coming to Him, who is the Infinite Portion and the Everlasting Rest. That wearied, vexed, and pained head requires a pillow. Is it not time to rest? Have you not pursued long enough the vanities of the world? Are you willing to be for ever repeating the old experiment, with the same resulting disappointment? Shall not the increasing cares of life teach you to seek consolation? When you were younger, you thought, perhaps, that wealth would give you tranquillity: now that you have attained it, you find the care of it as perplexing as the acquisition. Or if still in the turmoil of worldly business, you need but an hour of serious reflection to make you sure that neither this, nor aught like this, can insure your peace. The voice still cries, "Return." The Father whom you have abandoned in your sin and folly is still willing to receive you—to see you at a distance—to fall upon your neck and kiss you. The way of return you know, for you know Him who saith, "I am the Way, the Truth, and the Life." In this view, how can we ever be thankful enough for the truth, that Jesus Christ is the most accessible being in the universe! He is ever standing within his door of mercy, ready to throw it wide at the first and feeblest knock. He does not wait for us to ask leave to petition, but says to us, Ask—seek—knock! It is his province to give the weary rest, and to conduct to the Father for that purpose. There is no other way, and if you are seeking others, you are wasting your time, and laying up disappointment. What shall you do to gain this desired repose? Let me hasten to tell you. Dismiss all other concerns, which you can intermit without sin, and devote yourself to this. What would you do, if your estate were balancing on a point—if your life were in jeopardy? You would forsake all, for this one thing. Is any thing more precious than your soul? Is any thing longer than eternity or greater than God? The charge which we have to bring against the children of this world is, that in respect to religion, they turn their backs on all the safe maxims which regulate their actions in lesser things. If a man's property is endangered—if his investments are insecure—if his house is dilapidated—if his business is unproductive—if his family is diseased—these, or any one of these secular troubles engrosses his attention. He turns his mind upon this single point as his great study. He is not content to consider it now and then, in intervals of business, when other persons speak of it—when some friend urges it upon him;—I mean to say he does not treat this great worldly topic as you are habitually treating the salvation of your soul. No! He broods over it. He sets apart time for it. He takes advisement on it. It becomes his fixed idea, in his house and by the way; it retires with him; it awakens him in the night; it rises with him; it hangs over him as a cloud, and darkens all his prospect. The feast is no longer joyful; the cup no longer exhilarates; the music has no melody, and day no sunshine, till this importunate, haunting anxiety is satisfied and dismissed. And let me assure my readers, just so, *just so*, will you be affected, if at any time the care of your soul shall become an object of pursuit as really as your earthly interest now is. You have possibly seen a man so unsettled, as to let his business, health, and family go to destruction, while in his infatuation, he has left all to chance, and thrown himself away. Precisely thus you are doing with your soul. Is it not so? Do you ever bestow on this transcendent interest one hour of sober planning? And yet you complain that you cannot attain to rest! Pursuing your present course, it is certain you never will. O be persuaded to consider and to return! When shall you begin? Now! This moment! The path, though infinitely important, is, in respect to time, short.

CHRISTIAN JOY EXPELLING THE DISTRESSES OF THE SOUL.

VIII.

THE blessed Spirit of God is wont to destroy evil principles in the heart, by implanting such as are good; to wean the affections from the world, by attaching them to heaven; and to take away the sense of great trials, by shedding abroad the love of God in the heart. This mode of operation is obvious. If we can be made glad, our sorrows pass away; and to say that any one rejoices, is to say that he has full consolation. If, therefore, the most inveterate case of suffering, in a forlorn old age, could only be visited by the smiles of God's countenance, no more would be necessary, in order to entire relief.

In looking at little children—those delightful objects to which Christ has condescended to direct our eyes—we cannot fail to be struck with their joys, and to contrast them with the pleasures of after years. In their gambols there is the ebullition of a gladness, that is unsought, unfeigned, and heartfelt. Very different are the mirth and excitement of more mature life. After the natural elasticity of youth is gone, men try every mode of artificial stimulation. But with all their endeavours, there are dregs at the bottom of their most foaming cup. Their best excitements are the short-lived flame of some light, transitory material. May not the appeal be made to every reader? As you go on in life, you find, disguise it as you may, that the susceptibility for high pleasures is abated. You discover yourself to be grave, when all around you are in laughter. You are ready to judge austerely of the hilarity of youth, and to wonder how they can be so enchanted with a bubble, when, forsooth, your own bubble is only larger and heavier and duller. Now and then you pause before some scene or object, which, twenty years ago, set all your pulses in motion; you are loth to confess it, but all within you is dead. In vain do you endeavour to reproduce the romance of your childhood; to rekindle the fire among your embers; to restore the faded colours on the canvas. Your eye fastens itself on the long procession of departing youthful joys, growing smaller and dimmer in the distant perspective. The truth is, earthly joys are every day diminishing, and the susceptibility of pleasurable excitement from earthly causes grows less and less, with the decay of natural sensibility. This would be a melancholy truth, if we had no resource but terrestrial things, and no world but this. But thanks be to God, there are susceptibilities which do not grow old, and capacities which increase with exercise. And while earthly excitements lose their power, those which are heavenly grow stronger and stronger. Hence, an old age without religion involves the loss of both worlds.

There is no class of words more abundant in the Scriptures than those which express the varieties of joy. And this affords a new proof of God's infinite benevolence, that he has made it our religion to be happy. In calling us to leave the world, he is only calling us to heaven. In exhorting us to believe, and hope, and love, he only summons us to that harmony of the powers, which tends to their most blissful exercise. And hence, in the tender and affecting discourses which the Lord held with his disciples after the Eucharist, he principally speaks of the Indwelling Comforter, as the Author of their promised happiness. Having promised them peace, his own peace, he goes on to promise them joy, even his own joy. "These things have I spoken unto you, that my joy might remain in you, and that your joy might be full."

We may consider, first, the beginnings of this joy, in those who are effectually called; secondly, and as our chief topic, the progress of joy, in the habitual walk of God's people; thirdly, in few words, the power of joy to overcome earthly troubles; and, finally, the unspeakable blessing of joy on the bed of death. And, as we proceed, it should be our prayer, that even careless and worldly readers may be led to see that there is here a pearl of great price, for joy whereof, a man might well sell all that he hath, to make the purchase; which may God grant!

"Joy is a delight of the mind, from the consideration of the present or assured approaching possession of a good." Religious joy is the same delight of the mind, as caused by religious good. It is a fruit of the Spirit, and is, therefore, called joy in the Holy Ghost. It is the subject of our meditations for a little time.

I. *Early Joy* demands our attention. There is a joy which is altogether new, at the time of conversion. "We joy in God, through our Lord Jesus Christ, by whom also we receive the atonement." The degree of this heavenly gift varies exceedingly, with diversities of character and dispensation; but where God gives faith and hope, he usually gives some joy. You, who now peruse these pages, call to mind that day of rejoicing, when God gave you the garment of praise for the spirit of heaviness. It was emerging from the troubled delirious dream of a long illness. Doubtless there are those also who can remember great joys, seasons of exultation, when the day broke, and the dayspring arose in their hearts. Let us not doubt or condemn those whose experience does not altogether tally with this, or make that a test of piety which Christ has not made such; but let us, nevertheless, be thankful, that God does communicate these tokens of favour. And let those who seek God's face, and desire the light of his countenance, look forward to this, as a blessing which is not too great to be asked. These tranquil pleasures cannot be fully represented by earthly emblems, not even by the calmest vernal day, or the most glassy seas. There are many concurring sources of this joy. There is, for example, the exulting transport of escape. Shall the rescued mariner exult when he stands dripping upon his rock among the fragments of a shipwreck? And shall not the rescued sinner rejoice, when God has freely pardoned all his sins? There is joy in safety. There is joy in feeling for the first time in life that one is in his true orbit, moving in his right direction, and with powers engaged agreeably to their intent and creation. There is joy in opening the eyes on new heavens and a new earth; in joining the band of new companions; feeling the pressure of their ardent hand; catching the enthusiasm of fellowship, and wandering onward in paths strewed with mercies, and overshadowed with graces, and clustered over with fruits of benignant love. There was joy in the outburst of gratitude, and joy even in the tears with which you bedewed the sacred feet of Him who raised you in his arms, and freely forgave you all. But, having now touched on the beginning of joys, I reserve for another head of remark, those manifestations which are common to both.

II. *Joy in Progress* is next to be considered. It would be a great blessing, even if it ceased: but it goes along with the believer. Its source is perennial. It is *His joy*. It is his joy which "remains in them." The spiritual Israel have all drunk of that Spiritual Rock, which follows them, and that rock is Christ. It is a part of that communion in grace, which the members of the invisible church have with Christ, partaking of the virtue of his mediation; first in their renewal, and then in these blessings which manifest their union with him. Thus united, they have communicated to them, even in their life, the first-fruits of glory with Christ, as they are members of him their head, and so in him are interested in that glory which he is fully possessed of. As an earnest of this, they have some measure of joy. Hence, when we hear of conversions at Antioch, we read, "And the disciples were filled with joy and with the Holy Ghost." Acts 13 : 52. The difficulty here is to keep within bounds. Through the tender mercy of our God, the sources of religious joy are almost as numerous as the parts of religion itself. Among such a wilderness of delights, we must be brief, and must classify a little. The joys, then, of the believer, may be arranged in a threefold division. For they may be those which come home at once and directly to his own private happiness—or they may be those which he receives through the happiness of others—or they may be those which come from his new-born interest in the glory of God; exulting in God, and in the accomplishment of his will.

1. The joy of a Christian heart is sometimes the joy of *knowledge*. To the stupid uninquiring mind, this seems strange: yet even to the natural intellect the acquisition of light brings ecstasy. Hence the enthusiasm and self-martyrdom of scholars and discoverers. Think you any sensual pleasure ever equalled that of Archimedes, when he hung over

the theorem from which only death could tear him; or of Franklin when he touched the pendant key, and gave the spark which opened a new world to science? Who can picture the transport of early philosophers, or inquiring Jews, when they first welcomed the great Christian revelations? The truths which are common-place to us, were to them the very lights of heaven. There is sweetness in the acquisition of knowledge, especially of religious knowledge. God's word is sweeter than honey and the honeycomb. With a meager revelation, compared with ours, David could sing: "I have rejoiced in the way of thy testimonies, as much as in all riches;" and "I rejoice in thy word, as one that findeth great spoil;" and "thy testimonies have I taken as a heritage for ever: for they are the rejoicing of my heart." This will be yet more apparent, when it is considered, that in the august and glorious character of God, the believer has an object of knowledge, which infinitely surpasses all others, and is indeed all-comprehensive. The prayer of every saint will be that of Moses: "I beseech thee, show me thy glory!" We must include in this, the serene enjoyment which is experienced in the contemplation of the Divine Excellence, when intellectual acts are lost in the devout vision of Him whom angels worship. Here are pleasures which have in them nothing selfish, and which may even leave far behind all respect whatever to our own personal interest. God himself is the happiness, the joy, the life of his people. "This is eternal life, to know thee, the only true God, and Jesus Christ, whom thou hast sent."

2. Thus we are imperceptibly led to the joy of *communion*. The bond of connection is Christ. Through him we have access to the Father. He is continually approachable at the mercy-seat. Faith beholds him, devotion cleaves to him, love enjoys him. The disciple can rejoice that God is a reconciled Father, and that nothing can separate from his love. After union by the covenant, each separate attribute becomes a source of delight; and he rejoices in the very being of Jehovah; that he is, and such as he is. "The Lord reigneth, let the earth rejoice!" And when there is added to this, the unparalleled exhibition of divinity, in the plan of grace, and the blending of all God's perfections at the cross, nothing further need be added. God himself, I say, is the Joy of saints. They "rejoice in the Lord," and "glory in the Holy One." Is. 41. "I will greatly rejoice in the Lord, my soul shall be joyful in my God: for he hath clothed me with the garments of salvation, he hath covered me with the robe of righteousness, as a bridegroom decketh himself with ornaments, and as a bride adorneth herself with her jewels." Is. 61:10. This is a joy which remains, as Christ's gift, with his people, as long as the covenant of peace remaineth.

3. The *Joy of Worship* is but a step removed, and is common to all believers. It is in worship, that these exalted views of God are obtained. Meditation may lay the wood and the offering: but devo-

tion kindles the fire of the altar. To pray to such a God, so beheld, is to rise in joyfulness towards heaven. To praise him, under any true apprehension of his excellency, is joy unspeakable and full of glory. Employ this, beloved, as a test of Christian character. To the unrenewed mind, prayer is always a task, if not a burden; it may be performed, but it is never enjoyed; a needful remedy, perhaps, but not a refreshment or a delight. But if the testimony of your heart is, that prayer is among your chosen comforts—if your closet is a beloved refuge—if you feel the loss or interruption of this intercourse to be a cross and a trial—if even sometimes your affections overflow and your heart flows out towards Christ: then, my prevalent thought is, that you are a child of God, and an heir of grace. The hypocrite will not always pray. It is worship which makes the joy of Sanctuaries. When the whole congregation rises in prayer, and the united, respectful, adoring, exulting exercises of many souls goes along with the voice of him who leads; or when all voices of a great assembly send up the sound of psalmody, without the exception of a single organ that has the capacity; then are granted moments, long to be remembered, as an antepast of heaven. Here is the great attraction of God's house, which caused the psalmist to cry (Ps. 43 : 3) : "O send out thy light and thy truth; let them lead me: let them bring me unto thy holy hill, and to thy tabernacles: then will I go unto the altar of God, unto God my exceeding joy," or more literally, "unto God the gladness of my joy." And it is predicted, as part of the glory of a latter day, when foreign tribes shall take hold of God's covenant, I will bring them "to my holy mountain, and make them joyful in my house of prayer." Is. 56 : 7.

4. *The Joy of a new nature* is too important to be omitted. It is the misery of the wicked that he is an instrument out of tune; and the discordant strings are so many nerves, vital and sentient, and carrying anguish to the centre of feeling. But when the harp is new-strung; when the hand of grace moves over the harmonious chords; when the consciousness of the sanctified heart testifies that unity and love are at least preluding the choral joys of heaven, it is a breath of Heaven's health. Conscience, being pacified, allows the affections to rise and mingle in their strength. Every good thought, feeling, word, or work, is accompanied with such a measure of complacency as may consist with humility and penitence. " Beloved, if our hearts condemn us not, then have we confidence toward God." 1 John 3 : 21. Then it is that the believer can add: "We are in him that is true, even in his Son Jesus Christ: this is the true God, and eternal life." 1 John 5 : 20.

5. Then follows the *Joy of Possession*. There can be none greater than when the soul can say, "My Lord and my God;" "my Beloved is mine, and I am his;" "I know whom I have believed." This is not merely to know God, but to know him ours; to behold his perfections ranged on our

part; to enter into his fulness and partake of his love. Then the heart finds its true, inexhaustible portion, for which it was made, to which all its capacities are suited, and which will constitute its eternal heaven. " Whom have I in heaven but thee? and there is none upon earth that I desire beside thee." Ps. 73 : 25. "Far be it from thy servant (says Augustine) who confesseth to thee, O Lord, far be it from thy servant to rejoice in any other joy, so as to make it his happiness! For there is a joy which is not given to the wicked, but to those who serve thee freely, of whom thou art thyself the very joy. And the true happy life is to have joy towards thee, concerning thee, on account of thee;* this it is, and not another." Or in the words of a modern saint :† " Offer up thyself wholly to Him, and fix the point of thy love upon his most blessed increated love; and there let thy soul and heart rest and delight, and be as it were resolved and melted most happily into the blessed Godhead; and then take that as a token, and be assured by it that God will grant thy lovely and holy desires. Say, 'I am nothing, I have nothing, I can do nothing, and I desire nothing but ONE.'" These higher exercises may be wanting, and yet true piety may exist.

6. To these modes of renewed emotion must be added the *Joy of holy Excitement.* Man was not made to be stagnant. The sails are for the breeze, and for progress. There is no Castle of Indolence in all our goodly land. There is no languid happi-

* Gaudere ad te, de te, propter te.   † Leighton.

ness, no lethargic Christianity. He who would steer clear of all excitement may as well bid adieu to the coasts of joy, which is the highest excitement. The stream of human passions is admitted into a new channel, but it runs full. There is enough in gospel motives to carry the tide to its utmost. Scripture expressions lead us to think that it was so in the early day. "These things," said Christ, "have I spoken unto you that your joy might be full,"—a sentiment echoed thirty-three years after by the beloved disciple: "And these things write we unto you that your joy may be full." 1 John 1: 4. The powers must be on the stretch, in order to give the highest joy. The muscle must be in action, or suffer. And hence a life of Christian activity is the greatest means of enjoyment. Christ's chief joy is not for the couch, unless, indeed, it be the couch of weakness or pain sent by Him; and then suffering in all respects takes the place of action. "They also serve who only stand and wait;" but Christ's chief joy is in the conscious putting forth of grace; when the soul can say: "I know both how to be abased, and how to abound: I can do all things through Christ which strengtheneth me." Phil. 4:12.

In speaking of the height to which joyful Christian experience may rise, even in this life, it is allowable to adduce one or two instances from the recorded exercises of eminent Christians in different periods of the church. But we must do this with a caution premised. These attainments are unusual and extraordinary, and are not to be regarded as common to all believers. The consideration of them should not dishearten those disciples who have been called to walk in lowlier paths. The genuine faith of God's elect may exist without these raptures. Yet they serve to magnify the love of the Spirit, and to show how rich the effusions of grace may be when the sovereignty of the Giver so decrees.

The first instance which shall be cited is that of the learned orthodox and pious John Flavel, a man every way remote from credulity and superstition. In a treatise of his on the soul of man, he gives the following narrative, which, though in the third person, has always with justice been considered to relate to himself: "I have," says he, "with good assurance this account of a minister, who being alone in a journey, and willing to make the best improvement he could of that day's solitude, set himself to a close examination of the state of his soul, and then of the life to come, and the manner of its being, and living in heaven, in the views of all those things which are now pure objects of faith and hope. After a while, he perceived his thoughts begin to fix, and come closer to those great and astonishing things than was usual; and as his mind settled upon them, his affections began to rise with answerable liveliness and vigour.

"He, therefore, while yet master of his own thoughts, lifted up his heart to God in a short ejaculation, that God would so order it in his providence that he might meet with no interruption from company, or any other accident, in that journey, which was granted him; for in all that day's journey he neither met, overtook, nor was overtaken of any. Thus going on his way, his thoughts began to swell and rise higher and higher, like the waters in Ezekiel's vision, till at last they became an overflowing flood. Such was the intention of his mind, such the ravishing tastes of heavenly joys, and such the full assurance of his interest therein, that he utterly lost sight and sense of this world, and all the concerns thereof, and for some hours knew no more where he was than if he had been in a deep sleep upon his bed. At last he began to perceive himself very faint, and almost choked with blood, which, running in abundance from his nose, had discoloured his clothes and his horse, from the shoulder to the hoof. He found himself almost spent, and nature to faint under the pressure of joy unspeakable and unsupportable; and at last perceiving a spring of water in his way, he, with some difficulty alighted to cleanse and cool his face and hands.

"By that spring he sat down and washed, earnestly desiring, if it were the pleasure of God, that it might be his parting-place from this world. He said, death had the most amiable face, in his eye, that ever he beheld, except the face of Jesus Christ, which made it so; and that he could not remember (though he believed he should die there) that he had once thought of his dear wife or children, or any earthly concernment. But having drunk of that spring, his spirit revived, his blood stanched, and he mounted his horse again; and on he went, in the same frame of spirit, till he had finished a journey of near thirty miles, and came at night to his inn, where being come, he greatly admired how he had come thither; that his horse, without his direction, had brought him thither, and that he fell not all that day, which passed not without several trances of considerable continuance.

"All this night passed without one wink of sleep, though he never had a sweeter night's rest in all his life. Still, still, the joy of the Lord overflowed him, and he seemed to be an inhabitant of another world. The next morning being come, he was early on horseback again, fearing the divertisement of the inn might bereave him of his joy; for he said it was now with him as with a man that carries a rich treasure about him, who suspects every passenger to be a thief. But within a few hours he was sensible of the ebbing of the tide, and before night, though there was a heavenly serenity and sweet peace upon his spirit, which continued long with him, yet the transports of joy were over, and the fine edge of his delight blunted. He, many years after, called that day one of the days of heaven, and professed he understood more of the life of heaven by it than by all the books he ever read, or discourses he ever entertained about it. This was, indeed, an extraordinary foretaste of heaven for degree, but it came in the ordinary way and method of faith and meditation."*

To this may be added an account which Presi-

* Flavel's Works, fol. vol. i. pp. 501, 502.

dent Edwards gives of some remarkable manifestations of divine favour to himself: Attention is asked to those exercises of placid delight, for this reason among others, that the subject of them was no less eminent as a philosopher than as a Christian, and was versed in discriminating between what is false and what is true in religious experience.

Writing of his early religious life, he says: "Holiness, as I then wrote down some of my contemplations on it, appeared to me to be of a sweet, pleasant, charming, serene, calm nature, which brought an inexpressible purity, brightness, peacefulness, and ravishment to the soul. In other words, that it made the soul like a field or garden of God, with all manner of pleasant flowers; all pleasant, delightful, and undisturbed; enjoying a sweet calm, and the gentle and vivifying beams of the sun. The soul of a true Christian, as I then wrote my meditations, appeared like such a little white flower as we see in the spring of the year; low and humble on the ground, opening its bosom to receive the pleasant beams of the sun's glory; rejoicing as it were in a calm rapture; diffusing around a sweet fragrancy; standing peacefully and lovingly, in the midst of other flowers round about; all in like manner opening their bosoms to drink in the light of the sun. There was no part of creature holiness that I had so great a sense of its loveliness as humility, brokenness of heart and poverty of spirit, and there was nothing that I so earnestly longed for. My heart panted after this, to lie low before God, as in the dust, that I might be nothing, and that God might be ALL; that I might become as a little child." And again; "Sometimes only mentioning a single word causes my heart to burn within me, or only seeing the name of Christ, or the name of some attribute of God. And God has appeared glorious to me, on account of the Trinity. It has made me have exalting thoughts of God, that he subsists in three persons; Father, Son, and Holy Ghost. The sweetest joys and delights I have experienced have not been those that have arisen from a hope of my own good estate, but in a direct view of the glorious things of the gospel.

"Once, as I rode out into the woods, having alighted from my horse in a retired place for divine contemplation and prayer, I had a view that for me was extraordinary, of the glory of the Son of God as Mediator between God and man, and his wonderful, great, full, pure, and sweet grace and love, and meek and gentle condescension. The grace that appeared so calm and sweet, appeared also great above the heavens. The person of Christ appeared ineffably excellent, with an excellency great enough to swallow up all thought and conception; which continued, as near as I can judge, about an hour; which kept me the greater part of the time in a flood of tears, and weeping aloud. I felt an ardency of soul to be—what I know not otherwise how to express— emptied and annihilated: to lie in the dust and to be full of Christ alone; to love him with a holy and pure love; to trust in him; to live upon him;

to serve and follow him; and to be perfectly sanctified and made pure, with a divine and heavenly purity." *

All that has been urged might be summed up in the statement, that Christian joy is produced by whatsoever brings Christian principle into life and action; and holiness gives happiness in its very exercise, which may suffice, in regard to those joys which come home directly to the believer's private happiness. But in the progress of his joys, we arrive at others, which are reflected, or which rise out of sympathy with fellow-men. Christianity is not insulated. No man is regarded by the Master, or should regard himself, as having a separate interest. "Look not every man on his own things, but every man also on the things of others." Phil. 2 : 4. Hence a new class of joys spring up beyond the selfish circle. "Rejoice with them that do rejoice." Rom. 12 : 15. If I am rightly affected, that which brings good to my brother brings good to me. And as a large part of Christianity consists in acts of benevolence, every one of these is a means of joy. If we would be happy, we must love. We must do good and communicate. The man who, like his Master, goes about doing good, walks in a path perhaps of some sorrows, yet of more joys than any other on this side heaven. See how remarkably this was the source of Paul's comforts. He could not be happy, unless men were saved, so he presses truth on the Philippians (2 : 16), "that I may re-

---

* Edwards's Works, Ed. 1844, vol. i. pp. 21, 24.

joice in the day of Christ, that I have not run in vain, neither laboured in vain." And, in the same strain, to his beloved Thessalonians (1 Thess. 2 : 19): "For what is our hope, or joy, or crown of rejoicing? Are not ye in the presence of our Lord Jesus Christ at his coming? for ye are our glory and joy." The more we enlarge the circle of our benevolence, even until it take in the whole race of man, the more do we widen the field of our enjoyment; it is an extension of the sentient surface. It may, it must bring its pains, but it brings pleasures which the luxury of the worldling has never surmised. Every cup of cold water given to the thirsty—every helping hand offered to the weary—every tear shed over the desolate—every almsgiving to the worthy or visit to the dying—every page of the gospel sent to the ignorant—and every word whispered to the fainting, come back with a returning wave of joy to the soul which by grace has originated them. Nowhere, however, is this sympathetic communication so delicate or so quick as in the mystical body. The web is a texture all alive to the electric current. God has so framed the structure of his people, that there is no insulation; 1 Cor. 12:26, "that there should be no schism in the body; but that the members should have the same care one for another. And whether one member suffer, all the members suffer with it; or one member be honoured, all the members rejoice with it." Do we, brethren, so rejoice? The more we increase, therefore, in philanthropy and brotherly-love, the more will our joys increase, until, at length, we shall find nothing extravagant in the strong expressions of Paul, concerning the Corinthians (2 Cor. 7 : 13), when he thus alludes to the good news he had from them: "Therefore we were comforted in your comfort; yea, and exceedingly the more joyed we for the joy of Titus, because his spirit was refreshed by you all." The reason our joys are few is that our love of brethren is small.

There is still in the progress of Christian happiness a class of joys which are more directly for *God's sake;* when we rejoice in virtue of our connection with God, feeling as children for the honour and interests of a father. How can it be otherwise? The son and subject has now exchanged his own poor little interests for those of God. The filial spirit has come in. The spirit of loyalty has come in. The kingdom of Christ has swallowed up other regards. He would gladly suffer all and spend all for Christ's crown and covenant. And hence his joys, both of hope and possession, take their colour from the rising of Christ's standard in the world. This was felt in ancient days, even by the children of the captivity, at the waters of Babylon, when they said (Ps. 138 : 6): O Jerusalem, "if I do not remember thee, let my tongue cleave to the roof of my mouth; if I prefer not Jerusalem above my chief joy." "The zeal of thy house" (said the Psalmist and said the Messiah) "hath consumed me." In Christian days, the love of Christ's kingdom leads to high exultation at its increase; when one sinner repenteth there is (Luke 15: 10) joy among angels; when multitudes are saved, shall there not be joy among men? Where a minister of the gospel is a regenerate person, this is one of his records: "I have no greater joy" (said the aged John) "than to hear that my children walk in the truth." And it is a happiness which may rise to unusual heights, under great successes, as when Paul exclaims (2 Cor. 2 : 14), "Now thanks be unto God, which always causeth us to triumph in Christ, and maketh manifest the savour of his knowledge by us in every place!" This makes cheerful energetic labour, and sheds a holy oil on every wheel: for as Nehemiah said (8: 10): "The joy of the Lord is your strength." It is a joy which must brighten, as years roll on, bringing new and augmented evidences of Christ's advance to triumph over all his enemies; when the latter psalms shall be the significant and appropriate hymns of the Church, and the voice shall be (Ps. 149): "Let Israel rejoice in him that made him; let the children of Zion be joyful in their King; let the saints be joyful in glory; let them sing aloud upon their beds." We have thus considered, in a very imperfect manner, the progress of Christ's joy, as communicated to his people, in their progress toward the everlasting rest.

III. For a third topic, let us bestow a few moments on *Joy amidst Sorrows*. This is at once the most extraordinary and the most welcome part of the doctrine. Ancient fable tells us of a stream which passed through the salt sea, and reappeared in Sicily, without losing its freshness: but here we have a joy which flows unchanged through the midst of troubles. It may be a paradox; but if there is any thing undeniable in Christian experience, it is this. We could call ten thousand witnesses, from the martyr in his chain to the palsied or consumptive pauper, dying on his straw. Christian joy has triumphed over every variety of external distress. And the reason is, that it rests on nothing that is sensual, earthly, or fading. "He builds too low, who builds beneath the skies." I am fully persuaded, that no man is independent of trials but the Christian; and that there is no kind or degree of outward trial, against which grace may not furnish a perfect solace or support. It is a joy which flows from the very Head of the mystical body, and which remains and is full, when other fountains have gone dry. Hab. 3 : 18 : "Although the fig-tree shall not blossom, neither shall fruit be in the vines; the labour of the olive shall fail, and the fields shall yield no meat; the flock shall be cut off from the fold, and there shall be no herd in the stalls: yet will I rejoice in the Lord; I will joy in the God of my salvation." Observe how the great apostle to the Gentiles makes his way among contending tides of difficulty, like a sturdy swimmer striking out against a rapid sea. 2 Cor. 6 : 8 : "By honour and dishonour, by evil report and good report; as deceivers, and yet true; as unknown, and yet well known; as dying, and behold we live; as chastened, and not killed; as sorrowful, yet always rejoicing;

as poor, yet making many rich ; as having nothing, and yet possessing all things." Observe, again, how strangely the apostle James addresses the dispersed of the twelve tribes: "My brethren, count it all joy when ye fall into divers trials." Paul prays that the Colossians (1: 11) may be strengthened "unto all patience and long-suffering with joyfulness:" and he knew it to be possible; for he writes to the Corinthians, 2 Cor. 7: 4: "I am filled with comfort: I am exceeding joyful in all our tribulation." It was his constant testimony concerning this joy; for after enumerating the things which the world most dreads, namely, tribulation, distress, persecution, famine, nakedness, and sword, he adds, what the world can never say, "In all these things we are more than conquerors, through Him that loved us." Ah! that is the secret reason. It is the joy of Christ, according to our apostle. It is joy in the Holy Ghost. Isa. 61: 1-3: For the Spirit of the Lord was upon him, anointing him, "to comfort all that mourn, to appoint unto them that mourn in Zion, to give unto them beauty for ashes, the oil of joy for mourning." Enough has therefore been said, to convince us that this joy is immeasurably distant from all the joys of the present world, and is able to surmount all its troubles. But I have reserved, for brief notice in a last particular, the crowning triumph of this grace.

IV. There is *Joy in the hour of death*. We say not composure, simply, or fortitude, or patience, or resignation, but joy. It may not be given to all but it is possible, it may be prayed for; nay, blessed be His name, it is common. In the last words of the last canonical epistle, Jude (v. 24) exclaims, addressing believers: "Now unto him that is able to keep you from falling, and to present you faultless before the presence of his glory with exceeding joy." This light sometimes begins in the dying chamber. Paul awaited such a close of ministry and life, saying (Acts 20: 20) to the elders of Ephesus: "None of these things move me, neither count I my life dear unto myself, so that I may finish my course with joy, and the ministry which I have received of the Lord Jesus." In view of this salvation, Christ is still the grand object and source of hope. 1 Peter 1: 8: "Whom having not seen, ye love; in whom, though now ye see him not, yet believing, ye rejoice with joy unspeakable, and full of glory: receiving the end of your faith, even the salvation of your souls." Yes, with clay-cold hands, we receive this salvation from him who died for us! Though it is ranked among Jewish fancies, yet it is a beautiful thought of Maimonides, that the soul of dying Moses was taken from him by a sacred kiss of God. Of such joy, it would be difficult to find a more striking example than that afforded by the late Dr. Payson. "Were I," says he, "to adopt the figurative language of Bunyan, I might date this letter from the land of Beulah, of which I have been for some weeks a happy inhabitant. The celestial city is full in my view. Its glories beam upon me, its breezes fan me, its odours are wafted to me, its sounds strike upon my ears, and its spirit is breathed into my heart. Nothing separates me from it but the river of death, which now appears but as an insignificant rill, that may be crossed at a single step, whenever God shall give permission. The Sun of Righteousness has been gradually drawing nearer and nearer, appearing larger and brighter as he approached, and now he fills the whole hemisphere, pouring forth a flood of glory, in which I seem to float like an insect in the beams of the sun; exulting, yet almost trembling, while I gaze on this excessive brightness, and wondering, with unutterable wonder, why God should deign thus to shine upon a sinful worm. A single heart, and a single tongue, seem altogether inadequate to my wants. I want a whole heart for every separate emotion, and a whole tongue to express that emotion."*

In closing the discussion, and seeking to point some application to the mind, I shall not ask the reader whether he is in or out of the visible church, but exhort him to lay hold on this exceeding joy, by drawing nearer to Him who bestows it. There is a class—and he may belong to it—who have received from heaven no less commandment than this, repeated again and again: Rejoice—rejoice always: and again I say, Rejoice. The message of divine love is therefore well called, "Tidings of great joy." And we live in gross ignorance or error, when we think of Christianity as abridging our comforts, or encouraging depression and gloom. When we, who

* Life of Payson, p. 355.

profess Christ, are sad and disheartened, it is because the flame of grace burns low. Were we duly seeking the face of God, "with joy" should we "draw water out of the wells of salvation." More elevation of our gladness would make us better Christians. It would wing our flight into higher regions. It would throw this tempting earth into ignominious shade. It would cause our face to shine, and lead the men of this world to say (Zech. 8 : 23), "We will go with you, for we have heard that God is with you." But inasmuch as God is pleased to deal with churches in their collective capacity, it is not common for high enjoyments to be felt by individuals, when the community of believers is in a state of torpor. What prayer, then, can be better for any particular church, than that of the sons of Korah, Ps. 85 : 6: "Wilt thou not revive us again: that thy people may rejoice in thee?" In order to insure such joys, there must be great prayer, great love, great activity, and great holiness. The path before us is therefore plain. We should be unitedly engaged in seeking again the revival of our graces. Nothing short of a general and copious effusion of the Holy Spirit on our churches, will reach our case. Each one should lament, and pray, "Restore unto me the joy of thy salvation, and uphold me by thy free Spirit: then will I teach transgressors thy way, and sinners shall be converted unto thee." Then shall we begin to hear the voice of inquiry renewed. Then shall numbers of our beloved youth, who are still fascinated by the false joys of sense, be found coming into the church. Then shall strifes and heartburnings be banished, and heavenly elevation shine from every countenance. Then shall the heart of the fathers be turned to the children, and the heart of the children to the fathers. "The meek shall increase their joy in the Lord." Our "wilderness shall rejoice with joy and singing." And that shall be true of us, which was said of Samaria, when it received the gospel: "And there was great joy in that city." For a time of revival is a time of great joy, in all those varieties of it which we have detailed: joy in ourselves; joy in the good of others; and joy in the glorifying of Christ's name. And many a pastor feels the tender force of an expression used by Paul (2 Cor. 1: 24), in application to himself and to all ministers: "Not that we have dominion over your faith, but are helpers of your joy." Such help we would fain render. For as the same apostle says (2 Cor. 2: 2), every faithful pastor may say: "If I make you sorry, who is he then that maketh me glad, but the same which is made sorry by me?" for, adds he, "my joy is the joy of you all." Our interests are identical. An extended blessing on the word preached will reach to him who ministers, and "to you, and your children, and to all that are afar off, even as many as the Lord our God shall call." Sowing and watering, without harvest, is toilsome employment; but let God speak the word, and our whitening fields shall be covered with golden sheaves, full of the rewards of joy: John 4: 36: "He that reapeth, receiveth wages, and gathereth fruit unto life eternal; that both he that soweth, and he that reapeth, may rejoice together." And I trust we have the prayers of many a reader, that this promise of Christ, which we have been considering, may speedily be fulfilled to this whole religious community.

CONSOLATION DERIVED FROM THE USES

OF CHASTISEMENT.

IX.

IT is only in the Word of God that we learn to consider affliction as a blessing. The utmost which the most refined philosophy can effect is to remove from our sorrows that which is imaginary, to divert the attention from the cause of distress, or to produce a sullen and stoical resignation, more like despair than hope. The religion of the Gospel grapples with the evil itself, overcomes it, and transforms it into a blessing. It is by no means included in the promises made to true Christians that they shall be exempt from suffering. On the contrary, chastisement forms a necessary part of that paternal discipline, by which our heavenly Father fits his children for their eternal rest in glory. The Psalmist asserts the blessedness of the man who is chastened by the Lord, with this qualification as necessary to constitute it a blessing, that he is also instructed in divine truth. Psalm 94 : 12. By this we understand that the influence of chastisement is not physical; that mere suffering has no inherent efficacy; but that the afflictions of this life are, in the hand of God, instrumental in impressing divine truth upon the heart, awakening the attention of the believer to the consideration of his own character and situation, the promises of the Gospel, and the rewards of heaven. The child of God is assured that all things work together for his good; in this is plainly included the pledge, that chastisements and afflictions shall eventually prove a blessing; and this is verified by the experience of the whole Church.

The subject can scarcely ever be inappropriate. We are all familiar with suffering, in our persons or the persons of those whom we love: we are either now enduring, or shall at some future time endure severe afflictions. Among our readers, it is natural to suppose that some are at this very moment labouring under burdens of grief. Some, it may be, are experiencing the infirmities and pains of a diseased body, others are mourning over the loss of friends and relatives, and others are still living in the dread of trials yet to come. There are few of us therefore to whom the inquiry may not be interesting, How is affliction a blessing?

The question may be thus answered. The chastisements which God inflicts upon his children are profitable to them, as they tend under the Divine blessing to promote piety in the heart. Or more particularly, chastisement is useful, because it convinces the believer of his helplessness and misery when left to himself, and of his entire dependence on God; because it leads him to renew his repentance, puts his faith to the test, and strengthens his Christian graces; because it contributes to the exercise of filial submission, and fixes the mind upon

THE USES OF CHASTISEMENT. 215

the heavenly inheritance. Let us, with prayer for Divine assistance, meditate upon these truths.

1. Chastisement is useful, because it tends to convince the believer of his misery, and shows him that without Christ he cannot be happy. And in order to bring this subject more directly before the mind, let us for a moment consider our readers as suffering under the pangs of some great affliction. You will at once agree with us in the position, that if you had more faith, you would have less trouble of mind; or rather that if you had faith sufficient, you would be altogether clear from the deep impressions which lie upon you. Because we very well know from our own experience, that there are cases in which the most severe bodily pains, or mental distresses, have, so to speak, been neutralized by considerations of a spiritual kind. This is exemplified in the history of the whole Christian Church, and of every individual believer, and most remarkably in the sufferings and deaths of the Martyrs. There is then a certain point of elevation in divine trust, confidence in God, reliance on the providence, grace, and promise of God: that is, a certain degree of faith, which would entirely free you from these trials of mind. We take it for granted that you heartily concur in this, and that you feel, at this very moment of suffering, that no gift of God would so effectually bless you, as this gift of Faith. Your trials and afflictions, therefore, produce in your soul a deep feeling of want. You are now sensible that you need more of the presence of Christ; that your piety is not in sufficient exer-

cise to make you happy under your chastisements. In the moments when forebodings and fears become most oppressive, you are most strongly impressed with the truth, that you still lack a great deal; and your desires are quickened for that measure of faith which shall enable you, with filial confidence, to leave all in the hands of God.

If these are your feelings, you are now ready to acknowledge that chastisement has already produced in you one part of its intended effect. You are brought to feel that you are totally dependent on God for your comfort; that nothing but high measures of piety can render you independent of these clouds of trial, and that the attainments which you have made are insufficient to this end. You are brought to desire of God that grace which shall be sufficient for you, and to say with the disciples: "Lord, increase our faith!" This is one great end of chastisement, to humble man from his self-sufficiency, and make him feel, in the most profound manner, that in God he lives, and moves, and has his being. Afflicted brethren, you never felt in your hours of ease (we venture to affirm) so fully dependent upon God's will, as you do at this present time. Perhaps, if entire prosperity had continued, you would never have felt this persuasion; thus a most important point is gained in your spiritual progress. It is so in this respect, it prepares you for receiving the blessing. It is not God's method, in the ordinary economy of His grace, to give favours of a spiritual kind, until the soul feels its need of them. He "will be in-

THE USES OF CHASTISEMENT.

quired of for these things," even when he purposes to vouchsafe them. It is in answer to earnest longings, pantings, hungerings and thirstings of the spirit, that the Lord manifests himself in the most remarkable manner. You have been brought by chastisement to the very point, where you ought to desire to be brought; and where perhaps nothing but this affliction would have brought you, the total renunciation of your own strength, and the casting of yourself upon the strength of God. Now you begin more deeply to feel your need of Christ. Now you are convinced that something more is necessary than that vague and intermitted trust which you commonly indulge; that Christ must be embraced by your faith, and not visited merely by occasional devotions; in a word, that you must constantly be "looking to Jesus."

If these things are so; if you are persuaded that nothing except strong faith can heal your wounded spirit; if you are conscious that you still lack such faith; if you earnestly and constantly desire it; the question becomes exceedingly interesting to you: "Can I attain it?" And if this could be at once answered in the affirmative, to your full satisfaction, it would go far towards an entire banishment from your soul of these poignant distresses. Now in proportion as your soul is engaged in seeking this inestimable blessing, in just that proportion will your acts of faith be increased. As Christ becomes more and more present to your mind, you will, with more and more confidence, lean upon him with son-like assurance. And, therefore, without endeavouring to resolve the question, when, how, or in what precise manner, God will give you the grace which you need, it is sufficient for our present purpose to know, that one great end of your affliction is answered, when you are led to commence and persevere in a faithful and earnest application to Christ, as the great Physician.

Long have you wandered, it may be, long slighted this benevolent Redeemer. Like Israel in prosperity, you have forgotten your Deliverer, and have grown restiff and rebellious in the rich pastures of his goodness. While the skies were clear, and all around you was smiling, you were remiss in duty, irregular in devotion, lukewarm in affection. Your mountain seemed to stand strong, and in the delights of present enjoyment you could say, "To-morrow shall be as to-day, and much more abundant." Jesus Christ, the Master to whom you had so solemnly, so unreservedly given yourself, has been cast into the shade by the worldly things on which you have doted. Ah! how little do Christians ponder on the truth, that by their lives of carelessness they are rendering afflictions necessary! While they are at ease in Zion, forsaking their first love, and declining from the path of strict piety, the cloud is gathering darker and darker over their heads; that cloud of judgment and of mercy which is to drive them up from their unlawful resting-places, and alarm them into a renewal of their pilgrimage. Afflicted brethren! Ye thought not, while ye were at ease, that these trials were in reserve for you, though often forewarned by the preachers of the Gospel, and the experience of your brethren. The trial has now come; you have now to retrace your steps; you now feel that none but Christ can bring you back to happiness; and you are humbly asking for the blessings of his hand. Thus it is that chastisement convinces the believer of his misery, and shows him that afar from the Saviour he can never be at peace.

2. Chastisement is useful, as it leads the believer to see and feel his exceeding sinfulness. It is one of the strongest proofs that our sanctification is imperfect, and our self-love inordinate, that we are wrought upon so much more readily by stripes than by favours. Though the Lord's goodness ought to lead us to repentance, yet we generally observe that the heart grows hard under the smiles of Providence, and thus loudly calls for the necessary strokes of God's correcting hand. It is a favourable indication of reigning grace, when any soul, in the sunshine of great worldly prosperity, is considerate, humble, and constant in walking with God. In too many cases, it is far otherwise. And when sudden affliction breaks in a storm upon the head of one who has been relapsing into carnal security, the surprise and consternation are great and almost insupportable. After the first tumult of the soul, it is natural to look around for some solace or support; and in the case of a true Christian, the resort will at once be to the consolation of religion. Like the little child which strays from its watchful and tender parent, during

the hours of play, but hastens back at the approach of alarm, so the believer, overtaken by calamity, awakes from his dream, and endeavours to retrace his steps to the neglected mercy-seat. But ah! in how many cases does he here learn his lamentable distance from God; and how mournfully is he made to cry, "O that I knew where I might find Him!" He who is habitually walking with God does not suffer this, for the whole armour of God protects him from the most unexpected assaults: "he is not afraid of evil tidings, his heart is fixed, trusting in the Lord:" but the slumbering and lukewarm professor sinks disheartened. In vain does he apply himself to earthly solaces for alleviation of his grief. With shame, and pain of conscience, does he endeavour to ask deliverance of his offended Father. Every petition that he utters, is accompanied with a sense of weakness. The blessedness which once he spake of is gone; the habit of devout waiting upon God is suspended; the way to the throne of grace is obstructed. How confidently would he offer his petitions, if he were persuaded of his own acceptance: how gladly would he plead the promises, if he felt his title to them secured in Christ. But alas! it is not with him as in days that are past, when the candle of the Lord shone on him. His mind has become attached to the earth; his views of the blessed Redeemer are indistinct; he is convinced that his strength has departed, that his faith languishes, and that he is defiled with sin.

Now his repentings are kindled; now he knows

how evil and bitter a thing it is to forsake the Lord, and to depart from his fear; and when he considers how long God has borne with him, how many favours he has received, and how brutish has been his ingratitude, his heart is broken, his tears flow, he seeks the lowest place in the dust of abasement, wonders that affliction has not long since overtaken him for his carelessness and neglect, and bows before the Lord without a murmur. At such a time, the language of the afflicted soul will be: " Wherefore doth a living man complain, a man for the punishment of his sins? Let us search and try our ways, and turn again unto the Lord. Let us lift up our heart with our hands unto God in the heavens. We have transgressed and have rebelled: thou hast not pardoned. Thou hast covered thyself with a cloud, that our prayer should not pass through. Mine eye trickleth down and ceaseth not, without any intermission, till the Lord look down and behold from heaven."

Christian brethren, who have known affliction, and have been chastened of the Lord, that you should not be condemned with the world; who have suffered the loss of friends, of health, of property, of reputation, how often has one hour of such trials done more to show you your sins, and humble you in penitence, than months of ordinary self-examination, or stated means of grace!

When chastisement has its proper operation, the Christian will seek not to be comforted merely, but to be taught of God. "Blessed is the man whom thou chastenest, O Lord, and teachest him out of thy law." He seeks to know why God contends with him, and lies very low in contrition, when the still small voice of the Lord says to him, "The Lord hath a controversy with his people, and he will plead with Israel: O my people, what have I done unto thee? and wherein have I wearied thee? testify against me." Micah 6. And this exercise leads to godly sorrow which is not to be repented of. It is under deep affliction that we feel most deeply the connection between sin and misery, and acknowledge that the connection is just and holy. Smarting under the rod, we know that the Lord hath not dealt with us after our sins, nor rewarded us according to our iniquities; and that it is of his mercies that we are not consumed.

It was not immediately upon the commission of his atrocious crime, that David was humbled; but when he was chastised and smitten to the earth, hear how he mourns, not so much over his sufferings as his sin: "Have mercy upon me, O God, according to thy loving-kindness; according unto the multitude of thy tender mercies, blot out my transgressions. Wash me thoroughly from my iniquity, and cleanse me from my sin. For I acknowledge my transgressions, and my sin is ever before me. Make me to hear joy and gladness, that the bones which thou hast broken may rejoice. Hide thy face from my sins, and blot out all my iniquities. Create in me a clean heart and renew a right spirit within me. Cast me not away from thy presence, and take not thy Holy Spirit from me." Psalm 51.

Times of affliction afford some natural facilities for cultivating repentance. Occasions of sin are then removed; the world is excluded. The man confined to the silence of the sick room, or the house of mourning, cannot by idle pursuits divert his mind. He is forced to think; and to think of his sins. He considers his ways, bewails his transgression, and renews his covenant. He learns to confess, "Surely it is meet to be said unto God, I have borne chastisement, I will not offend any more; that which I see not teach thou me: and if I have done iniquity, I will do no more." Job 34: 31.

Now, in these experiences of the afflicted, there is a real consolation. Such tears are sweet, and it will probably be the unanimous testimony of all true penitents, that they have enjoyed a tender and refined delight in those moments of grief, in which they came to God as a forgiving God, and heard him say to their souls, in accents at once of gentle rebuke and comfort: "Behold, I have refined thee, but not with silver; I have chosen thee in the furnace of affliction," "for mine own sake will I defer mine anger." "For a small moment have I forsaken thee, but with great mercies will I gather thee. In a little wrath I hid my face from thee for a moment, but with everlasting kindness will I have mercy on thee, saith the Lord thy Redeemer." Isa. 54.

3. Chastisement is useful as a trial of faith.

To use the expression of Bishop Hall, "untried faith is uncertain faith." There often is in professors of religion enough of the semblance of piety to lull their consciences while they are prosperous, but not enough of the reality to support them in time of trial. Adversity makes the exercise of faith needful, and puts the strength of that faith to the test. It is compared to the fire, the furnace, the fining-pot or crucible, because it not only purifies, but tries; it not only consumes the dross, but ascertains the gold.

There is no true believer who does not desire this trial. The very supposition of being found wanting at the day of judgment fills him with horror. His daily supplication is: "Search me, O God, and know my heart; try me, and know my thoughts; and see if there be any wicked way in me, and lead me in the way everlasting." Christian reader, give a moment's thought to this question, Is your faith sufficient to support you in the hour of death, if that hour (as is very possible) should soon and suddenly arrive? Are you not ready to sink under ordinary afflictions? How then will you bear this greatest of trials? To adopt the language of Jeremiah (12:5), "If thou hast run with the footmen, and they have wearied thee, then how canst thou contend with horses? And if, in the land of peace, wherein thou trustedst, they wearied thee, then how wilt thou do in the swellings of Jordan?"

This trial of your faith is plainly important, and it is the office of chastisement to constrain you to such a trial. If your standing in the covenant is so firm, through humble trust in God, that you can say, "But he knoweth the way that I take: when he hath tried me I shall come forth as gold," you are happy indeed. But this conviction is not likely to be strong in those who have not passed through the furnace. The apostle Peter, in comforting the dispersed saints, explains to them this end of their chastisement, "If need be, ye are in heaviness through manifold temptations, that the trial of your faith being much more precious than of gold that perisheth, though it be tried with fire, might be found unto praise, and honour, and glory, at the appearing of Jesus Christ."

We have already seen, in the course of our meditations, some of the ways in which faith is tried by affliction. If any be afflicted he will pray. But there can be no comfort in prayer, where there is not a belief that prayer is heard, and will be answered. The supplication of one who pours out strong crying and tears, in a great fight of afflictions, is a very different thing from the formal addresses of one at ease. The sufferer cannot be consoled until he finds that God is his friend; he cannot find this without faith; and in this manner, most directly, chastisement convinces the soul, that it is still unprovided with the shield of faith, or awakens the exercise of this grace, with great and unspeakable satisfaction. And thus the tribulations which have succeeded one another through life, give us stronger and stronger reliance on God, for the approaching hour of death. At some future day it will be sweet to remember how the Lord sealed us with his Spirit of adoption, in these times of trial. Therefore, "beloved breth ren, think it not strange concerning the fiery trial which is to try you, as though some strange thing happened unto you, but rejoice, inasmuch as ye are partakers of Christ's sufferings; that when his glory shall be revealed, ye may be glad also with exceeding joy."

4. Chastisement is useful, as it strengthens faith, by leading the believer to the promises, and especially to the Lord Jesus Christ.

There is no expression in the word of God better suited to reconcile the Christian to trials, than that of the Apostle Paul: "He [that is, God] chastens us for our profit, that we may be partakers of His holiness"—partakers of His holiness! What words are these! This is the very summit of your desires. This you have been toiling for, and longing after. This you have earnestly implored, and are you now ready to shrink from the very means by which your Father in heaven is about to promote your sanctification? By no means will you be led to relinquish this appointment of God for your good. Now it is by these very trials that your graces are to be invigorated.

We have seen that these trials disclose the reality and degree of our faith. We may go further, and observe that faith is greatly increased and strengthened by the same process. Faith is strengthened by exercise. As the touch, or any natural faculty, becomes obtuse and often useless by want of exercise, or the removal of its proper objects, so faith languishes and seems ready to perish, when those truths which are to be believed are long kept out of the mind. The most valuable truths of the Christian are "the exceeding great and precious promises." He does not feel his need of these promises while he is indulging in that self-pleasing which usually accompanies prosperity. In penning these lines we say advisedly, no man can fully value health who has not been ill, nor appreciate the services of the kind and skilful physician, until he has been healed by him. And thus also, no man can fully prize, or fully understand the promises of the Scriptures, until they are made necessary to his support in adversity. Many of the most precious portions of revelation are altogether a dead letter to such as have never been exercised by the trials to which they relate.

The believer who is in sufferings or straits of any kind, comes to God by prayer; and in attempting to pray, seeks some promise suitable to his precise wants. Blessed be God! he needs not to search long—so rich are the treasures of the word. These promises he takes as the very truth of God. He pleads them at the throne of grace; he believes them, relies on them, rejoices in them. This is faith; these exercises are vital exercises of the renewed soul. So long as the Christian is oppressed with affliction, these exercises must be continual; and in proportion as the trial is great, must the faith be great also, so that he often finds every earthly support cut away, and is taught, with implicit trust, to hang on the simple word of Divine faithfulness. This is em phatically the life of piety; and it is encouraged, developed, and maintained in time of trial.

Affliction is sanctified when we are made to feel that nothing can satisfy us but God, and when we actually wait upon God, and rely on Him as our only hope. It is then that the Christian finds the promises confirmed to him: "Whom the Lord loveth he chasteneth, and scourgeth every son whom he receiveth." "No chastening for the present is joyous, but grievous," &c. Then he rolls his burden on the Lord, commits his way to him, leans upon Him, trusts in Him with all his heart, so that with a meaning altogether new, he can sing with the Church: "God is our refuge and strength, a very present help in trouble: therefore will we not fear, though the earth be removed, and though the mountains be carried into the midst of the sea."

Some appear to entertain the mistaken opinion that the only relief which is afforded to the Christian in suffering, must arise from some hope of speedy deliverance or escape. This is so far from being true, that perhaps the greatest solace under afflictions is derived from direct acts of faith upon the Lord Jesus Christ, and communion with Him; in which the soul is so much absorbed that the present suffering is forgotten, and the mind wholly occupied in its exercises of piety. And herein the chastisement is profitable. In pain, and despondency, and grief, we go to Jesus as to a friend that sticketh closer than a brother: we pour our sorrows into his friendly ear, and ask his aid, and then, when he reveals to us his love, and speaks his promises, and unveils his face, even though he give no assurance that we shall be set free, he does more,—he gives us *Himself*, and faith is refreshed and nourished by receiving him. And shall we not regard as a mercy, that illness, or that bereavement, or that alarm, which so embitters the world's cup, as to lead us to Christ, that we may see his beauty, and be filled with his love?

Prosperity leaves us to wander, and offers temptations to wandering. Afflictions alarm us and drive us back to the right path. Prosperity casts a glittering but delusive veil over divine realities, and encourages unbelief. Afflictions rend and destroy this covering, and show us the truths of another world. Prosperity seldom leads to increase of faith. Affliction, by God's blessing, is in many cases made the instrument of sanctification to such as are truly pious.

Dear Brethren, that God who "doth not afflict willingly, nor grieve the children of men," offers you in your trials these "peaceable fruits of righteousness." Taste of the sweetness of his promises, and each of you shall say with David: "It is good for me that I have been afflicted."

5. Chastisement is useful, because it leads the believer to exercise entire submission to the Divine will.

It is an undeniable truth, and one of which the child of God is very deeply convinced, that "the Lord reigneth;" that it is infinitely right and fit that he should reign; and that the first duty of every intelligent being, is to submit promptly, cheerfully, and unreservedly to every ordinance and dispensation of God. It is not very difficult to keep the soul in correspondence with this truth, so long as our self-love is not interfered with, nor our present happiness invaded; but when the sovereignty of God is manifested in despoiling us of our most precious possessions and delights, our souls are often ready to falter, and our weakness betrays itself, when with hesitating lips we endeavour to say, "Shall not the Judge of all the earth do right?" It is common to hear those who are ignorant of the Scriptures cavilling at the representation of Job as a man of eminent patience; but where, except in his biography, shall we look for the instance of a man, suffering in one day the total loss of immense wealth, and of ten beloved children, and still saying, "The Lord gave, and the Lord hath taken away, blessed be the name of the Lord."

Without exercise, Christian graces do not grow, and severe afflictions are probably intended to cultivate this important grace of entire submission. Nothing is more common than for persons under chastisement to indulge in such thoughts as these: "I could endure almost any affliction better than this; it is that which I have most dreaded, for which I was least prepared, and now it has overtaken me! It is so strange, new, and unexampled, that I am unmanned, and my soul sinks within me." These are the symptoms of a rebellious and unsubdued will; the murmurings of a proud and stubborn heart, which must be humbled in the dust. This is just the trial by which, perhaps, God graciously intends to bring down the imaginations and high thoughts of your soul into captivity to the obedience of Christ. And patience will not have had its perfect work in any case, until the afflicted soul is prepared to make no reservation, to claim no direction, but to give up all into the hands of the most wise, most righteous, and most merciful Creator. If the suffering were less, it would not have this humbling efficacy, and he mistakes the nature of the covenant, who supposes that such peculiar trials are excluded. It was, no doubt, a visitation sudden and alarming as a stroke of lightning, when Aaron beheld his sons consumed by fire from the Lord. It was an awful sanction to that rule, "I will be sanctified in them that come nigh me, and before all the people I will be glorified." Yet, on seeing and hearing these things, the bereaved father "held his peace." Lev. 10 : 3. It is a bitter medicine, but the soul which is convinced of God's justice and goodness, lays down every thought of rebellion and discontent.

When, in the time of the Judges, the children of Israel gave themselves up in a shameless manner to the worship of idols, they fell under the wrath of God, and were eighteen years oppressed by the Ammonites and Philistines. Still, when they came to themselves, and cried to the Lord, they joined to their repentance lowly submission, and said, "We have sinned; do thou unto us whatsoever seemeth good unto thee." Judges 10.

This is the temper which sanctified affliction al

ways begets, so that the prostrate soul dares no longer to impose terms on Jehovah, but yields itself to his sovereign discretion. There is peace in such a surrender, a peace which is altogether independent of any expected mitigation of the stroke.

Wave after wave often goes over the child of God, before he is brought to this state of self-renunciation. Murmuring may for a time prevail, yet the Great Physician, who applies the painful remedy, cannot be baffled, and triumphs to his own glory and the unspeakable benefit of the believer's soul. The Scriptures afford us striking examples of this yielding up of every thing into the hands of God; particularly in the case of David, whose history and experience are given in detail. One of the sharpest inflictions which fell upon this pious man, was the rebellion of his unnatural son, Absalom; and one of the most affecting scenes in the course of this transaction, is the flight of the aged king with the ark: 'All the country wept with a loud voice, and all the people passed over." Now, what was the language of David under these circumstances? "The King said unto Zadok: Carry back the ark of God into the city; if I shall find favour in the eyes of the Lord, he will bring me again, and show me both it and his habitation; and if he thus say, I have no delight in thee, behold here am I, let him do unto me as seemeth good unto Him." 2 Samuel 15: 26. Now, we have here exemplified the very frame of soul which each of us should endeavour to maintain under chastisement. For we are not to speak thus,

"I can bear this because it cannot be avoided, or, because I hope it is the last of my sufferings." No, my brethren, we are not thus to limit the Holy One of Israel; but let each of us with filial homage say, "Lord, I am in thy hands, in the best hands, I deserve thy stripes, I yield myself to thy dispensations, thy will be done!" Happy is he who, like David, can look back upon chastisements and say, "I was dumb, I opened not my mouth, because thou didst it." Ps. 39.

"Humble yourselves, therefore, under the mighty hand of God, that He may exalt you in due time;" yet, if his rod should long abide upon you, if you are ready, like Job, to cry, from repeated and continued strokes, "He hath set me up for his mark. He breaketh me with breach upon breach. He hath fenced up my way so that I cannot pass, and he hath set darkness in my paths;" yet even then, "remember the patience of Job, and the end of the Lord," and say, "Though he slay me, yet will I trust in him."

Some may be disposed to think, in the time when all God's waves and billows go over them, that they could acquiesce and be comforted, if they perceived any way of escape, if they could reasonably expect deliverance: and this is the whole of what is sometimes called Christian resignation. Yet the comfort in this case is merely worldly. The grace of God can do more than this; it can make you willing still to endure, and in enduring still to praise.

Say not, "I could be content if I were sure of

deliverance." God has not promised absolutely to remove the chastisement. Perhaps it is his holy will not to deliver. Perhaps it is this very thing in your afflictions which is to insure you the blessing from the Lord. The apostle Paul earnestly desired, and thrice besought the Lord to deliver him from that trial which he calls the thorn in his flesh, the messenger of Satan to buffet him. Yet, as far as we are informed, it was continued to the end of his life. But mark the glorious indemnification: "My grace is sufficient for thee, for my strength is made perfect in weakness." Upon this declaration, which we shall presently consider more in detail, he goes forward under his burden, singing as he pursues his pilgrimage: "Most gladly, therefore, will I rather glory in my infirmities, that the power of Christ may rest upon me; therefore I take pleasure in infirmities, in reproaches, in necessities, in persecutions, in distresses, for Christ's sake, for when I am weak, then am I strong." The sweet support under every possible calamity is, that God can turn it into a blessing, and that if we have faith he will do so. With respect, therefore, to the use of afflictions, "all things are possible to him that believeth."

6. Finally. Chastisement is useful, because it leads the believer to look for complete happiness in heaven only.

And at this stage of our reflections, let us rejoice, dear brethren, that the consolation offered is liable to no exception or abatement; it is adapted to every case; perfect and entire. If the comfort which you need depended upon the hope of deliverance in this world, there would be many cases which we should be forced to leave as hopeless: for there are many in which no expectation of exemption in this life can be indulged. But let the worst, most lingering, and most aggravated instance of suffering be presented, and the hope of heaven is still sufficient to mitigate its ills. You may have been reduced to hopeless poverty; you may have suffered from the treachery and ingratitude of supposed friends, from cruel mockings and persevering calumny; you may labour under incurable disease, or follow to the grave beloved objects of your affections, who can never be replaced in this world. Still, there is a country, and you are rapidly approaching it, "where the wicked cease from troubling, and the weary are at rest." It is well if you have learned to look beyond all secondary, earthly, imperfect comforts, to 'God, the source of good, and to that world where all tears are wiped away. It is well if the trial of your faith has enabled you to say, "I know whom I have believed, and am persuaded that he is able to keep that which I have committed to him against that day."

This is a benefit of affliction, which is striking and great in proportion to the failure of earthly consolation. For it may be doubted, whether any man fully yields himself up to the view and prelibation of heaven, until he is disentangled and rent away from all hope of blessedness on this side the grave. It is natural to seek resting-places by the way; and trials, losses, sufferings, bereavements, are thrice blessed when they engrave upon our hearts that we have here no continuing city, but must seek one above. So long as we can flatter ourselves with any refuge in this world, we are prone to lean on an arm of flesh, and to look upwards only for the supply of what is deficient here. But let all expectation of worldly peace and satisfaction be cut off, and the released soul which is truly sanctified and full of faith, rises like a bird from the snare, and rejoices to say, "My soul, wait thou only upon God, for my expectation is from him. Then shall I be satisfied when I awake in thy likeness!" Think not, however, to enjoy this fruit of chastisement, while you cast longing and lingering looks on that country whence you came out. Nothing but the hope of a glorious resurrection upheld the apostle Paul, when troubled on every side, perplexed, persecuted, cast down, and (as to the outward man) perishing. Hear the method of his escape out of sorrow: "Our light affliction, which is but for a moment, worketh for us a far more exceeding and eternal weight of glory."

He is the happy man who dwells most on the thoughts of heaven. Like Enoch he walks with God. Like Job he can say, "I know that my Redeemer liveth," &c. Like David he glories, "Thou wilt show me thy salvation." Like Paul he triumphs, "For I am now ready to be offered," &c.

This happiness we sometimes witness; but where have we found it? In the house of prosperity, where death has never invaded the family circle; where all have more than heart could wish; where health, and opulence, and honour unite to expel all care? No! but in the hovel of the poor, where one affliction hath followed another, till earthly hope is almost extinct. In the darkened chamber of mourning, whence all that was most loved and cherished has taken its last flight. In the bed of lingering, incurable disease, and in the very gasp of death! Here religion hath set up her trophies; here is happiness, here, where things hoped for are substantiated to the believing soul, where things unseen are evidenced to faith by divine influence.

In every case of suffering it is the prime wisdom of the Christian to fix his eyes upon the heavenly crown. In every other hope you may be disappointed, in this you cannot. Try, as you may, all other fountains for your solace, there is a time coming when you must be driven to this. Become familiar with the meditation of heavenly glory! Daily contemplate that joyful deliverance from evil, that indissoluble and ecstatic union with the Lord Jesus Christ! Then, when death lays upon you his cold hand, you can say, "I am prepared for this hour. I have longed for this deliverance to meet my Lord in his temple. I have lived in communion with the blessed Lord of heaven." "Lo, this is my God, I have waited for him, and he will save me; this is the Lord, I have waited for him; I will rejoice and be glad in his salvation."

THE HOLY SUBMISSION OF CHRIST'S
WILL CONSIDERED AS A SOURCE
OF CONSOLATION.

X.

THE very name *Gethsemane* carries remembrances which sadden the demeanour and fill the eyes. How can we draw near to it? Especially, how can we withdraw the curtain and expose the divine humiliations of that hour, when we know so well how many have already gazed carelessly on every pang of the Son of God, until they are hardened like the nether millstone? And this is one reason why we shall not attempt a picture of that scene; but after a hurried glance at the series of events, will single out one expression as our theme. Every reader will remember that the disciples had risen from their couches in the guest chamber of Jerusalem, and joining in a hymn, had descended into the little valley, which on the east separates the city from Olivet; and in that valley had found, at the foot of the hill, the garden now so memorable. It was just out of Jerusalem, over the brook Kedron, between the brook and the place where the mount begins to ascend. It was a spot to which Jesus was accustomed to resort for solitude and devotion: and the fact is connected with his betrayal. He caused the eleven to sit down and pray, while he went further onward to pray also. Three of the number were more privileged. They went to his more secluded retirement, and were witnesses of his agony. The terms which describe this have an awfulness which belongs to no other words in Scripture. "His soul was exceeding sorrowful;" immersed in sorrow; in death-sorrow. It was an indescribable and unearthly suffering, mingled with tears, and cries, and blood, and angelic appearance. It was an hour of agony—*the* hour. Mark 14 : 35. He was fallen on the ground, and the unseen cup was at his lips. All the struggles and wrestlings of the universe are nothing to this. Here is Divinity in conflict with itself. Here is the Father bruising the Son. Here is God the Saviour, as it were, contending with God the Just, lest the sinner should have what he deserves. Here is manhood exalted to be the vehicle of divine atonements, and Godhead upholding the only nature that could die. Here is the fainting, sinking, forsaken Messiah, still looking up, and crying, "Abba, Father." "Abba." It is the word of the babe, when first in that dialect he knows the filial language, and reads the father's soul in his eyes; the simplest articulation of language; the most trustful outburst of affection—"Abba, Father." It is the recognition of supreme power and Godhead: "All things are possible to thee." It is the cry of nature suffering in its profoundest depths, and exclaiming for help, or rescue, or alleviation, in the moment of anguish, and pressed by unutterable woes. "Take away this cup from me!" It is, nevertheless, the total, instant, absolute subjection of the whole spirit to Jehovah: "Nevertheless, not what I will, but what thou wilt!" The proposition to be considered is this: *The submission of Christ's will to the will of God is the great atoning act, and the motive and pattern for our submission, and the source of our consolation.*

1. *The person here humbled is to be regarded.* It is not the absolute Jehovah, who has neither parts nor passions, and who is to all eternity insusceptible of change or pain. It is not any one person of the adorable Triune Godhead, considered absolutely, separately, and in respect to his divine nature. Such acts and sufferings as those to which we ascribe atonement seem to have required a suffering adjunct, that is, a human body and soul, in order to be possible; and such acts and sufferings alone vindicate the Incarnation. Nor yet was it man, simple, naked man: no, not the greatest, best, purest, holiest, loveliest, heavenliest of mere men; priest, king, or prophet;—it was not a bare teacher, a superior Jew, Jesus, son of Mary, who was subjecting himself to God. Such subjection as this would indeed have been good and admirable, but finite, and unworthy of occupying this distinct, prominent, and mysterious place in the gospel annals. A thousand martyrs have suffered, without a murmur, like this; yet their sufferings had nothing vicarious, nothing penal, nothing meritorious. The personage who here submits his will to the will of absolute Divinity, that is to Law, in its sublimest sense; to infinite right; the personage who endures and obeys; who

shrinks in torture, and yet looks up in love; who dies of a thousand griefs, yet bathes with tears the Father's hand which smites, is without any complete parallel in heaven or earth, in time or eternity. He stands alone; for the exempt case, the unprecedented juncture in the world's history, demanded the appearance of one unlike all others. Hence the impossibility of explanation in regard to this mystery. All explanation lifts up the mind to the desired height by means of some truth of likeness, some analogy, some similitude. Here there is no analogy, no similitude: likeness fails, and so does explanation. God may be likened to God, and man to man; but the resulting CHRIST—God and man in one ever-abiding union—is comparable, in regard to this union, to nothing in this world or that which is to come. The very term *Person*, not found in Scripture, but adopted by catholic usage, from a very early age, testifies to the necessity felt for some new phrase to mark a new relation, and guard against a new error. Hence the early creeds multiplied words to prevent any one from supposing either that there was but one nature in Christ, as if the divine and the human were intermingled, so as to leave no human nature and no divine nature, but a third essence betwixt the two; or that there are two persons, a personal Godhead united to a personal manhood—a God *and* a man; these early formularies opposed themselves to both errors, maintaining the truth with a fulness which savoured of tautology. "Who, although he be God and Man, yet he is not two, but one Christ. One, not by the conversion of the Godhead into flesh, but by taking of the manhood into God. One altogether, not by confusion of substance, but by unity of Person."

In contemplating this holy mystery we must not look too closely into the ark, nor endeavour with niceness of scholastic distinctions to separate what is divine from what is human in the person or the work of our Lord Jesus Christ. To us, and for our salvation, he is " *One Lord*," and it is enough for us to look on his deeds and atonement as proceeding from one indivisible and glorious Person, the Lord Jesus Christ. In a sense, all he does and all he suffers is divine, inasmuch as the divinity sustains all, the divinity concurs in all, and the divinity gives merit and infinitude to all. It is the Son of God, who prays. Standing as Mediator, between all that is purely God, and all that is purely man, himself God-man, he offers up the tribute of a will absolutely and unspeakably surrendered to the infinite will. The prayer which He himself prompted was never so uttered as by him in the garden, "Thy will be done !" Which leads me to remark,

2. There was in our Lord, in the garden, *a struggle between his innocent nature and the will of the Almighty Father*. The words are plain — "Take away this cup from me; nevertheless, not what I will but what Thou wilt." If there was no struggle there could be no meaning in such words. There was a cup, brought to his lips, which he was expected to drink, and which the Almighty Father

commanded him to drink, but which nevertheless was so repugnant to all the instinctive feelings of nature, as to be the cause of those ineffable fears and griefs and astonishments. There was present a suffering nature, a part which could sigh and grieve; a voluntary nature, which could accept or reject; a loving nature, which could yearn with godlike affection and ,pity for the salvation of a world of believers; and a subdued and holy nature, which gave up all for the honour and glory of infinite justice. It was a vicarious work from first to last in which Christ was engaged; that is, he was acting for others, not for himself. Human nature would never have been assumed, unless to lift up that human nature from its sunken condition. To carry man up to God, it was necessary for God to become man. It was not enough that God should decree the sanctification of the fallen. Something besides sanctification was demanded, something more than the present, actual holiness of the creature. This, it is true, was intended, as a grand result; but before this something must be done. A legal obstacle lies in the way, which must be removed. There is a claim of Law, which must be satisfied. For this sanctification the Son of God became man; to satisfy in the nature which had offended. The will of the race has become opposed to the will of God : this is only another way of saying the race has sinned. There is an awful and irreversible penalty. Not for an instant will I admit that God's threatenings are meant only for alarm and not for execution. They are executed, with direful condign vengeance in the fall of Lucifer, in the fall of Adam, in the Deluge, in the cities of the plain; as they will be in the retributions of the Last Judgment. In all and each of these, Divine Justice burns forth to the execution of threatened penalty. In none of these instances would such penalty be inflicted, if threatening could be set aside without fulfilment. Perfect subjection of will in our Surety, without any struggle, would have been infinitely holy, would have been immeasurable obedience, and would have fulfilled the law in a way of active righteousness; but it would not have been endurance of legal pains; it would not have answered the vindicatory part of the law, and it would not have exhibited to the universe the high spectacle of the Son of God subjected to anguish for the sinner's sake. Hence the necessity for the struggle of which we have spoken. The yoke is borne, and it is felt to be a yoke. The cup is bitter, or it would not be a cup of atonement. The genuine though perfect humanity of the Redeemer, having all the instinctive love of ease and hatred of pain which belongs to humanity, turns pale and shudders, and sinks and groans and dissolves in blood, before it drinks this cup:—yet drinks it! A total instantaneous subjugation of Christ's will to the will of God, of such a nature as to overwhelm and drink up the native propensities, such as to cast out all pain—would not have been endurance of penalty. Hence the need of shrinking, repugnance, and struggle, in the suffering subject. Hence was there wrung from our divine Redeemer the cry—"Father, if it be possible, let this cup pass from me!" In our view, that which is essential to atonement is the bearing of sin, that is, the bearing of penalty. And we stop short, and content ourselves with light, insufficient views of the part sustained by Christ, when we do not include in our thoughts the crushing of the human nature (which would have been its annihilation but for the sustaining power of divinity), under the weight of legal pains endured representatively and vicariously. There was a force drawing the will of Jesus away from the cup of anguish, which force we must in some degree appreciate, before we can duly esteem the glory of his drinking it up. This was the struggle of Christ's will, in Gethsemane.

3. Notwithstanding this struggle, *there was a perfect submission of Christ's will to the will of the Father.* "Nevertheless, not what I will, but what thou wilt." The length of foregoing repugnance is a matter not revealed. That there was no moment in which the holy submission of our Saviour gave way, is certain. That the grace of a loving subjugation to law transfused itself through the whole of the sinkings and agonies of nature, so that the two coexisted at every instant, is most probable. Through the whole, there was so much of weakness as to insure pain, our sacrificial pain: through the whole, there was so much of acquiescence as to insure obedience, our vicarious obedience. And who does not know that even in the lesser world of human affection, and in

many a domestic hour, love and pain may be so blended as to be the very warp and woof of our heart's existence; pain being still pain, yet embraced even with transport, and chosen without a lingering hesitation, for the sake of the beloved object; as when the mother suffers for her offspring—the father for the son—the wife for the husband—the brother for the brother! And shall we wonder when He in whom are gathered up the glory and beauty of all virtues, graces, and exalted benignities, stoops to taste the cup which our sins had prepared! It is the crowning act of his life of submission, on which he is now entering. In a certain sense, the whole period, from his birth till his resurrection, was one series of humiliation, one subjection to covenant, one tribute of obedience, one satisfaction to law, and one Righteousness. In the same sense, this whole period was one submission of will; because there is no obedience but of will. But, nevertheless, this permanent obedience of our Mediator for our sakes does at certain epochs reach a point of overflowing, which reveals the same more fully to us; as in the garden, the arrest, the trial, and the cross. Infinite are the mysteries of that piacular suffering and submission, which were passing within the darkened chamber of Christ's soul, and which no finite mind can ever comprehend! Not more private and inaccessible was the *Sanctum Sanctorum*, than this Holy of Holies of our Atoning God and Elder Brother. The little that we know is, that he suffers and submits.

This is enough. This is the bowing down of the
will, the federal, vicarious, mediatory will, to the law
which we had injured; to the law in its twofold power,
as commanding and as smiting. It is the will, the
stubborn, impious will, which in us fights against God,
and by all human power is unconquerable. It is
the will that does all of sin that is active, that
rejects salvation, and that damns the soul. It is
the will, the God-defying will, which now, this
day, in some who read, deliberately sets itself
against the Most High God. It is the will which
Jesus Christ, amidst an ocean of contending griefs,
offers up, steeped in death and humbling, pure and
unresisting, unto God for us. And though he made
this offering a thousand and a thousand times during
the course of his mediatory tabernacling among us,
and though there was no instant in which he made
it not; yet at certain moments he did more formally
and observably consummate this surrender of self;
and this is one of them. It is the completest, as it
is the most stupendous, oblation unto God which the
universe has beheld. In all its parts, it forms the
theme of eternal thought and songs. "Not my will,
but thine be done.". In a certain sense it might
have been avoided; for God the Father is omnipotent; but not in any sense which would not have
left us in hell. In regard to the manner of help, it
might have been avoided. "Thinkest thou that I
cannot now pray to my Father, and he shall presently give me more than twelve legions of angels?"
Matt. 26 : 51. "Put up thy sword into the sheath;

SUBMISSION OF CHRIST. 251

the cup which my Father hath given me, shall I not drink it?" John 18 : 11. It might have been avoided, in respect to power, but not in respect to love. "Abba, Father, all things are possible unto thee: take away this cup from me; nevertheless, not what I will, but what thou wilt!" What THOU wilt! Here is the supreme and infinite and eternal will which binds the universe. What THOU wilt! Here is the divine will which, if unopposed, would have kept an eternal universe in happiness, but which was violated by sin. Here is the will, which all nature obeys, but which devils and men have outraged and defied. Here is the will which is dear to all holy intelligences, and infinitely dear to the Son of God, the holiest of intelligences; to this will, therefore, he submits himself at once and irrevocably, though it costs him the greatest sacrifice which has been known in all worlds. This obedience, even unto death, is the ATONEMENT. It is a satisfaction of infinite value made to the will of Jehovah, that is, to Justice. It is an oblation both of doing and of suffering. It fills the cup of duty; it exhausts the cup of penalty. It meekly says to Almighty Justice, "Thy will be done." It does this, not in some remote planet, or distant circle of heaven; though in such regions there are perpetual tributes to the Infinite Will. Such would have been pleasing to God, but would have availed nothing to our earth. Here, on this accursed orb, the satisfaction was rendered. It is not a submission of will, by some super angelic being unrelated to ourselves, nor a declaration solely of God's hatred against sin: it is an offering up of an immaculate, law-fulfilling, covenanted obedience of act and suffering, in our human nature, by one who is chosen as the head of our human nature; who assumed our human nature for this very end, and who in every deed, groan, tear, pang, and drop of blood, acts in and for our human nature; so that for all purposes of atonement, we then and there obey and suffer in Christ, as truly as in Eden we disobeyed and suffered in Adam. So far, therefore, from being unjust for God to impute to us the acts and expiatory pains of Christ, his subjection of will to God as (if they were) our own acts and pains, it is beautifully and gloriously and infinitely just, inasmuch as these are the acts and pains of One who is our Head. Christ performs the whole mediatory work as the head of a great moral person, his Church. He is as truly connected with all the members as our head or heart is with our extremities. Christ's satisfaction is our satisfaction. "If one died for all, then all died."* If one lives, all live. When that glorious submission of will to God takes place, the law is satisfied by a federal compliance, which for ever cuts off all payment of that debt by those means.

4. The submission of our Lord amidst this inconceivable struggle is *the pattern and motive for our submission to God's will.* So beautiful a sight, to those who account moral perfection the greatest beauty, was never presented, as in the spot

* See the original.

less obedience of Jesus; and so pre-eminent a part of that obedience is nowhere displayed as in this closing night and day of his life of humiliation; and in these hours of agony, no single moment is more intensely hallowed and subduing than that in which he cried, "Nevertheless, not what I will, but what thou wilt."

I seem to behold all heaven bending down towards a world on which for forty centuries there has not been one immaculate object, to concentrate its gaze on the "Man of Sorrows." "These things the angels desire to look into:" they cannot imitate, though they admire. They "adore and burn;" but such stretches of benevolence are beyond their reach. Angels cannot suffer: they have not become incarnate. Such struggles are wondrous to them. Gladly does one of them descend to Gethsemane, and appear "strengthening him." This is a love which has been the grand attraction of the church in all ages, and which we celebrate in a sacrament. It is love in its highest exaltation; suffering love; tearful, bleeding, dying love. As you drew near and meditated on it at that table, did your heart melt, O my brother! to consider that it was for you and for your sins that this unexampled act of submission was put forth? And as you ventured to stretch out your hand to the bread of the sacrament and the cup of blessing, did you try to measure your obligation? Ah, you found it immeasurable! By all the legal submissions of Jesus Christ your Lord, and especially by all the untold agonies of that hour of darkness, when the sword of Jehovah awoke against his fellow, and smote the Shepherd; by all his profound obedience of soul, you lie bound also to obey. From every drop of that precious blood, the voice comes to you, "Submit yourselves unto God." No thunder of Sinai can so move the will as these gentle groans of your beloved Saviour in his woe. That rebellious will, which is perpetually offending and resisting, and which you mourn over as your chief calamity, the plague of your heart, the serpent in your bosom, never, never yields to bare Law. Obligation may be felt; it is felt in hell; it produces the fear of hell: "the devils also believe and tremble;" but obligation does not convert. If you have ever fled to Jesus with the intolerable burden of your sins, you know this. You know that the denunciations of penal vengeance, often repeated, produced only sullen aversion, and maddened your sense of inability, sometimes even to despair. You became afraid to look toward the fiery mount and the tables of the law; for so often as you looked, you sinned; and so often as you strove to amend, you sinned the more; and though your conscience was lashed into exacerbation of remorse, your heart acknowledged no true submission to the God whom you had offended. But when from the mount that might be touched, and that burned with fire, and blackness, and darkness, and tempest, and trumpet, and terrible words, which made you exceedingly fear and quake, you were gently led aside, and brought to this Zion, to Jesus the Mediator of the

New Covenant, and to the blood of sprinkling; when here you were made to behold the incarnate Son of God bending his will (at vast, unspeakable cost of glory and happiness) to that law which you would not fulfil, obeying that precept which you had trampled under foot; and himself enduring those pangs which you had merited; and when, in addition to all this, and above all this, you saw this same Jesus turning to *you*, (ungodly and rejecting sinner as you were,) and as it were drenched in the blood which you had shed, and offering to you the full value of the atonement to which you had constrained him; then, then, the mountain of ice began to melt; then the full soul began to flow down in rivers of penitential tenderness. Christ had conquered, and you were his; and as he bore you away in triumph, subdued by the power of his compassions, you vowed that after the example of this divine submission, you also would submit your will to God. For Christ's submission is not only our motive, but our pattern. Here is our example; here we learn that greatest, hardest lesson of Christianity, to say, "Not as I will, but as thou wilt." It is particularly learnt in time of affliction and bereavement; in the chamber of illness and mourning; in the altered scenes of sudden depression and overthrow; in the downhill of friendless old age and poverty. Then you hear God saying: "Should it be according to thy mind?" If God had let you have your own way; if he had let your riches remain; if he had spared those whom you are now mourning for; if he had confirmed your health; if he had put an end to your fears; if he had granted you all your fond desires, how, I pray, my dear, suffering fellow-Christian, could you ever have learnt that lesson which you are now learning? How could you ever have had any sympathy with the submissive Son of God? You sometimes think thus, I dare say: "O if I could only do some great work for Christ! If I could only strike some blow, achieve some exploit, brave some peril." But let me assure you, you may as certainly and fully glorify Christ by submission as by act. Make sure that you are *called* to suffer, and you may even glory in it by submission. I could repeat to you the famous old heathen saying, that "a good man struggling with adversity is a sight worthy of the gods;" but I prefer to say, that you are never so pleasing to God, and hence so like your adorable Redeemer, as when you are surrendering yourself unreservedly to the providential hand of Him who doeth all things well. Still say, though all his waves and his billows go over you, "Though he slay me, yet will I trust in him!" When trials grow heavier and more frequent, remember Him, who under the greatest and heaviest trial, still looked up, and said, "Abba, Father, all things are possible unto thee: take away this cup from me; nevertheless not as I will, but as Thou wilt!"

Let me, in conclusion, entreat those who feel themselves ignorant of these experiences, to reflect on the opposition of their will to God. See what a change has yet to be wrought in you. Is it not time to begin? Is there not motive to begin? What is it that is ruining you? If (as is probable from your present habit of mind) your soul should be among those at the left hand of the Judge at the last day, what, so far as you now can judge, will have been the cause of your condemnation? What is it that is now dragging you hellward with so dire a fascination? What is it for which you are selling your soul? Seek for it in your morning thoughts; seek for it in your musings by the way; seek for it in your watches and your dreams. Bring out to view that which you are choosing before Christ; and when you have looked at the idol, whether of lust, or pride, or power, or money; ask yourselves whether in this you have reasonable cause to trample on the blood of a dying Redeemer, and to forswear the heaven which he has purchased by his submission.

17

CONSOLATION FROM GOD'S PROMISE
NEVER TO FORSAKE.

XI.

AS if it were not enough that God has given us his Son, and with him all things, we are continually repining and distrusting. Not instructed by a thousand instances in our past lives, in which God has extricated us from difficulties, and been better to us than all our fears, and forgetful of the great fact in our history that not one good thing hath failed, of all that the Lord promised, we act over again the murmurings and the incredulity of Israel in the desert. "They forgat God their Saviour." "Yea, they despised the pleasant land, they believed not his word, but murmured in their tents, and hearkened not unto the voice of the Lord." Ps. 106. In such circumstances, it would be infinitely just in God, to take us at our word, and leave us to sink in our own unbelief, and suffer all we fear; but blessed be his holy name, his ways are not as our ways, nor his thoughts as our thoughts. He condescends to reason with the wayward, ungrateful child, and to bring his promises into view. So in that remarkable passage of the epistle to the Hebrews, in regard to anxieties about temporal support, the apostle says, "Be content with such things as ye have; for He hath said, *I will never leave thee nor forsake thee.*" It is not certain what particular passage of the Old Testament is here quoted, for such are the riches of promise that the meaning is found in many passages. The reference may be to the case of Abraham (Gen. 28 : 15): "And behold I am with thee, and will keep thee in all places whither thou goest,—for I will not leave thee, until I have done that which I have spoken to thee of." Or to the case of collective Israel: (Deut. 31 : 6): "Be strong and of a good courage, fear not, nor be afraid of them; for the LORD thy God, he it is that doth go with thee; he will not fail thee, nor forsake thee."

There is a gracious mystery about covenant promises, which we should earnestly seek to understand. What God promises to any one of the Old Testament saints, he promises to every believer, with such modification as suits his particular case. For all these promises are different leaves of the same tree of life, different expressions of the same covenant of grace. In this sense, whatsoever things were written aforetime, were written for our learning, that we through scriptural patience and comfort might have hope. It is in this way that thousands of believers have drunk at the same fountain; and what God said to Abraham, Isaac, and Jacob has been the refreshment of many souls in all generations. This principle of interpreting promises is implied in the verse just quoted. The apostle clearly invites all Christians to receive, collectively and individually, that comprehensive promise, which may originally have been addressed to an individual or to "the church in the wilderness." He gives it a form so general that it is not so much one promise, as all promises in one. And he adds a force of asseveration, which our language cannot reach; for in the Greek these few words contain no less than five negatives; to give the full force of which we should have to read it thus: "I will never, never leave thee, I will never, never, never forsake thee." The precious truth therefore which I commend to you for all coming years, is this: God engages in covenant, to be with the believer, for all needful good, now, henceforth, and for ever.*

When God says that he will never leave, it is of course a promise to be ever present. But this means more than that omnipresence which reaches equally to all creatures. This indeed sustains their existence, but does not insure their happiness; because the worst and most wretched of men might say with the Psalmist, "If I make my bed in *hell,* behold thou art there!" It means more than that providential sustentation and help, in regard to which God causeth his sun to rise and his rain to fall, on the evil and the good. It is not only a benignant and bountiful but a gracious presence, founded on the provisions of the covenant of grace. God will not forsake his Son, the head of the mystical body, and therefore he will not forsake any one of those

* Οὐ μή σε ἀνῶ, οὐδ' οὐ μή σε ἐγκαταλίπω.

who are joined to his Son. Let us clearly apprehend this connection. There is no gracious dealing with any, but through the Mediator. There is no adoption of any, but in the only begotten of the Father. There are none reconciled, but through the Lamb of God who taketh away the sin of the world. There are none accepted, but "in the Beloved." All the wealth of blessing is treasured in his hand; and in him all the promises are Yea, and in him Amen. Which will serve to answer a question that no doubt has been rising in the reader's mind, to wit, To whom is the promise of the text made? It is made to believers, and to none others. To all men, without exception, God is loving and bountiful; but his promise never to forsake is made to such only as by receiving Christ make all the promises their own. That God will leave and forsake the finally impenitent, and that to all eternity, is a truth which ought to thunder in the ear of every ungodly reader.

How can I expound such a promise as this? It is simple and clear as light. It needs not so much exposition, as belief and application. It is not the promise of one blessing, but of all. It does not so much say what God will do, as declare that there is nothing which he will not do. The Lord God is a sun and shield; no good thing will he withhold from them that walk uprightly. In these words he offers not simply his gifts, but himself. Whatever there is in God of help and comfort, is herein made over to the believer, through Christ Jesus: for he says, I will never leave thee nor forsake thee. It contains provision for body and for soul, in life, in death, and in eternity. It covers every instance, addresses itself to every character, and meets every emergency. Resting on the veracity of Jehovah, it needs no proof. Rising beyond all qualification and exception, it requires no elaborate comment. But it does require to be illustrated and amplified, so that it may be seen to apply to our several cases.

As originally urged, it was addressed to those early Christians who were in worldly straits. "Let your conversation be without covetousness; and be content with such things as ye have." To the Church, Christ says, "The poor ye have always with you." In primitive days, a large proportion both of preachers and hearers were literally poor. To the poor the gospel is preached. God hath chosen the poor rich in faith. It has been so in all ages; it is so at the present time. Some who read this at once make the case their own. At those seasons of the year, when careful persons look into their affairs, balance their books, take account of their stock, and provide for their liabilities, there are many whose hearts fail them. The future is very dark in respect to their daily bread. Such cases are not beneath the notice of Him who feedeth the young ravens; they should not be neglected by the Christian disciple. Let such rejoice to know that their accounts are audited in heaven. As their cry is, "Give us this day our daily bread," so the answer is, "Thy bread shall be given thee, and thy water shall be sure." Cast all your care upon him, for he careth for you, and gives you this as the primary and literal meaning of the promise, "I will never leave thee nor forsake thee."

But the supply of food and raiment is not the only temporal blessing which a believer may want. Other things there are, connected with health and illness, cheerfulness of temper, place of abode, safety by land and sea, treatment by friends, neighbours, or enemies, social relations, connections in life, among parents, children, husband and wife, master and servant, education, learning, good name among men, strength for labour; in a word, all the lights and shades of our common journey; all these awaken our solicitude; and in regard to all, our only security is in having God with us. This he graciously promises. It is our part to lay hold on this immutable word. It has been the stay of thousands—it is strong enough to be ours.

Mark well the nature and extent of the promise: God does not say you shall have no afflictions, or that you shall never fear, or that his presence shall never be doubted. Indeed, in other places, he says the very reverse. "In the world ye shall have tribulation, but be of good cheer, I have overcome the world." Ah, brethren, we are sometimes brought into perils, where we need a new, special, and divine application of the promise to our hearts, or we sink into despair. The trial seems unlike all we ever had before, and all that others have endured. The enemy whispers, "There is no help for him in God."

GOD WILL NOT FORSAKE.

The sun of your common day has set in clouds. The stars of your common night are hidden. The wind howls tempestuously, and the sea is chafed into deadly fury. Your helm is broken, your sail rent, and your bark all but foundered. The only light is the lurid flash, and perdition opens its chasm to swallow you up. I specify not the sort of affliction: your own heart will tell you that; and it makes no difference here. One in ancient times, in such a case, could say, "For thou hadst cast me into the deep, in the midst of the seas; and the floods compassed me about; all thy billows and thy waves passed over me. Then I said, I am cast out of thy sight; yet will I look again toward thy holy temple." The thought of God in such moments affords the only hope. And it is heard, above all the commotion of the elements, saying, "It is I, be not afraid!" God does not forsake his people in their extremities; if he should do so, all would be despair. As if to prepare them for extraordinary encounters, he often throws his promise into a form which indicates great and sore trial; thus showing us that no one is to be dismayed, or to doubt his loving-kindness, because danger is great and imminent. It is not said, Thou shalt never be in pestilence; but it is said, "A thousand shall fall at thy side, and ten thousand at thy right hand, but it shall not come nigh thee!" It is not said, Thou shalt never go through fire and flood; but it is said, "When thou passest through the waters, I will be with thee; and through rivers, they shall not overflow thee."

You may not promise yourself that you shall never be an orphan; but you may declare assuredly, "When my father and mother forsake me, then the Lord will take me up," that is, he will never leave me, nor forsake me.

The promise before us fully justifies the persuasion that there is no variety of character, no stage of life, no peculiarity of temporal distress in which the believer may not count on God's presence, protection, aid, deliverance, and comfort. And a believing view of this will give our religion such a cast, that it will be our habit of soul to rejoice in God himself, rather than in his gifts. Still the song will arise: "Although the fig-tree shall not blossom, neither shall fruit be in the vines; the labour of the olive shall fail, and the fields shall yield no meat; the flock shall be cut off from the fold, and there shall be no herd in the stalls; yet I will rejoice in the Lord, I will joy in the God of my salvation."

That God does not forsake his people is a foundation-truth of religion, established by the history of all saints, in Scripture, and in the later Church. Innumerable are the instances in which their greatest extremity has been the juncture of his gracious interposition. So it was with Abraham, when his hand was stretched out over the son of promise, in his greatest earthly trial; and ever since the name of the place has been a holy watchword, *Jehovah-Jireh:* "In the mount of the Lord it shall be seen." If this presence had a single moment of intermission, that might be the moment of ruin; but "I will never, never leave thee." The presence and the power are unintermitted and perpetual, reaching to the smallest cares as well as to the greatest terrors. "Such honour have all his saints." And this is the grand consolation of life.

But this promise has a bearing, yet more important, on our spiritual life. We need not wonder that God should continue to stand by the new creature in all its emergencies. His plan is not to be disappointed; nor does he lay hold of a resisting rebel, and subdue and transform him, in order to be baffled by the adversary. If we had nothing stronger than the persistency of human will to depend upon, our reliance would be on the weakest of all causes. One moment of caprice or carelessness might ruin the soul for ever. But grace is determined to complete what it has begun, and to perform the good work unto the day of redemption. The whole church is given to Christ in covenant, and every individual believer has his share in the blessed security. Looking at the internal strength of the church, we may say it is endangered; but looking at the covenant, it is safe. "In that day sing ye unto her, A vineyard of red wine. I the Lord do keep it; I will water it every moment: lest any hurt it, I will keep it night and day." God's honour is concerned to bring the disciple through, in spite of all enemies. This is felt in time of temptation, when the sound of unearthly hosts marshalling around us is heard on every side; "for we wrestle not against flesh and blood, but against principalities, against powers against the rulers of the darkness of this world, against spiritual wickedness in high places." Let God forsake us but an instant when thus beleaguered, and we should be torn to pieces by the fiery talons of a thousand hellish destroyers. But still the voice is, "I will never leave thee nor forsake thee." What else saved Peter in the hour of darkness? "I have prayed for thee, that thy faith fail not!" Precious words, which are applicable to all of us in our times of temptation! "The devil, as a roaring lion, walketh about, seeking whom he may devour;" and all the fold would be a desolation were it not for the good Shepherd, who knoweth his sheep, and is known of them. The more deeply we drink of gospel grace, the more shall we value this assurance of God's never-ceasing help, as knowing that we are not sufficient of ourselves so much as to think a good thought; but that all our sufficiency is of God.

There are moments of despondency in which the believer is ready to take up David's lamentation and cry, "I shall one day perish by the hand of Saul." But the promise gleams forth among the stars of heaven, and he rejoices in the sure mercies of David. It is wonderful how Scripture makes provision even for these moods of weakness and distrust in the Church. Out of the clouds and darkness, the well-known voice is heard, saying, "For a small moment have I forsaken thee, but with great mercies will I gather thee. In a little wrath I hid my face from thee for a moment; but with everlasting kindness will I have mercy on thee, saith the Lord thy Redeemer. For the mountains shall depart, and the hills be removed; but my kindness shall not depart from thee, neither shall the covenant of my peace be removed, saith the Lord that hath mercy on thee." It is this covenant which still remains as the foundation of confidence. Yet the individual believer may take up the language of Zion in the hours of desertion: "The Lord hath forsaken me, and my Lord hath forgotten me! Can a woman forget her sucking child, that she should not have compassion on the son of her womb? yea, *they* may forget, yet will I not forget thee." Come what will, God's mercies cannot fail, nor his presence be removed. Even sin, his abhorrence, and our greatest enemy, shall not be allowed to break the hallowed alliance. This is a delicate point in Christian experience, and one which requires to be treated with caution. It is no part of the covenant, that the believer may live as he lists, and yet have God's favour; that he may continue in sin, that grace may abound; that God does not hate and chastise his sins; or that he may walk in unholiness, and yet persevere. This were to assert contradiction, absurdity, and impossibility. "Sin shall not have dominion over you." "This is the will of God, even your sanctification." To be left in sin is to be forever forsaken of God; it is to secure your deliverance from sin, that he says, "I will never leave thee nor forsake thee." Indwelling corruption may rear its head, and sometimes threaten to prevail, but the presence of the Holy Spirit, working repentance and faith in the soul, will crush the monster. God is perpetually carrying on a hidden but mighty process to this very intent; and there is no aspect of the promise which is more acceptable to the true disciple, who, having these promises, is induced to lay aside all filthiness of flesh and spirit, and to perfect holiness in the fear of God. Though the Master may leave the gold in the furnace, he does not abandon it. The flames may rage, but they are only consuming the dross; and at length the refulgent mass issues from the glowing heat fit for the use of its Lord.

There are conjunctures in the soul's history when there is a combination of enemies, and when God seems departing. External affliction presses in unexpected forms; to increase the anguish, Satan and his angels assault the soul with manifold temptations; and to complete the calamity, treachery is found within, and the will begins to yield consent to evil. Job was in such case, as was also David. But he that is with us is mightier than they that are against us. The conflict would be fatal if God now were to depart; but he abides. It is agreeable to his covenant so to do. How insufficient would the favour be if he were to cling to us in our outward distress, and leave us to ourselves in the infinitely greater hazard of spiritual assault! Such is not the manner of his grace. In the present endurance of such evils, and in the expectation of those that are future, we are authorized to assure ourselves, that he will never leave us nor forsake us. "There hath no temptation taken you but such as is common to man; but God is faithful, who will not suffer you to be tempted above that ye are able; but will with temptation also make a way to escape, that ye may be able to bear it."

My fellow-Christians, in looking forward towards infirmity, old age, and the decline of life, you have sometimes sunk in spirit, and feared lest the stock of strength which you now possess might not be sufficient for that sad and disheartening part of the pilgrimage. To clear away such doubts, you need only hearken to the paternal voice, which says, "Even to old age, I am He, and to hoary hairs will I carry you;" that is, "I am he whose promise hath been given, I will never leave you, nor forsake you." Combine in your imagination all the forces of outward distress, poverty, weakness, pain, desertion, and despondency; all the temptations of a cruel and experienced foe; all the surviving evils of your own partially sanctified nature; all shall prove unable to break the covenant. And as you go down the harsh descent into the last valley, though fears may be in the way, you shall still say, "Who shall separate us from the love of Christ? Nay, in all these things we are more than conquerors through him that loved us!"

And then, in that dreaded trial which awaits us all, what is our assurance for the death-bed, but this same declaration of God's gracious purpose? Can we rely on any powers of which we are now conscious for the conflict with the last enemy? Thanks be unto God, he has not left us to so feeble a source. If there is on earth a spot where his covenant mercies are especially shown, it is the dying chamber. There, when friends have fallen back, because they cannot help; when earthly sights have failed before the glassy eye; when earthly sounds, even of devotion and love, have ceased to reach the ear; when the soul, almost free from a body that is cold and stiffening, almost reduced to that nakedness and loneliness with which it is to explore the unknown future, is already forsaken of all that is created, a gentle, well-remembered whisper is saying to the inward sense, "I will never, never leave thee: I will never, never, never forsake thee." And the accomplishment of all is just at the door; for when the last breath is wasted, and the silence around is broken by sudden wailing and preparations for the tomb, that spirit, nearer to God than ever before, is rapt for ever in the embrace of love, no more to fear, to sorrow, or to sin. O ye who have no God, and who know ye are afraid to die, it is worth your instant labour and importunate prayer; it is worth toils and sufferings of a lifetime to be prepared for such a departure.

This, indeed, is vast and glorious, but is this all? Does God conduct his beloved child to the gate of bliss, and then cancel his promise, and abandon it? O no! All that precedes is but a single momentary breath before a lifetime. We have arrived at the true birth of the soul. Now it emerges

GOD WILL NOT FORSAKE.

into tracts of endless expansion, where there is no danger, because there is no evil. Perfect holiness is perfect bliss, and both are increasing for ever. Now the union of the soul with God, often sighed for, is consummated; and so shall they "be ever with the Lord." Such is the value, my brethren, of the truth here revealed, that God engages to be with the believer, for all needful good, now, henceforth, and for ever.

It would not be difficult to show the consolatory bearing of this sacred truth on some particular cases of trial which are common among God's suffering people. For example, these pages may fall under the notice of one who has been bereaved of the guide of her youth, and is left to pursue, in solitary weakness, that part of the journey in which the support of a loving friend is most needed. The stay has been removed from the sinking frame. The best, and nearest, and most sympathizing counsellor is removed. He upon whom the great burden of responsibility was so constantly devolved that it was scarcely felt, is no longer present. That heart, which of all others had most forbearance and compassion for her weaknesses and sorrows, no more beats on earth. To this may be added, in some cases, the pressure of poverty, the failure of health, and the infirmity of age. It is not to be denied that this is a moment of unusual affliction. But God has not left it without promise; since he has named himself the "Judge of the widows." He will plead their cause; he will never leave them nor forsake them. However desolate in regard to human prospects, the widowed heart may confidently throw itself upon the tender mercies of him who is at once Maker and Husband. A thousand testimonies might be adduced, if departed saints could speak, of God's faithfulness in this very relation, to daughters of afflictions who have fled to him for succour, and have been sustained and cheered throughout the days of forlorn and otherwise hopeless pilgrimage.

In general, it may be asserted, that the gospel covenant secures to us the presence and support of God, for all the future. Let no moody clouds obscure this prospect, nor any temporary adversities discourage us from hoping boldly in our all-sufficient Helper. The worst that shall ever befall us, if we are within the pale of his grace, shall be so ordered in time and measure, as only more distinctly to show that his purposes are full of mercy. Let go this confidence for a moment, and we become wretched indeed. But it is not to be omitted, that God not only gives this promise, but causes his servants to believe it. Without this the word of assurance, however certain of fulfilment, would for the time being be a dead letter. And the suffering soul is sometimes allowed to reach the very brink of such a despondency. But he who worketh in us both to will and do of his good pleasure, utters the word of promise, opens the wistful ear of woe, pours in the grace of believing, irradiates the soul's chamber with the light of hope, and lifts up the head that was hanging down in apprehension. Then it is, that amidst the reverberation of the tempest Christ's own voice is heard, giving peace and assurance. From which we learn the value of faith, as an instrument of consolation.

Preparation for trials yet to come is a principal part of Christian prudence. It is too late to make ready the safeguards of the vessel, when the storm has begun to rage. He who is wise will bethink him of the hour of darkness, long before its arrival. He will store his mind with provision of truth from the word of inspiration; above all, with promises adapted to each emergency of this changeful life. He will, in ways already indicated, seek to make his calling and election sure; lest in the time of peril he be plunged into doubt respecting his own acceptance, and thus into an incapacity of receiving comfort from the most explicit promises of the Scripture. And he will, by repeated acts of faith, acquire such a habit of mind as shall not be shaken from its moorings when winds prevail upon the sea. It is therefore earnestly to be pressed upon the consideration of all professing Christians, that their support in affliction will bear proportion to their vigilance and holiness in ordinary times. All observation of religious experience tends to verify this remark. None are so immediately prostrated by a great distress, none so prone to exclaim that God has forsaken them, as those who have been conformed to the world, and have lived as if God were not their portion. Melancholy indeed is the case of that servant of Christ, who is surprised by some desolating stroke, at the very time, when, backsliding and carnal, he is in full pursuit of earthly idols. Even him, supposing that he is a child of the kingdom, God will not forsake. But fearful must be the paroxysms of fear and compunction, through which his way of return will lie to the confident reliance of the heavenly word. Whereas, he who walks humbly with his God, delights in him, communes with him, and enjoys him, as the daily tenor of his life, sees the night of adversity darkening around him without consternation. His apprehensions of God's nature and providence, his relation to Christ as his covenant head and ever present advocate, and his certainty that no jot or tittle of promise shall remain unfulfilled, avail to lift his head, when the waves run highest. In these shakings of the earth and sea he does not behold the tokens of a departing God. On the contrary, he can sing with the psalmist, "God is our refuge and strength, a very present help in trouble. Therefore will not we fear, though the earth be removed, and though the mountains be carried into the midst of the sea: though the waters thereof roar and be troubled, though the mountains shake with the swelling thereof." Psalm 46 : 1, 2, 3.

THE BELIEVER SUSTAINED BY THE STRENGTH OF CHRIST.

XII.

A SENSE of weakness is one of the first impressions of which the convinced soul is conscious. There was a day when the believer fondly imagined that all things were possible to him, by his own unaided endeavours. Therefore it was, that he put far off the day of repentance, believing that at any moment of alarm or illness, or even in the article of death, he might gather his powers and cast himself by a happy effort into the kingdom of God. Practically denying the need of divine assistance, he deferred until a more convenient season that work which multitudes have never performed to the entire satisfaction of their souls, even during a lifetime. But no sooner is any one convinced that he is miserable, and not only miserable, but guilty; that he is condemned, and not only condemned, but dead in trespasses and sins, cut off from all succour, and absolutely helpless and undone—than he begins to see the meaning of such declarations as these, "No man can come to Christ, except the Father draw him." He acknowledges indeed that the barrier is his depravity, his sin, his alienation from God, the want of a holy nature and disposition; and he feels him self on this account justly condemned; yet just as strongly is he impressed with the insurmountable greatness of this hinderance. The change of heart which he knows to be necessary is a change which no human philosophy can persuade him is within the power of himself or any creature; and the more he enters into the solemn reality of this his entire helplessness, the more will he cry out with unutterable anguish of spirit, "Lord, be merciful to me a sinner."

"This heart of mine," he says, "is too hard to be melted into love by any influence but the baptismal fire of the Holy Ghost: yet am I not thereby justified—for as a matter of right I dare not ask of God to rescue me. I am an enemy of the ever blessed Jehovah. My chains are the chains of sin; and sin is in its very essence alienation from God or opposition to God, and cannot be my excuse. I lie at the mercy of Jehovah, and even though I pray and strive, I do but see more and more this plague of my own heart: I do but feel more and more my own weakness. If I am ever saved, it must be by the very energy of the Almighty. I am unholy. I partake with devils in that abominable thing which God hateth. I must be born again or perish. I must believe on the Son of God or remain condemned. The condemnation is just. I have no excuse for not loving supremely the most blessed and glorious and beneficent Jesus, no apology for not relying upon his offered mercy. I lie athirst by the fresh fountain of the water of life: still I cannot stoop and drink; and this very reluctance is my sin—the sin of obstinately rejecting Christ and his salvation. Whither shall I look for help? No power can remedy my disease, but one which can reach this stubborn principle of depravity—and there is no such power but that of God."

These are common exercises, and this struggle is more or less protracted in all cases of conviction. In order to feel that salvation is all of grace, it is just as necessary to be convinced of our dependence on God for every right thought, as to be convinced of guilt and condemnation. The work of our regeneration is not, in any part of it, man's work. For although man is active in believing and repenting, and loving and obeying, yet the co-operation, or rather the primary and effectual operation, is of God. When the withered hand was stretched out at the command of Christ, the poor sufferer was active, yet we all know that it was Divine energy which wrought in and by this volition. No man can say at his conversion, "I will do thus much; I will go so far.; I will meet the advances of God on some middle ground—and then—when I have done my utmost, in my own strength, God will accomplish the remainder, and come to the aid of my weakness." No, my brethren, when a perishing sinner is most in earnest in working out his own salvation, he does it with fear and trembling. And why this fear and trembling? Because he knows that a sovereign and holy God holds his very being at his own pleasure, and may or may not, as he will, work in him both to will and to do of his own good pleasure.

We are now able, in a measure, to account for the length of this agonizing struggle in certain minds: and to give one reason why a heavy-laden soul cannot at once come to Christ, when the free overture of salvation is made. It is mainly because the person convinced of sin, is still unconvinced of the perfect freeness of the proffered gift. He is still desirous of arriving at some deeper conviction—some more poignant grief—some terror or earnestness—of being melted into greater floods of tears or fixed in firmer resolutions. He is, in short, not yet convinced of his dependence on God for every right thought, feeling, and action. He will come to Jesus when he has made his heart better, and he even dreads to believe now, to cast himself now upon the open arms of Christ, lest it should be too soon. His struggles are suffered by the wisdom of God to continue, that he may find his own weakness, and, after having wearied his soul in going about to establish his own righteousness, may submit himself to the righteousness of God.

The belief of our dependence on God, as the source of all spiritual strength, grows with our Christian growth. The newly converted person may, in the wonderful path of God's most wise discipline, be permitted for a season to walk in his own strength, and left as the tottering infant is left by the parent to prove its own limbs; but he is soon made to cry out, "I am not sufficient of myself so much as to think a good thought, but my sufficiency is of God." The believer does not receive at his ingrafting into Christ, a supply of vital energy sufficient to influence him in a holy manner all his life long. The branch must abide in the vine. There must be a union, not only formed, but kept up. New streams of grace must flow, hour by hour; and if for a moment this communication is interrupted, he begins to languish; like the twig or the bough which is robbed of its life-giving sap and moisture. "Without me ye can do nothing." This is the lesson which we are constantly learning. God is glorified when we are apt scholars in this school.

It is true there are habits of piety; but not such habits as render us independent of the divine influences. If God withhold his hand the habit ceases. If he hide his face we are troubled. The most experienced Christians are most aware of being themselves unable to stand a moment, and of the danger of self-dependence. They are taught of God that the glory must not only be, but appear to be of Him. If they are faithful, it is because Christ by his holy Spirit replenishes their souls with his grace. They live by faith, and not only so—it is by constantly renewed acts of faith that they live. The child of God is no more able to put forth acts of faith now, than he was when he first passed from darkness to light, except so far as he has divine aid.

The life that he now lives is the same life which was communicated at his effectual calling. Though an abiding, it is not an independent principle. He cannot say, I live now because God once raised me to newness of life and then left me to keep my own soul alive. No, "I live, yet not I, but Christ liveth in me; and the life that I now live, I live by faith in the Son of God." We live, my brethren, but not independently; "our life is hid with Christ in God." God is the author of the vital action, Christ is the vital centre, the very heart of the system, from whom, and in correspondence with whom, every pulsation of spiritual being is made. It is important that those who profess godliness should be led to consider this peculiarity of true religion. They that are Christ's feel that they are in the exercise of grace, only so long as Christ lives in them; that the true method of cultivating piety is to cultivate a sense of dependence on Christ; that if we desire to grow in grace and to glorify God, we must look above and beyond all means, all instrumentality, all ordinances, to Jesus Christ as our living head. To the believer Christ says, "Because I live, ye shall live also." There are some who have a name to live while they are dead. They are numbered among the people of God: they are punctual in the outward performances of religion. They have felt some sorrow and tenderness and compunction, and subsequent to this, some peace and joy, and they believe themselves safe in the ark—though it may have been very long since they knew what it was to experience any near communion with their Redeemer; and though they are seen by the world to "mind earthly things" and to love the world, and to be ashamed of Christ—and though they bridle not their tongues—and speak evil of brethren—and indulge in pride and hatred, in ambition and avarice in folly and levity. Now such persons, though they are frequently so much blinded by their sin as to think that they are rich and increased in goods and have need of nothing, are really poor and miserable, and naked, and actually in need of the principal thing in religion. The great attainment they have not reached. They do their works and attend their duties without Christ. Their sufficiency is never felt to be of God. The mystery of union with the Redeemer, abiding in him, being complete in him, feeling strong in him, walking, living, and triumphing by faith in him — this delightful mystery of godliness has never been revealed to their souls. Such religion as this is a mere shell, without the kernel. It is legal—it is Christless—and however great the zeal, or bustling the activity of those who possess it—it is such as will not honour God, or give comfort in the hour of death. Now the faithful servant of God owns at every step that if having been once blind he now sees, it is all of the Spirit. "By the grace of God I am what I am." Not one movement can be made towards the end of his course without assistance. "Looking unto Jesus" the author and finisher of his faith, he runs with patience the race that is set before him.

This dependence is felt very sensibly by the believer, while engaged in the active duties of life. Is he a parent? He knows that his teaching and correction and discipline can in no way avail to the salvation of his household without the blessing of Christ. Is he a minister? He sows the seed and administers the truth, as one who can do nothing efficaciously toward the increase. He feels that all his sufficiency is of God; and while he plants in many soils, and waters with many tears and prayers, he lifts to heaven his eyes, which often fail for grief, and says, "My soul, wait thou only upon God, for my expectation is from him." Is he using those means which lie within the reach, and belong to the duty of every member of Christ's body, to promote true religion? He depends on the arm of Jehovah. The battle here is not to the strong; whatever his zeal, his talents, his assiduity, all the increase must be of God. He acknowledges that he is nothing—feels that he is nothing—desires to be nothing—delights to be nothing—that Christ his Saviour may be all in all. His longing desire is to set the crown of all blessing, honour, glory, and power, upon the head of Immanuel.

When the Apostle Paul says, in writing to the Philippians, "I can do all things through Christ which strengtheneth me," there is in his words a total renunciation of all dependence on his own strength. Though he could say, with regard to his brethren, that he laboured more abundantly than they all, yet he thus speaks; "Not that we are sufficient of ourselves to think any thing as of ourselves, but our sufficiency is of God." And he elsewhere states the reason of this to be, "that the excellency of the power may be of God and not of us." Whatever employment or labour, my dear brethren, you may be called to undertake, whether within or without, of soul or body, for yourselves or for your fellow-men, great or small, new or accustomed; whatever burdens, temptations, or afflictions, you have to endure; whatever pleasures or sins you are commanded to deny yourself or forbear—in every case, and at all times acknowledge and feel that you are without strength. Yes, so true is this, and so important, that you cannot feel it too strongly. You may, indeed, cherish a false and counterfeit impression of your own weakness—a sentiment which is wrong in kind, which is sinful and hateful to God. You may say in your hearts, "I can do nothing, and therefore I will do nothing I am helpless, and therefore I will not seek divine help. God calls me to duties, but I am unable to perform them, and I will sit still, fold my arms, and wait upon the Lord without effort." This is rebellion, for it is in effect saying, "The Almighty is a hard master, reaping where he hath not sown, and I will not attempt to obey." This is the form of depravity which rages in the souls of those who are unconverted. Because they profess to believe that they are dead, they will not come unto Christ, that they may have life. And very often these very persons have less genuine belief of their impotence than all others. But you who believe that the law of God is holy and just and good; you who delight in it after the inner man, and desire to obey it, and strive to be holy, and at the same time render to God the praise of every right thought, every momentary view of the truth, every contrite sigh; you who lament that when you would do good evil is present with you, and groan being burdened, because ye cannot do the good ye would, and sink into nothing in the consciousness of your feebleness and corruption;—you, beloved, cannot too much encourage such renunciation of your own strength.

You are taught already by your daily experience that the belief of this truth does not make you listless. Never does the believer work for God with so much confidence, and activity, and perseverance, and zeal, and success, as when he knows that all his works are wrought in God: that God is fulfilling in him all the good pleasure of his goodness, and the work of faith with power.

Are any ready to say, If we have no strength except in Christ, we might as well make no efforts until the energy of God falls upon us and bears us away irresistibly to the performance of duty? To such we reply: This might be reasonable, if man were a mere machine operated upon by the Holy Spirit, as the ship is moved by the wind. But no. Man is essentially active. How God works in us and by us we know not; neither do we know how an act of our will sets in motion the muscles of our bodies. This, however, we do know, that God works and that we work also. The only revealed connection between the two operations is such as we just stated. We are to put forth strong efforts—as strong as though there were no aid required; but at the same time feeling that every such act is spiritual and acceptable and useful, only so far as Christ strengthens us. These efforts are as truly our own as any thing conceivable is our own. God in great mercy rewards us for them as our own. They are as truly effects of God's agency as the creation is such. Observe the order of the ideas in the words of Paul already cited. 1st. I can do all things. This is the expression of a resolution to work, to attempt all duty. He does not say, I will wait until I see and feel the breathing of the Spirit of Christ, I will be inactive and supine until I can be so no longer. No; I will arise and confidently do every act which is commanded—endeavour the utterance of every good word—the performance of every right action. 2d. Through Christ which strengtheneth me. This is the expression of faith in Christ's strength, of actual belief that Christ does strengthen. This is being strong in the Lord, and in the power of his might. When Paul thus spoke, he felt that he was strengthened with all might according to His glorious power.

We learn this truth, then, as to the order in which these ideas arise in the mind of a Christian. First, We set ourselves about the work of piety. Secondly, The Spirit of Christ makes this work effectual. So, also, in another passage the same order is observed: 1st, Work out your own salvation; 2d. It is God that worketh in you to will and to do.

I have endeavoured to set forth in all its fulness the doctrine of human dependence, in order to show that it is not only consistent with human agency, but is an incentive to it. For who will so readily undertake the Lord's work as he who expects the Lord's assistance?

The words just cited express a desire and purpose to be intensely active. This is the man who felt that in him, that is in his flesh, dwelt no good thing. Yet now he exultingly says, "I can do all things; I can act; I can suffer; I have learned in whatsoever state I am, therewith to be content; I know both how to be abased and how to abound; every where and in all things I am instructed both to be full and to be hungry, both to abound and to suffer need; yea, I can do all things through Christ which strengtheneth me."

And how consoling to hear from Paul an expression of humble confidence, that Christ will strengthen. I am ready to attempt without delay whatever my Master calls me to undertake or to endure. However mortifying or afflictive the trial, here am I, Lord, send me. However uncertain the prospect of what is to be demanded, I am ready, "Lord, what wouldst thou have me to do?" Is it to rebuke an Apostle? He is withstood to the face. Is it to enter again the persecuting seat of Jewish malice? "Behold, I go bound in the Spirit unto Jerusalem, not knowing the things that shall befall me there; save that the Holy Ghost testifieth in every city, saying that bonds and imprisonments abide me; but none of these things move me." Is it to publish the news of a crucified Galilean in the imperial metropolis? " I am ready to preach the gospel to you that are at Rome also." Is it by his apparent enthusiasm to risk being thought insane? " Whether we be beside ourselves it is to God, or whether we be sober, it is for your cause, for the love of Christ constraineth us." Yes, brethren, this was the motive, and the strength of Christ sustained the Apostle, and sustains in the same manner all that are true believers.

"Through Christ which strengtheneth me." From whatever part of the world of grace the believer looks, his eye will always fasten itself upon the great Sun of Righteousness. As it is only in Christ that we see and know the Father, so the supplies of divine aid are all conveyed to us through the mediation of Christ. The Holy Spirit is the gift of Christ. His influences are bought for us by the blood of Jesus. And our great High Priest, who bears our names upon his breast, looks from heaven to see us toiling here with manifold trials; and obtains and sends down upon us the strengthening influences of this adorable and glorious Teacher and Comforter. The operations of the Spirit are invisible and secret, and known only by their effects. These effects are various. They are not always elevated emotions, or sensible raptures, frames of sorrow or of joy. There is reason to believe that the blessed Sanctifier often works by immediate impulses to Christian action, without at such particular times, filling the soul with self-evidencing pleasure. We may grieve the holy Spirit of Christ if we defer our duty, if we neglect the doing of any enjoined act until we feel that we can do it joyfully, until every feeling of mortified pride, or spiritual cowardice, or sloth, or unbelief is expelled. This would be to look for the triumph before conflict. If we love Christ, we shall do his will so far as it is known to us, now, without delay. Are we destitute of the proper feelings? This aggravates but cannot excuse the sin of disobedience. To believers, and also to unbelievers, the command is, Do the will of God; do it now; do it with such strength as you have. Christ gives strength while we are in action. It can scarcely be necessary to prove this. You do not surely expect a dormant stock, or magazine of graces, a hoarded capital of piety in your souls, sensibly manifesting its presence before you begin to do those acts which make these graces necessary. Put the slumbering muscles in action: not till then can you know whether you have or have not strength. Stretch out the withered hand: not till then shall it be made whole.

Look back upon what your own experience has taught you, and you will find that these statements are correct. Remember you not the time when you have been awakened to see that some great Christian duty had been neglected, such as the duty of confessing Christ before men; of defending his truth; of reproving sin; of warning your impenitent friends; of confessing your faults to those whom you had of fended; of obeying Christ, by casting out of your soul every unkind or unforgiving temper, and making advances of reconciliation towards those who had offended you? Have you not struggled long with your rebellious heart, before you could be persuaded to do what you seemed to hear God so plainly commanding? perhaps, until you were alarmed to think that, continuing in known sin, you could no longer consider yourself as any thing more than a self-deceived formalist? Have you not dreaded to attempt the duty; and have you not at length, with unutterable distress, taken up the cross; and then, in the very moment at which you thought to fail, found a pleasure, a delight, a peace of conscience, a holy joy, an ease and satisfaction, in this dreaded duty? Is it not so? At that moment Christ, by his Spirit, was strengthening you; and thus it will ever be. "Draw nigh unto God, and he will draw nigh unto you." Go forth in his name, and he will reveal himself as present with you when you are least of all expecting it. Begin now, I earnestly beseech you, to do those things which you see to be your manifest duty. This is an exhortation which brings false professors to a safe test. Whatever you may feel of soft emotions, whatever you may do, or forbear to do, you are in danger of condemnation if your heart can turn away from the light of the law, or your soul rebel against known duty. Your faith, if it do not teach you to do the will of God, so far as you know it, is dead, being alone. It is a glorious truth, that we are not saved by our works; but it is as salutary and as certain a truth that, "he that saith I know him, and keepeth not his commandments, is a liar, and the truth is not in him."

Your dependence on the Spirit of Christ will never be so great as when you are actively employed in his service. Then you will feel, when in labours most abundant, that you can do nothing. Yet, my brethren, we must receive into our minds the whole of the idea, without separation. Dependence on God does not mean simply a doubt of our own strength; but further than this, and principally, a belief in the promised strength of Christ. You may have your minds filled with worldly thoughts, and your lips with worldly conversation, and your lives with worldly pursuit; thinking, saying, doing nothing for Jesus Christ, and may still cry out, "We are poor, weak, dependent creatures."

This is not Christian dependence. Such feelings do not tend in any degree to holiness, while there is no looking to God for help. Such is not the dependence of Paul. Hear him: "I can do all things through Christ which strengtheneth me." It is as much your duty to trust in Christ's strength as to distrust your own. You attempt nothing for the honour of God and the good of your neighbour; and why?—Because you are weak, and of yourselves far from all good. True; and such you will ever be until, with a pure heart, you address yourselves to the joint work of prayer and action. Christ will not give strength to any man to lie unapplied in his bosom. He gives grace when it is needed, and it is needed in the hour of action. Continue to do nothing, and you shall, in all probability, die as you have lived—waiting, waiting for the moving of the waters, when Christ stands ready and says, " Wilt thou be made whole ?"

Again, let every reader be exhorted to contemplate this Christian paradox: When most active, most dependent. When most sensible of weakness, then most abundant in labour. When stretching every power to honour Christ, then sinking most deeply into the lowliness of self-distrust, and rising most triumphantly in trust upon the Lord. When convinced that without God's immediate agency no duty can be performed, no soul converted; then attempting, with unwearied effort, to come up to the help of the Lord against the mighty. Let us pray for large measures of this grace of dependence on Christ: let us seek it by labouring for Christ. This is the secret of being useful and yet humble. Would to God that we could acquire it.

There is an awful solemnity in the thought that our strength is of God; that our acts, if Christian acts, are wrought by the Holy Spirit.

When I am weak then am I strong. Let us be encouraged to undertake whatever we consider our plain duty, with holy boldness, knowing that God calls us to nothing in which he is not ready to assist us. No man ever undertook a duty, in reliance on Christ's aid, who was left to struggle in his own strength. Those only are ignorant of this who have no knowledge of the aid of the Spirit. Those are most ready to attempt new enterprising and hazardous services for religion, who have been oftenest upon the forlorn hope of the Christian host; or rather—as the expression applies not to Christ's army—none can do more for Immanuel than those who have hazarded the most. Dare we cast ourselves on the simple word of divine promise: "Commit thy way unto the Lord, and he will direct thy steps?"

Let us leave this discussion with the belief that there is no service or suffering so great or trying, that Christ cannot and will not strengthen his people to enter upon and accomplish. We are complete in him.

THE COMPASSION OF CHRIST TO THE WEAK, THE SORROWING, AND THE SINFUL.

XIII.

THE world is deceived by the glare of seeming greatness; but those things are not always the best, which make the most violent impression. The common sun and air, the dews and rains of heaven, the fertilizing river, and the silent growth of fruits and harvests, which are the benignant influences of our world, are less awakening and vehement than the storm, the volcano, and the earthquake. The work of destruction is often more startling than the progress of merciful and happy benevolence. It is much the same in the moral world. The welfare of society is promoted by a succession of quiet acts, scarcely heeded as they pass, and often unseen, while the murderous deeds of warfare and outrage are loud and sudden. It is too much the case, that we fall into the same error with regard to spiritual character and the interior life of religion. We set great value on the outbreak of passionate feeling, or the acts which inflame the multitude, while we account but little of ten thousand gentle thoughts, words, motions, and habits, by which God is honoured, and the soul is carried forward toward the heavenly state.

Yet when we imagine the condition of ransomed spirits, we picture to ourselves a world of peculiar serenity and repose, where no paroxysms break the equable flow, and where the very ecstasy of love and praise is a constant, uninterrupted, and balanced glory. So we judge of the blessed angels; and so we hope for ourselves, when we anticipate perfect holiness. Rest and Peace are the names of such a paradise. That we form such conceptions, is a token that in our sober hours we set a superior value on those religious states which are permanent and unobtrusive.

The same thing appears in the only model we possess of human excellence. In the character of the Lord Jesus Christ there is nothing of spasmodic and convulsive action. The greater portion of his life was spent in retirement. The hills and vales of Galilee, and the borders of the lake of Cinneroth, beheld the silent loveliness and rapt devotion of the Son of Mary. His precursor and kinsman after the flesh, as he uttered the voice of Elijah in the wastes of Judah, seems never to have had a personal knowledge of him whom he proclaimed. And even when these two great personages met at the waters of Jordan, though the voice from heaven vouched the legation and the sonship of Jesus, the multitude knew him not. He is hurried away by the Spirit into the wilderness, in order to conflict with Satan; he dwells among the wild beasts (Mark 1: 13), and is ministered to by angels. These are long and secret preparations for a kingdom which cometh not by observation. When John points him out, he expressly adds, "There standeth one among you whom ye know not." And when again he points him out, as the great propitiation, the Lamb of God, not the thousands of Israel, but only two Galileans, follow in his way. When the third convert, Philip of Bethsaida, makes known his discovery to his guileless friend, Nathanael answers: "Can there any good thing come out of Nazareth?" What may have been the feelings of his near friends we know not. At the entertainment at Cana, where, by the "beginning of miracles," he "manifested forth his glory," we are informed of the unguarded zeal with which the blessed Virgin would have drawn him out to a premature development of his majesty. But his hour was not yet come. And after this sudden and transient flash of his divinity, he went back again into the shades of home: "He went down to Capernaum, he, and his mother, and his brethren, and his disciples." John 2 : 12.

By all this we are reminded of God's method of preparing for great actions. Moses was forty years in the tomb-like palaces of Egypt; despising their treasures, but treasuring up their learning; and then forty years more in the desert of Midian, before he was commissioned for his great work.

Even after the public manifestation of Christ, there is a singular reserve as to fuller disclosure of his greatness. His most explicit revelations are made in private and to humble individuals, as to the woman of Samaria, and the man that was born blind; and even his miracles were left to work their principal effect, as evidence, when he should be risen from the dead. Now and then, indeed, he breaks forth into signal demonstrations of authority, as when he scourges out the profaners of the temple, and feeds the multitudes; but more usually there is no proclamation of his greatness. He calls the humblest men, one by one, or in pairs, from fishing-boats and money-tables. After transcendent miracles, he rises before dawn, goes into a solitary place, and prays. "All men seek for thee;" but he goes at once to preach from town to town, notwithstanding their importunities. Matt. 8 : 17. He heals a leper; but it is with the injunction, "See thou say nothing unto any man;" and when the sensation through the country side brings crowds around him, it is expressly said, "Jesus could no more openly enter into the city, but he went without to desert places, and he withdrew himself into the wilderness and prayed, and they came to him from every quarter." Secrecy and devotion are the beloved retreat of holy minds. Humility and contemplation and lamenting love, all seek the shade, where, like the turtle dove, they grieve and are unseen.

Though our Lord must have come into contact with a very large portion of the inhabitants of Palestine, he retreated from public show, and the acclamations of the mass. "I receive not honour from men." He did not covet the ostentatious conflict of the foolhardy martyr of fanaticism. When he knew of conspiracy, "he withdrew himself with his disciples to the sea"—that beautiful sea, which is ever since consecrated in the recollections of believers. "Great multitudes followed him, from Galilee, and from Judea, and from Jerusalem, and from Idumea, and from beyond Jordan: and they about Tyre and Sidon, a great multitude, when they had heard what things he did, came unto him. And he spake to his disciples, that a small ship should wait on him, because of the multitude, lest they should throng him. For he had healed many; insomuch that they rushed* upon him for to touch him, as many as had plagues; and he healed them all"—as well those who cast themselves upon him in the frenzy of agonizing importunity and headlong craving, as those who besought him at a distance, with the homage of an awe which feared to profane the hem of his garment—"he healed them all. And unclean spirits, when they saw him, fell down before him, and cried, saying, Thou art the Son of God! and he straitly charged them that they should not make him known." Not that his mighty works could remain absolutely private, or that he desired them to be buried in oblivion. This had been to defeat the very end of his mission. The intention of the miracles was to attest his divine legation. But from various passages we learn that the grand revelation of the body of evidence was postponed until a critical point in his mediatorial history—the resurrection from the dead. This, as it was in itself the visible

* Margin.

seal of Heaven on his teaching, was that which brought to recollection, and so to public view, the tide of beneficent and supernatural wonders which had been flowing together for several years, as so many streams, to form a torrent of evidence, which at the appointed time should burst forth with irresistible conviction. By the sea of Galilee, however, he chose to repress the untimely fame, and to complete the quiet lowliness of his humiliation; for we read that it was agreeable to the oracle of Isaiah, 42 : 1 : " Behold my servant whom I have chosen ; my beloved in whom my soul delighteth: I will put my Spirit upon him, and he shall show judgment to the Gentiles.' He shall not strive nor cry, neither shall any man hear his voice in the streets." His entrance was with no flourish of heraldic trumpets; no kingly harbingers forewarned the multitude of the entrance of a king; no voice of murmuring thousands accompanied the progress of their deliverer; no clamour of contention broke from his lips, even in behalf of his down-trodden country. Rebellion found no countenance from his meek and holy presence. The Herodians, and such as refused tribute, heard him remand them to Cæsar. In his very walks of love, as he went about doing good, while the largesses of his charity flowed to thousands, he fled from the thanks and praises of his beneficiaries, and stole away, again and again, from the captivated populace, to cast himself before his Father, in the cold recesses of the mountain or the strand. His voice was ascending to heaven in solitary interces-

CHRIST'S COMPASSION.

sion: it was not heard in the streets. "A bruised reed shall he not break, and smoking flax shall he not quench."

There is here a transition of a natural and pleasing kind, from the gentleness of the Messiah's character to the feebleness and insignificance of his people. That feebleness and insignificance he will not despise or crush, but will uphold it as a means towards his victory. Though the King of Glory, at whose approach the everlasting gates are lifted up, he stoops to the lowest and most burdened. It is the same connection of ideas which occurs in that matchless invitation, "Come unto me, all ye that labour and are heavy laden, and I will give you rest: take my yoke upon you, and learn of me; for I am meek and lowly, and ye shall find rest for your souls." It is by reason of this meekness, this lowliness, this serene and retiring and silent compassion, that the shrinking, and the self-condemned, the fainting and the unprofitable, are emboldened to draw nigh. The encouragement might be less cheering if it had not been inscribed centuries before the advent, on the very scroll of his prophetic and regal commission, and if we had not heard it among the ancient titles of his Messiahship: "A bruised reed shall he not break, and smoking flax shall he not quench."

The reed is at best an ignoble growth in the vegetable world; having no rank among the sturdy trunks of the forest; rejoicing in no verdure of shady foliage, and scattering no flowers or fruit into the lap of toil. It may minister support, as the most slender staff, or solace a weary hour as the shepherd's pipe; but it can never be the weapon of war or the timber of architecture. Springing in fens and marshes, it is an image of weakness and poverty. Thus, " the Lord shall smite Israel as a reed shaken in the water," 1 Kings 14 : 15—a mean, defenceless thing of nought. The Egyptians, as a useless resort, are " a staff of reed to the house of Israel." Ez. 25 : 9. And John the Baptist, for his firmness and constancy, is contrasted with " a reed shaken of the wind." But a broken reed is something viler still. Of small value in its integrity, it is below notice when crushed. Who will look upon it, or pick its broken stem from the highway, or the water side? It can picture nothing better than the weakest and lowliest of all whom Christ relieves. Shall the bruised object be trampled down and left? The foot of pride might so deal with conscious wretchedness; but such is not the dealing of infinite Love: "He shall not break the bruised reed." The prophet employs another and a kindred metaphor, drawn from the common lamps of the Hebrews, in which the humble wick was of nothing better than flax. The office of the lamp is to blaze and give light; but when instead of this it barely smokes, it is of all household objects one of the most useless, noisome, and offensive; and we hasten to extinguish it. Not so the benign Redeemer: he does not extinguish even that which flickers in the socket, and is ready to die out. The smoking flax he shall not quench. It is part of his Messiahship to spare the perishing and rejected, the outcast reed, the half-quenched lamp. Blessed be his name! his princely advent is accompanied with a proclamation fitted to "revive the spirit of the humble, and to revive the heart of the contrite ones." Is. 57 : 15.

From the whole imagery of that text and context, we derive the truth, that the Lord Jesus Christ in his princely work as Messiah, looks with forbearance and compassion on the weakest and most despised of his people. It is a topic not inappropriate to our series of consolations; for it is well known that humble, tempted, and desponding persons are often ready to doubt their own welcome, and to deny themselves the blessings which constitute the portion. I mean therefore to inquire, who those characters are, designated by the bruised reed and the smoking flax.

And First, *The weak are such.* Their type is the reed, and the reed almost crushed. Such a one often comes to the sanctuary in the spirit of the Syrophenician, unable to claim any thing, yet pleading with irrepressible desire: Yea, Lord, but the dogs do eat of the crumbs from the Master's table. The soul trembles, lest this debility of grace be the want of title, and almost hears the words: ' 'Friend, how camest thou in hither—not having a wedding-garment." Or can scarce lift up the eyes to the place of emblematic propitiation, but is ready to smite the breast, crying, "God be merciful to me a sinner." Others may be pillars in God's house, but

I am but a rush, a reed, a bruised reed; of little value to my neighbour—of no value to my Lord. I am feeble in knowledge. There is more in Scripture that is dark than light to my understanding. I am in doubts and perplexities. I am low in faith. The frames of high assurance which others enjoy, are not mine. Scarcely can I write myself among God's people. I am weak in purpose, and failing in resolution; weak in conflict, and often flying before the enemy; weak in fortitude, and sinking under my cares. The grasshopper is a burden. I faint in the day of adversity, and my strength is small. Others may think well of me—but I know myself better. My light is dim—not a lamp of the golden candlestick—not a torch in a sheaf—not even a candle to give light to all in the house. So small is my wisdom, so dull my example, so hesitating and infrequent and fearful my words of grace, that I am no more than a dying wick, repulsive and useless. These are not uncommon exercises; though they seem such to the subjects of them. Every Sabbath the doors of the sanctuary open to some of this class. They love God's house, and resort to God's altars, as the timid, affrighted sparrow to her nest. They dare not refuse Christ's dying invitation—while they dare as little claim the children's bread. And I ask particular attention to the statement—that these persons are sometimes among those who make no public profession of faith.

They are deeply humbled at the knowledge of their own deficiencies, both in nature and grace;

and never harbour a thought of seeking any advantage by their merits. Not for an instant do they fancy themselves rich, increased in goods, eminent saints, harmless people whom God will not condemn: not for an instant do they stand and thank God that they are better than the publican, or rehearse prayers, alms, and fasts. Not for an instant do they look on their house as made ready for the Master: "I am not worthy thou shouldest come under my roof." To take the tearful place of Mary, the sinful woman, at his feet—they would consider heaven. They cannot look at Sinai: they cannot look at the law: they cannot look at themselves: "Unclean! unclean!"—the cry of the leper, is their cry. They think not of lessening their sins; their best prayer is, "Pardon mine iniquity, because it is great." They confess judgment, and have not a word to say why sentence should not pass to execution. In view of God's righteous demand, and their account, they are dumb in their insolvency, when rigorous Justice takes them by the throat, saying, Pay me what thou owest! Mark this. It is characteristic. It is critical. It distinguishes the broken spirit from the loose sinner who desires and attempts no holiness, and from the starched, complacent, moral, respectable, well-doing Pharisee, who feels no want. These are God's poor. Hearken to the voice of silver notes from the mount of the Beatitudes: "Blessed are (not the rich but) the poor in spirit, for theirs is the kingdom of heaven. Blessed are (not the proud but) the meak, for they shall inherit the earth. Blessed are (not the full and sated but) they which do hunger and thrist after righteousness, for they shall be filled." Even through the courts of God's house there do stalk some, whose elation and spiritual self-esteem will scarcely be beholden for any thing, even to Jehovah. "There is a generation that are pure in their own eyes, and yet are not washed from their filthiness! There is a generation, O how lofty are their eyes! and their eyelids are lifted up." Prov. 20 : 12, 13. There lived in the days of Christ, "certain which trusted in themselves that they were righteous, and despised others." They live in our day, and in our churches. But they are not bruised reeds, or smoking flax: and their hopes are not in this promise. The word which sounds here from the gospel, is a "word to him that is weary." God resisteth the proud and giveth grace unto the humble. The sense of weakness, provided it be deplored and bewailed, is no disqualification for receiving free gifts. Grace is gratuity. "Salvation is of God." Heaven has no seats for those who earn eternal life. It is into the empty vessel, that the divine favour pours its fulness. It is to kindle the expiring lamps, that He who walks among the golden candlesticks comes into his tabernacles this day.

The figure of our text designates the *sorrowful*. I see their very image in the bruised reed, which has been rolled over by the wheel of pride— the smoking flax, which sobs away its strength and gives no light, because it has none. There is a phi losophy of this world which keeps itself comfortably cool and calm in a land of misery, by a method of abstraction which makes no man's sorrows its own. It sees many a man lying half-dead by the wayside, but it must maintain its dignified equanimity: it passes by on the other side. Hear its lectures of worldly-wisdom: "You must not be so soft-hearted—repress your sympathies—they are childish—they are womanish. Admit a little pang for your own family, or your immediate circle—but do not lend an ear to every cry of distress."

Knock at no such door! Child of misfortune, seek not to melt that polished marble heart! Tempt not the sneer of such condescending selfishness. O, bruised reed, go to Christ! There, there is the heart which made every human ill its own. Go to the followers of Christ: "Who is weak, and I am not weak? who is offended and I burn not?" Go to those whose maxim is, "Rejoice with them that do rejoice, and weep with them that weep." It is the spirit of Messiah. He came to exemplify and communicate it. While on his triumphal progress to judgment and victory, he beholds the downtrodden object in his way, stays his victorious wheels, descends from his car, takes the bruised reed, and cherishes and erects it into health and vigor. And where self-important man would extinguish the failing light, he approaches the flax which scarcely smokes, and breathes new life into the flame.

If the gospel were not a message to sufferers—to great sufferers, to sufferers the most solitary.

neglected and abject—it would not be a message, my brethren, for us. If religion could not display its glories where there are great trials—among the aged, poor, infirm, sick, desponding, and disheartened, we might erase from the catalogue the larger part of Christ's friends. But to show that his religion was open to the wretched, and to show that for such it was a balm, the Redeemer of men took on him not merely human form, but human sorrows.

We sometimes come to take a glimpse of his humiliation. "Himself took our infirmities and bare our sicknesses." Behold the man! in pains, in sorrows, in degradations, in fears, in agonies—a man! bone of our bone and flesh of our flesh! Can he not feel? Can he not have a fellow-feeling? Did he not bear the same shrinking fibre and nerve that thrills with our anguish? Behold the man! He comes forth, wearing the purple robe and the crown of thorns— weary, languid, fainting, spit upon, betrayed, condemned, all bloody from Gethsemane and the human scourge—about to bear his cross, and to be nailed to it, to thirst, to be excruciated, to die! Behold him, ye who are bruised. It pleased the Lord to bruise him; he was bruised for our iniquities—despised, rejected—a man of sorrows, acquainted with grief — stricken, smitten, afflicted, wounded — a slaughtered lamb travailing in woe—pouring out his soul in death! Surely he will not break the bruised reed. Though all men trample on it, yet will not he. He cannot—he doth not. And none better know this than they who suffer. They can venture to cast their burden on him, who denied them not the endurance of their agony, when it was demanded by the law.

The scriptural figure has been seen to include the weak and the sorrowful. I add, thirdly and lastly, it includes the *sinner*. If it did not, it would be all lost on us. Under the first head, the infirmity described was a sinful infirmity, and we consider moral obliquities and defects as a part of it. But the same depravity which we there viewed as weakness, we are here to view as sin. For this is the very stumbling-block of the troubled conscience, and so long as this lies across the way, there is no reaching the cross. In vain do I proclaim to the drooping culprit that Christ invites the weak and the sorrowing. Yes! I am indeed both; but I am more than weak, more than sorrowful. I am vile—behold I am vile! crimson and scarlet cover all my life. Iniquities prevail against me; one of a thousand would destroy me. The Master is, I know, compassionate, but he is holy. He will pity infirmity and wipe away tears; but sin is that which his soul hateth. I am excluded, because I am a sinner.

Let me plead with this unbelieving one. Jesus, who appears as a consoler, has a message for thee. You are a sinner, vastly worse than you have described or dreamed. *This man receiveth sinners*. It is the disease he came to cure. Will you go to the surgeon and hide your chief wound? Ah! you then deem it incurable! that is, you doubt the re medy. If you were better, you would apply for his touch. But what saith he? They that are whole need not a physician, but they that are sick. I am come to call not the righteous but sinners. I am not sent but unto the lost sheep. To the Pharisaic mind this is amazing; for its maxim is, that grace must be purchased, that Christ receives us on conditions. For generations the Jewish clergy had been walling themselves out from the unclean; they would not eat with them, or speak to them, or touch them. Jesus trode down and broke through all these partitions, and there was a doctrine in his practice which perplexed and disgusted the Jewish precisians. "Why eateth your master with publicans and sinners?" "Behold a friend of publicans and sinners!" Did he repel them? Nay, he said to the righteous ones, "The publicans and the harlots go into the kingdom of God before you." And the history adds, "the publicans and harlots believed him." Levi and Zaccheus and Mary embraced a gratuitous salvation.

The chief of sinners has part in the offer. It is worthy of all acceptation. Be not weary of the familiar truth; account it not as the "light food," the "manna" which the world rejects, while the "full soul loatheth the honeycomb." Come ye, buy and eat, yea come, buy wine and milk, without money and without price. It is the echo between the Old Testament and the New, "Though your sins be as scarlet, they shall be white as snow; though they be red like crimson, they shall be as wool."

CHRIST'S COMPASSION.

You are a professor, and have sinned in the church. It is so; it is dreadful; it is amazing; it is more black and damning than you think. You have broken vows; you have been unfruitful; you have hated your brother in your heart; you have denied your Lord. It is a bruise more serious than others—your crushing bruise. David felt it—Peter felt it. But he of whom we speak is Jesus; he shall save his people from their sins. He will not overlook the principal malady. The bruised reed shall he not break. He will not put out the expiring glimmer of your corrupt, offensive lamp; the smoking flax shall he not quench. If he came with healing for all diseases but one—this one—he would come in vain. Here is the hydra's head, and he strikes at it. Sin and sorrow came in together in Eden; sin and sorrow shall go out together at the Judgment. And during the interval, though they remain—though the sting is still sin—though there is a law in your members warring against the law of your mind—though it sometimes oppresses your living graces as a body of death—yet thanks be to God, who giveth us the victory through our Lord Jesus Christ!

The doctrine of this grace may be abused: the grace itself cannot be. The lamentations to which these truths are directed proceed from those who cry out, as they writhe in the mighty coils of their serpentine enemy. Whether in the church, or out of it, if you detest that which is closest to you—your sin—if this bruise of the spirit is your daily pain; if you long as importunately to be cleansed of your leprosy as to be pronounced clean by the priest; if you see in Christ's body and blood deliverance as well as pardon; then, no matter how great your sense of sins, your help is at hand. You may have lain long in the porches of Bethesda, among the great multitude of "impotent folk." You may have witnessed repeated seasons, when the angel descended into the pool and troubled the water. You may have had no man to put you into the pool. While you have been making the effort, others may have stepped down before you into the cleansing laver. Yet this day there is one among you whom ye know not. And as his benignant eye fastens on you, he says, "Wilt thou be made whole?" Nay, he says, "Take up thy bed and walk!" The smoking flax is almost dead, but here is "the Light of the World." It would indeed be a profanation beyond remedy if you should make the blood of Christ the encouragement to remain in sin; it would be turning the grace of God into licentiousness: it would be trampling on the crucified body of the Lord; if persevered in, it would be certain destruction. But it would be all this simply because it would be rejecting the offered salvation. The salvation is as truly from pollution as from guilt. The acceptance of it is not possible, except where sin is the burden from which the soul flies with abhorrence. The terms of the free gospel may be abused; they have been abused. But the danger does not lie in overrating the fulness, freeness, nearness, and accessible-ness of the invitation; nor is it to be avoided by annexing legal conditions to the grant. No atrocity of licentious Antinomian presumption can render the gift less free or Christ less compassionate. His immaculate holiness turns away, indeed, from the heaven-daring impiety of hypocritical professors, who resolve to venture on known sin, while they cry, "Lord, Lord," and plunge deeper in iniquity and guilt, because there is pardon for transgressors; from this, I say, the pure and righteous Saviour turns away with infinite repugnance; nevertheless, his divine, unbounded love abides unchangeable; and no malignancy of the wicked can avail for a moment to quench his compassions, or stay the hand of his relief. Though your grief, therefore, be sin itself; though your bruised spirit sinks most under the recollection and consciousness of sin; yet, if your inmost soul abhors the plague, and cries to be delivered from it, the Messiah of our prophetic word will not reject you. He will not refuse to lift you up because your distress is one caused by the greatest of all evils. And, in the language of Davies on this text, the desponding soul should thus think: "Has God kindled the sacred flame in his heart in order to render him capable of the more exquisite pain? Will he exclude from his presence the poor creature that clings to him, and languishes for him? No; the flax that does but smoke with his love was never intended to be fuel for hell; but he will blow it up into a flame, and nourish it, till it mingles with the seraphic ardors in the region of perfect love."*

Weak, and sorrowful, and sinful though you be, you are come to behold One who gives strength, peace, and righteousness; who died, and yet lives who "was made sin for us," in the manner exhibited in previous pages, and who "of God is made unto us wisdom, righteousness, sanctification and redemption."

---

* The fifth sermon of President Davies on this text is earnestly commended to the attention of all readers.

CONSOLATION UNDER THE JUDGMENTS
OF MEN.

XIV.

THE wounds of the soul are not always such as bleed outwardly, nor is the most poignant anguish caused by visible agents. When we speak of consolation, our minds naturally call up the images of illness, bereavement, or peril of life or limb. But man is so constituted, that an assault on reputation, or even a public or general censure of conduct and character, will often inflict as keen and lasting pain as the piercing of a sword. There are, moreover, some who could with more equanimity go to the cannon's mouth than withstand the voice of disapprobation, when proceeding from great numbers, or from persons of rank and importance. And when censure and rebuke actually fall, there is always an emotion of unhappiness, at least for a time, under which the supports of religion are as truly needed as under the more palpable inflictions which have passed so largely under our review. Nor is there any means of rising altogether above such suffering except that which is afforded by Christianity; because the true believer is the only man who can rationally and universally appeal from the judgment of man to the judgment of God.

To do right, to do always right, and to do it without concern as to the judgment of human creatures, belongs to the very highest degrees of moral culture, to the strong man in Christ Jesus. Yet we should strive after it, as indispensable as well to our holiness as our happiness. The contrary temper is continually brought to our knowledge in others and in ourselves. The world is to a great extent governed by a regard for human opinion. Instead of tracing all seemingly good actions up to the impulses of reason and conscience, we are frequently constrained to admit that their actors have done them in order to be seen of men. Even the truly Christian man, while in the main he follows the dictates of duty and of God, pursues this path through violent struggles, and at great expense of feeling. When by grace he has succeeded in accomplishing his duty against the opinion of many, perhaps of most, sometimes including highly valued and excellent persons, he is deeply conscious that he has come out of a conflict, and has barely escaped from yielding to the power which attracted in another direction. But this case is far too favourable. Multitudes are daily kept from doing or attempting what they know to be right, by the dread of what fellow-creatures will say or think. It is precisely this which keeps some from entering on a religious life, and owning the Lord Jesus Christ before men. And this is but one of a thousand obligations, which men neglect from fear of human judgment. In this there is such a weakness, that we are prompt to despise it, when presented in the abstract, or in the case of another, while we are perpetually incurring the same condemnation by our indecision and cowardice. As the character thus formed is insusceptible of true greatness, so it is liable to unspeakable misery. No man can lift up his head with manly calmness and peace, who is the slave of other men's judgments. It is, therefore, a matter of great moment, in our discipline of heart and life, to keep before our minds those considerations, which shall dispose and enable us to say with the Apostle Paul, in a notable instance, "With me it is a very small thing that I should be judged of you or of man's judgment." Let us, therefore, meditate on the means which, by God's blessing, shall lift us above this dependence on the thoughts, caprices, and censures of mankind, and shall console us when we incur them.

I. The first which I shall mention is a clear discernment of what our duty is. Here some will be disposed to say that every man knows what is right and what is wrong, and that the only defect is in the will to perform it. But this is one of those half truths, which often do the office of falsehood. In nothing do men differ more than in the distinctness with which they apprehend the line of duty. Conscience, though existing in all men, does not in all men exert itself with equal power. Conscience is often called the vicegerent of God in the heart; but this is not to be taken in such a sense as shall confound God and conscience. As a human faculty conscience is limited, improvable, or capable of development, and fallible. As the faculty of fallen man, it is sometimes dark and uninformed, and sometimes erroneous. The actings of conscience are twofold; first, to discern what is right and wrong; secondly, to recompense right or wrong action with correspondent pleasure or pain. In one of these functions it is combined with the understanding, and may therefore err, and be instructed. If it were not so, there could be no such thing as moral instruction, and no need of any revelation of God's will in the Scriptures. For it is plain, that if conscience were an umpire, immediate, infallible, and final, man would need no other rule, and would be a law unto himself. Experience shows that while conscience, like understanding, is universal, yet like understanding, it may act in ever varying degrees, and be stimulated to ever improving power. Experience shows that conscience may be educated, and that it may be perverted. Men differ exceedingly from one another in their views of duty. You shall find one man who sees clearly what is required of him. The line of his duty is obscured by no mists, but lies distinctly before him, as a path laid down with mathematical precision. He never wavers on the brink of an obligation. His principles of action are defined and unalterable, and as he advances in life, the lesser ramifications of duty are marked out with correspondent precision. You shall find another man who is perpetually staggering among the different roads which invite him. His principles are unfixed and conflicting. He judges that to be right to-day which he condemned yesterday. In a thousand cases, therefore, he fails to accomplish the highest good, by vacillating as to what is required of him.

It is very evident, that a person thus diseased and debilitated in his moral character cannot be greatly independent. Such a man needs the support of numerous companions. His rule of duty is very much made up of the opinions of those around him. Hence he diligently gathers such opinions and anxiously craves them. As the judgment of fellow-creatures is in good measure the rule of his conduct, he trembles at the censures of mortals. Perhaps few of us have sufficiently considered how directly this servile weakness is connected with dim and confused views of duty. If any one is continually trembling with suspense as to the right or wrong of actions, he will in the same degree set an undue value on public opinion, which may often cast into the balanced scale a preponderating weight. Throw light into the conscience of such a one; let the bounding demarcations of good and evil become sharp and obvious; let him see without a misgiving which way duty points; and thus far he begins to be what we justly denominate a man of principle. As when the mariner, after many days of cloud and dead reckoning, at length obtains a clear noontide observation, ascertains his position, and is ready to dart off in the direction of his course; so the perplexed mind, when duty is made apparent, no longer needs to be in concern about the judgments of men.

Mere decision of character, taken in a worldly sense, is insufficient to produce this greatness of character. What is further needed is a clear commanding view of duty, as one and unalterable, to be the polestar in the heavens. It is therefore hard to overrate the importance of cultivating this distinct and unclouded apprehension of right and wrong, as a permanent mental habit. In order to attain this, we must be often thinking of moral questions, and settling principles before the hour of trial. In this likewise men widely differ. Happy is the youth who begins early to meditate on such subjects, and to clear his notions, as to what he ought to do in given emergencies. He will find the bracing influence of such views, in moments when all are shaking around him. Looking only at the principles of eternal right, he will go serenely forward, even in the face of adverse popular opinion. While weaker minds are halting, to collect the votes of the masses, he will bare his bosom to the shower of darts, and march up to the requisitions of conscience, in spite of the instant tyrant, or, what is often more formidable, of the turbulent populace.

To acquire settled and available decisions respecting duty, a man must determine every question as in the sight of God. Help is here afforded in the book of revelation. "The commandment of the Lord is pure, enlightening the eyes." So far as Scripture is law, it is given for the purpose of in forming, directing, and strengthening the conscience. The study of God's word, for the purpose of discovering God's will, is the secret discipline which has formed the greatest characters—the Daniels, Pauls, Luthers, and Howards, of the church. Listening here, rather than to the shifting voice of human opinion, we shall gain a robust principle altogether unknown to the world. But this clear discernment of duty will not fall to the share of him, who remains undetermined whether to practise that which he discerns. Wherefore another means of acquiring Christian independence is now to be mentioned.

2. The second means of rising above undue regard for human judgments, is a determinate purpose to perform all known duty. This is just as much more valuable than the preceding, as practice is above speculation. An habitual disposition of the Will to keep all God's holy commandments, will effectually carry a man above any sickly anxieties respecting the opinion which fellow-creatures may form of his actions. It is one thing to know what is required; and we have seen the knowledge to be vastly important; but it is a very different thing, to comply. Indeed it is a fruit of the Holy Spirit in the new creature. There is no more sure mark of discipleship than a solemn determination to fulfil all that is demanded by our righteous Master. "Ye are my friends," said Christ, "if ye do whatsoever I command you." The resolution so to do is very strongly expressed by David: "I have sworn, and I will perform it, that I will keep thy righteous judgments." Wicked men sometimes suppose that they are ready to do whatever God enjoins; but a

careful examination of their lives and hearts will show that they daily and willingly break the law, in thought, word, and deed. As there is no sinless perfection in this life, even renewed persons have an inward conflict, which is one of their chief trials. They find a law in their members warring against the law of their mind. Still they would do good, even when evil is present with them. Each can say, "So then with the mind I serve the law of God, but with the flesh the law of sin." It is this mind, or settled purpose to live in holy obedience, which we are now considering. Different Christians, and the same Christian at different times, are subject to marked variations, as to the intensity of this determination to do what is right; but wherever it prevails, it begets the holy independence which we are seeking.

This will become more clear if we look for a moment at the contrary temper. Here is a man of what may be considered general good intentions; a professor of piety, if you will, but one who halts and wavers in his obedience. His mind is not made up to surrender himself unreservedly to God. He is not quite sure that if the will of God were clearly revealed he would have the heart to perform it. There are some questions of practice which he willingly leaves in the dark, afraid to examine too deeply what is duty in the case, lest upon trial he should be revealed to himself as purposing to abide in known sin. Now, what we affirm is, that a man thus situated is in the right mood to become the slave of other men's opinions. He looks around for company and countenance in his irregularities and shortcomings. He catches at excuses for this or that indulgence, derived from the sentiments of those who know him. If some great and holy act of high decision is proposed, as, for instance, to deny some appetite; to become reconciled with an offending brother; to yield up some sacrifice to Christ; to bestow munificently upon the Lord's cause; to throw himself into some gospel labour; he has no freedom or boldness to go forward. His feet are bound; his hand is palsied. Every whisper of worldly professors which can excuse his delay is welcome to him; for he lacks that high resolve which would bear him triumphantly over all the surges of adverse opinion.

What a glow of healthful strength and liberty, on the other hand, is felt by one who has made it the law of his life to do what God ordains at all hazards! His course is clear. What matters it to him whether man approves or disapproves? That which he seeks is not human approval, but the keeping of the commandments of God. When he has once discovered what his Master has required of him, all dubiety is ended. He will advance to the performance, though all the world should rebuke.

Cases occur in which one actually performs a duty, but at the expense of great inward pain and mortification, from the opposing judgments of friends. Now, such pain is relieved by the abiding consciousness of right. The voice of an approving conscience, uttered loudly in the bosom, overpowers and drowns all voices of rash censure. The reason, or one great reason, why we sometimes feel distress, even in the performance of right actions, is, that our purpose to risk all for the sake of what is right has not risen to the proper degree.

This was felt by the apostle Paul at the time of his conversion. He might have said: "How is it possible for me to break forth at once as a preacher of Christianity? It is to incur the hatred or the scorn of all my nation, and the indignant censure of all my friends. Universal judgment is against me To act thus is to incur the shame of a sudden unaccountable tergiversation. I shall become a proverb and a name of reproach to all the scoffers in Israel." But how did he act? Hear his own words: "When it pleased God to reveal his Son in me, ... immediately I conferred not with flesh and blood." Gal. 1:15. His purpose was immovable, to do what was right, come what would. This was in favourable contrast with the dissimulation of Peter at Antioch (2:11), who ceased to eat with the Gentiles, when "certain came from James;" and "separated himself, fearing them that were of the circumcision, insomuch that Barnabas also was carried away with their dissimulation." Let me say to my readers, if you would learn to consider the judgment of mortals a small thing, grow in your resolution to do all that God commands. Prefer it to honour; prefer it to pleasure; prefer it to life. It will be to you a perpetual commendation from the inward monitor;

and the sweet testimony of a good conscience toward God and man will enable you to smile serenely, though all the world, and many who are named Christians, condemn and reproach you.

3. A principal means to prevent too high a regard for human censure, is the conviction that the judgments of men are insignificant. This is the precise import of Paul's words—"It is a very small thing that I should be judged of man's judgment.". Here, my brethren, is the very point. This is the persuasion which we need to have deeply engraved on our minds. The reason why we are concerned and shaken by man's judgment, is because we consider it a great thing, when in reality it is contemptibly small, as I now proceed to show.

There is, perhaps, not one of our known actions which is not brought into review by some of our fellow-creatures—a self-constituted inquest for this purpose. The more elevated the person, the more public his sphere, the larger will be the number of his judges. Thus, when any great man is named for high office, how are his secret things sought out; how is his private life brought into review; how bitter, malignant, false, and foolish, are the awards of over-heated partisans on one side and the other! But no one of us is so humble as to escape. The very beggar at our doors, probably, stands in awe of some tribunal among his mendicant acquaintances, which sits in judgment on his acts.

Now, human judgments may be disregarded, because they are passing away. Nothing is more transient. They last but a moment. They are a breeze, which lulls or changes as soon as it is observed. Let wisdom teach you not to observe it at all. "All flesh is grass," and each generation of man is rapidly passing from time into eternity. But long before the persons depart, their judgments have ceased and been forgotten. Why should we be wounded or hindered by a breath that fleets away?

Again, human judgments are inoperative. They amount to nothing. They are arrows which do not reach us, except so far as we put ourselves in their way. The opinion of other men, of all men together, upon our actions and character, need not weigh a feather with us, except so far as they coincide with the decree of reason and conscience. They do not affect our happiness; they cannot reach the inward man. To tremble at them, or to shrink from duty on account of them, or to go haltingly and timorously on with duty from morbid regard to them, is to flee from a shaking leaf, and to turn pale at a shadow.

The judgments of men are, furthermore, in a great number of instances, pronounced with small opportunity for arriving at the truth. All are not wise who assume the censor's chair. Foolish and ignorant persons are apt to be most forward in venting their hasty conclusions, and these utterances go to form what is called public opinion. Wretched is the man who waits and hearkens for this, to guide his practice, or as if any thing depended on it. Man's judgment is very small, when we look at the authority possessed by those who claim to judge.

There is hardly any part of a weak and yielding man's character, for which he can make less reasonable apology than his deference to the opinion of men. Their words concerning him, and their rash judgments of him, are prompted in many instances by prejudice and malignant affections. They often utter more disapprobation than they feel, and as often disapprove from some secret spite or ignoble grudge. If we are to be pained, harassed, and obstructed in our course by the voices around us, we thereby put our happiness and our very usefulness at the mercy of our enemies and the enemies of truth.

Human judgments are of small moment, because they are conflicting among themselves. Ancient fable might teach us that no line of conduct will certainly please every one. The path of wisdom is to be regulated, therefore, without regard to the pleasing of men. "If I please men," says Paul, "I should not be the servant of Christ." Act as you will, some will be displeased. And no marvel; for as has been well said, how can we expect to please men, who are displeased with God, and not seldom displeased with themselves? The purity of an angel would not escape the tongues of those who denounced John the Baptist as a demoniac, and the Son of God as a winebibber. Surely it is not from the verdict of such a world, that we are to judge of our own actions. These very opinions are changeable as the moon, and they will condemn and acquit the same conduct, almost in the same breath.

But, above all, we must learn to undervalue man's judgments, when we consider how often they are erroneous, false, and displeasing to God. Human eyes penetrate but a little way. Man judgeth according to the outward appearance. We have only to look at what the world approves and disapproves, for a single day, to see that it is fallible, blind, and presumptuous. As well might we take our bearings from clouds or meteors, as regulate our conduct by the opinions of men. And no one will ever attain to any true greatness of character, until he comes to leave this absolutely out of view, in shaping his course through life. From earliest youth, all persons should be trained to look higher, and to settle questions of duty, on fixed moral principles, without recourse to these fallacious tests. Let a man take this lofty view of duty, which becomes a Christian, and he will no longer shudder when he finds his best actions exposed to obloquy. Those who are God's enemies will be his enemies, so far as he resembles God. He will remember the blessing pronounced on those of whom all manner of evil is spoken falsely; and the woe uttered against professors of whom all men speak well.

It is painful, but unavoidable, to add that the opinion even of fellow-Christians is not to be taken as our rule. To his beloved Corinthians, Paul says, "With me it is a very small thing that I should be judged of you." Good men may pass wrong judgments. From ignorance of facts and circumstances, from inattention, haste, or false report, from moral obliquity, from bias, from interest, from passion, from remaining unsanctified tempers, even believers may judge us amiss. Their opinion has not been made our rule. Sometimes we may be called upon to perform acts which even our beloved Christian brethren disapprove. It is one of the sorest trials of an honest and affectionate mind. In such circumstances we must remember the saying of the excellent Halyburton, that though God has promised to guide his inquiring child in the way that is right, he hath nowhere promised to make this way seem right to friends and neighbours. Yet if a man's ways please the Lord, he will cause even his enemies to be at peace with him. Viewed, then, in every light, the judgments of men concerning our conduct do not seem worthy of being taken into the account. And it should be the lesson of our life, to grow into a holy independence of every judgment which has not the sanction of conscience and of God.

3. The last and principal means of living in disregard of man's judgment, is to keep in view the awful judgment of God. That this was before the apostle's mind, in the case cited, is sufficiently manifest. "With me," says he, "it is a very small thing that I should be judged of you, as of man's judgment; yea, I judge not mine own self," *i. e.*, it is no self-approbation or self-condemnation which can carry authority with it. "For I know nothing by (or against) myself; yet am I not hereby justified: but he that judgeth me is the

Lord.* This is the controlling consideration. The opinions of poor, frail, erring, dying man, whose breath is in his nostrils, is nothing, is less than no thing and vanity, when I come to regard the great Omniscient Judge of the Universe. The honour which cometh from men, and which some are found willing to fight for and die for—what is it, compared with the honour that cometh from God only? Suppose men condemn me, and cast out my name as evil, yea, suppose all men unite in censure and reprobation; what is this, if He that sitteth in the heavens looks down with approval? This, my brethren, is the only true ground to take, in regard to the regulation of our conduct, to do all, as in the immediate presence of God and as subject to his animadversion. In his balances all our acts are weighed. Each word, each thought, as it rises into existence, is passed upon by him who is All-wise and All-holy. To live under such an impression elevates and purifies the character. How serenely, how loftily may

---

* It is worthy of notice that in two places in our admirable version, common readers are liable to miss the sense, from the great variety of meanings belonging to the English preposition *by*. The first is Acts 20 : 16, "For Paul had determined to sail *by* Ephesus." That is, as the Greek instantly shows, he would not make his voyage *via* Ephesus, but would pass it by. The other is the passage cited above, 1 Cor. 4 : 4, "For I know nothing *by* myself," οὐδὲν γὰρ ἐμαυτῷ σύνοιδα. That is, I am conscious of nothing *against* myself. Here the mind is misled by a use of the English particle which has long fallen out of the language. This is evident from collating the older versions; "For I am no thing ouertrowing to my silf."—*Wiclif*. "For I am not guilty in conscience of any thing."—*Rheims*. "Nihil enim mihi conscius sum."—*Vulgate*. Therefore correctly given by Doddridge; "I am not conscious to myself of any thing criminal."

a true Christian go on in the performance of some distasteful or unpopular duty, if he can say with assurance, "I know that the eye of my God looks down with approbation on what I am doing." This sustained Paul, and has sustained God's most faithful servants in every age; the thought and assurance of God as ever sitting in judgment upon every act.

The day is coming, very soon, when all the judgments of men, which now give you so unwise a concern, shall be blotted out, as clouds of the morning or turbid dreams of feverish delirium; and when you will be transfixed by contemplating the righteous, final, incontrovertible doom of the All-seeing and Almighty Jehovah. In those moments when you feel yourselves in danger of being unduly moved by human opinion, let your attentive thoughts hurry forwards to the time—behold it is at the door—when the trumpet shall sound, the globe shall tremble in the mighty hand of Him that made it, the graves and seas shall render up their dead, the throne shall be set, and the books shall be opened; when the Son of Man shall come in his glory and all the holy angels with him, and shall sit upon the throne of his glory; when all nations shall be gathered before him, and be separated on his right hand and his left; and when, in your presence, in your hearing, and addressing himself to you, he shall utter one of these solemn sentences—Come, ye blessed of my Father, inherit the kingdom prepared for you from the foundation of the world—or, Depart from me, ye cursed, into everlasting fire, prepared for the devil and his angels. At that awful juncture, which assuredly awaits you, at what value, think ye, will you hold the decisions of fellow-worms upon your conduct? With what degree of complacency will you look back upon the servile compliances, the shrinkings from duty, the doubtful indulgences, the worldly conformities, into which you have been tempted by regard for human approbation or censure? This, this—believe me—is the great commanding motive, which ought to keep you upright, amidst the conflicting voices of popular judgment. Let your souls be absorbed by the just judgment of God. Fear God more, and you will fear man less. And, in regard to others, be instructed by the words of the apostle, and "judge nothing before the time, until the Lord come, who both will bring to light the hidden things of darkness, and will make manifest the counsels of the hearts: and then shall every man have praise of God."

And O ye, who have been the slaves of human opinion, and have done all your works to be seen of men; what shall it profit you to have had the acclamations of the multitude, if, when driven away in utter nakedness and arraigned before the tribunal from which there is no appeal, you feel the eye of God piercing you to the heart, and the frown of God withering your disconsolate spirit! All things earthly are tending towards that awful consummation. All our days are preparing materials for the adjudication of "that day." And alas! how unprepared are some who read these words, for that appearance before God! Can it be possible that we remain unconcerned, when no voice has yet assured us whether the Judge shall place us on the right hand or the left? Yet on one or the other, must you and I speedily stand. The time is short. The days are hastening. The sands are falling. The doom is impending. "What meanest thou, O sleeper? arise, call upon thy God, if so be that God will think upon us, that we perish not." And I am bound, before I close, to declare, that no strength of bare human resolution, no philosophical dignity, no self-righteous purpose, will avail to produce this independent elevation of character. There must be an operation which shall reach to the inward sources of action, with revolutionary power. Ye must be born again. Ye must be at peace with God. What is imperatively demanded, is not merely new views, but a new nature. In which I find a mighty argument with which I may urge every reader, as here I do, to seek true vital piety, and to seek it without delay. Then—when the Holy Spirit shall take your heart into his moulding hand—you will be delivered from the mortifying experience of mean indecision, truckling to the demands of the world, broken resolutions, and a violated conscience. Christian brethren, let it be our daily prayer that we may cease from man, whose breath is in his nostrils, and look to God as the Judge that ever standeth at the door. "Therefore, my beloved brethren, be ye steadfast, unmovable, always abounding in the work of the Lord, forasmuch as ye know that your labour is not in vain in the Lord."

CONSOLATION DERIVED FROM A REVIEW

OF CHRISTIAN MARTYRDOM.

XV.

THE sufferings of Christ's faithful martyrs not only furnish an attestation to the truth of Christianity, but evince its power to support the soul under the greatest sufferings. And herein the study is one eminently promotive of consolation.

One of the great evils which have been wrought by Popery is that it has cast suspicion and rebuke on many good things which belong as much to us as to them, but which we can scarcely use with liberty for fear of superstition. This has remarkably been the case in regard to the sufferings of the saints. At a very early age, unsuspecting the evil which should follow, surviving friends began to honour the remains and frequent the tombs of the martyrs; hence followed, in irresistible progress, the consecration of set days, the doctrine of supererogatory merit, the canonization of saints, and the worship of relics. Notwithstanding all this, we, my brethren, have an interest in the heroic work of the martyrs: they are ours as well as Rome's; and we are not to be cheated out of our right to the example, proof, and incitement afforded by them, because a corrupt church has made their names the watchword of error. This has been beautifully expressed by one of the brightest luminaries of the modern Anglican church, who sufficiently proved himself the foe of Popery and its imitations. "It is likely enough," says the late Dr. Arnold, "that Gibbon has truly accused the general statements of exaggeration. But this is a thankless labour, such as Lingard and others have undertaken with respect to the St. Bartholomew massacre, and the Irish massacre of 1642. Divide the sum total of reputed martyrs by twenty—by fifty, if you will—but, after all, you have a number of persons, of all ages and sexes, suffering cruel torments, and a death for conscience' sake and for Christ's, and by their sufferings manifestly, with God's blessing, insuring the triumph of Christ's gospel. Neither, do I think, do we consider the existence of this martyr-spirit half enough. I do not think that pleasure is a sin. The Stoics of old, and the ascetic Christians since, who have said so, have in saying so overstepped the simplicity and the wisdom of Christian truth. But though pleasure is not a sin, yet surely the contemplation of suffering for Christ's sake is a thing most needful for us in our days, from whom in our daily life suffering seems so far removed. And as God's grace enabled rich and delicate persons, women, and even children, to endure all extremities of pain and reproach in times past, so there is the same grace no less mighty now; and if we do not close ourselves against it, it might in us be no less glorified in a time of trial. And that such time of trial will come, my children, in your days, if not in mine, I do believe fully, both from the teaching of man's wisdom and of God's."

When our Lord, in predicting the arrest and trial of his disciples, says to them, "And it shall turn to you for a testimony;" the meaning is, your persecutions, when foes shall lay their hands on you, *this* shall turn to you for a testimony: it shall afford you an opportunity to *testify* for Christ in the most striking circumstances, and with the greatest effect. The word rendered "testimony" is kindred to our word *martyr*, which is only the Greek for *witness*, one who bears testimony. Ye shall, by means of your faith and endurance, be witnesses for my gospel. Let me, then, call your attention to the lessons to be drawn from the testimony of the martyrs. But first, we must consider who and what the martyrs were.

I. A *martyr*, it has already been said, is a witness; but, in the language of the church, one who bears witness to Christianity by his death; while the term *confessor* was applied to those who, before persecuting magistrates, firmly hazarded punishment for confessing Christ. The confessor became a martyr by shedding his blood. In this sense we constantly speak of "martyrs and confessors." The ancient historians reckon exactly ten persecutions; but it is scarcely possible to confine the number to this. They arose from the iron determination of the heathen powers to suppress the true religion; for I pass over the earlier persecutions under the Jews, from Stephen onward. I desire to afford some glimpses of the scenes of martyrdom, confining myself to ancient authorities, and uncontradicted narratives. The name of Nero has a black celebrity. "Examine your records," said Tertullian, in his Apology; "there you will find that Nero was the first that persecuted this [Christian] doctrine . . . . . He that knows who he was, may also know, that Nero could condemn only what was great and good." It is believed that Paul was a martyr under Nero. I will not enter into the question as to the number of the martyrs. Though superstition has exaggerated in this point, we cannot deny the concurrent testimony of all ancient records, that thousands on thousands were slain for Christ's sake. Those who were lowest, such as paupers and slaves, escaped most easily; the ministers, the learned, and men of wealth, were sure to be summoned to this ordeal. The persecution, which was closed by the death of Nero, broke out afresh under his imitator, Domitian. Their names have come down to posterity besprinkled with the same blood. "Nero," says Tertullian, "was content to have executions, ordered at a distance; Domitian chose to have them under his own eyes." The mild and gentle Trajan was a persecutor. Happily there remains to us a portion of his correspondence with Pliny the Younger, who was, under him, governor of Bithynia. This gives us the assurance derived from Gentile testimony. Pliny writes to his sovereign to know what is to be done, when so many thousand Christians are willing to go to the stake. Hear the account given by this heathen magistrate; it forms part of a state paper, or official report: "I have taken this course with those who are brought before me. I asked them if they were Christians; if they confessed, I asked them, again, threatening punishment; if they persisted, I commanded them to be executed. The case demands your orders, from the vast numbers who are in danger; for many of all ranks and ages, both men and women, will be arrested, as the pestilence of this superstition has overspread, not only cities, but towns and country villages."

During this reign suffered Clement of Rome, Simon of Jerusalem, and Ignatius of Antioch. The last is memorable. He was condemned by Trajan himself, who ordered him to be sent from Asia to Rome, and there to be thrown to wild beasts. But his journey was a missionary tour, in which he probably did more than in all his life toward the strengthening of the brethren. "From Syria even to Rome," says he, "I fight with beasts, by land and sea, day and night; bound with ten leopards (that is, a guard of soldiers,) who are worse for the favours I do them. I pray that the beasts may despatch me quickly; but I know what is best for me. Now I begin to be a disciple, desiring nothing of things seen or unseen, that so I may gain Christ. Let fire, cross, droves of ravenous beasts, wounds and convulsions come upon me, so only that I may enjoy Jesus Christ."

Under Adrian, the successor of Trajan, an incident occurred in proconsular Asia which is instructive. Tertullian relates, that when Arrius Antoninus was beginning to persecute in a certain city, the whole of the population beset his tribunal, and openly avowed themselves to be Christians. He could only order a few to be executed as examples.

As, however, a far more distinct impression is made on our minds by a few particular incidents, than by general enumerations, I will dwell a little on the famous instance of the churches of Vienne and Lyons on the Rhone, in the second century. This persecution raged under the philosophic emperor M. Aurelius Antoninus, and we are better acquainted with the details, because the historian Eusebius has preserved letters written on the subject, by these churches, to their brethren in Asia Minor.* There is something very affecting in the letters of these simple-hearted people, penned amidst the very horrors of which they tell. The populace had been inflamed by the calumnies of the age which accused the Christian assemblies of licentious and bloody crimes. "The Christians," say the letters, "nobly sustained all the evils that were heaped upon them by the mob—outcries, blows, plunder, stoning, imprisonment. Then they were hurried to the Forum, and when examined by the tribune and magistrates, in presence of the multitude, they were shut up in prison till the arrival of the governor." "They seemed unprepared indeed and inexperienced, and too weak for the mighty conflict. About ten fell away, caus-

* Euseb. v. i. 55.

ing excessive sorrow to the brethren. We were filled with suspense and anguish lest the remainder should apostatize." There were arrests every day, till all the more zealous members of the two churches were collected. Particular mention is made of a poor servant-woman named Blandina. "For whilst we were all trembling, and her earthly mistress, who was herself one of the contending martyrs, was apprehensive lest by the weakness of the flesh she should not make a bold profession, Blandina was filled with such power, that her ingenious tormentors, who relieved and succeeded one another from morning till night, confessed that they were overcome, and had nothing more that they could inflict on her." "Wrestling nobly in the fight, this blessed saint, from time to time, found strength to say, 'I am a Christian! No wickedness is carried on by us.'"

From Sanctus, another martyr, no extent of torture could extort any declaration but this, "*Christianus sum!* I am a Christian!" Pothinus, a venerable minister, more than ninety years of age, and very infirm, seemed to live only that Christ might triumph in him. After being delivered over to the blows and indignities of the mob, he lay two days in prison, and then died of the injuries. On the last day of the gladiatorial games, Blandina, already named, and Ponticus (a Christian boy aged fifteen) were brought in, as they were every day, to see the torments of the rest. "Force was used to make them swear by their idols, and when they continued firm and denied the gods, the mob became outrageous, pitying neither the sex of one nor the youth of the other. Hence they subjected them to every horrible suffering, and led them through the whole round of torture, ever and anon striving to make them swear, but in vain. The boy (as the heathens could see) was encouraged and upheld by the words of a Christian sister; he nobly bore the whole sufferings, and gave up his life." I forbear describing the death of Blandina by a wild beast, though it is detailed. "Even the Gentiles confessed that no woman among them had ever endured sufferings as many and as great as these." Allow me to remind you, my brethren, that the essential thing in all these persecutions is, that these martyrs died testifying; it turned to them for a testimony.

Instead of pursuing the account of persecutions under successive emperors, let me add two testimonies of ancient writers; you will not fail to give them that weight which belongs to declarations recorded at the time. The first is by Sulpicius Severus, an elegant writer of the fourth century: "Under the reign of Diocletian and Maximian, for ten years the persecution constantly preyed on the Lord's people, during which the whole world was full of the sacred blood of martyrs. Never was the world more exhausted by wars, and never did we conquer by a greater triumph, than when with ten years' suffering we could not be overcome."

The other is Tertullian. "Good governors," said he, "you may torment, afflict, and vex us; your wickedness tries our innocency, and therefore God lets us suffer it; but all your cruelty is to no purpose; it is but a stronger invitation to bring others to our sect. The oftener we are mowed down, the ranker do we spring up again. *The blood of the Christians is the seed of the church.* Many of your philosophers have exhorted their hearers to patience under suffering and death; as Cicero in his Tusculans, Seneca, Diogenes, Pyrrho, and Callinicus; but they could never make so many disciples, by all their fine discourses, as the Christians have by acts. That very obstinacy you charge upon us serves to instruct others. For who, beholding such things, will not be moved to inquire what is the truth from which they proceeded? and when he has found it, will he not embrace it? and having embraced it, will he not desire to suffer for it? Therefore we give thanks for your sentence, knowing that the judgments of men do not agree with those of God; for when we are condemned by you, we are absolved by Him."

Without intending to enlarge on their history, I may add, that the principle is equally illustrated in the case of all those witnesses for the truth, in later ages, who have suffered under a wicked hierarchy, even down to the poor expatriated Portuguese, from the island of Madeira. Thus the Waldenses. They were just as really persecuted by the popes as ever their fathers were by the emperors. Between 1176 and 1226, there was such havoc of them, that even the Archbishops of Aix, Arles, and Narbonne, consulting with the inquisitors, expressed some pity at the multitudes who were cast into prison. In the year 1260, the number of Waldenses was reckoned at eight hundred thousand. The Albigenses were so numerous that they were made the object of a crusade. To recount the martyrdoms of Protestantism would be to recite the folios of the pious and laborious Foxe. The name of Smithfield can never be forgotten by descendants of Great Britain. In these, as in the ancient times, the arrest and persecution of God's people turned to them for a testimony; affording only so many new opportunities of publicly avowing the truth of Christianity. The general result is sufficiently clear, that in every age Christians have been found ready to hazard the greatest sufferings rather than deny Christ, and have gone out of the world in torments of body, but triumph of soul, declaring their belief of the gospel.

II. (1.) Among the invaluable lessons to be deduced from the sufferings of Christian martyrs, the first is this: *They furnish attestation to the truth of Christianity.* They thus turned to those who suffered for a testimony. The great foundation of the credibility of divine messengers is the miracles which were wrought to certify their legation. The Apostles and many of the primitive Christians attested the truth by martyrdom. This is a fact as undeniable as any in history. Do I hear you object, that martyrdom may be suffered for falsehood as well as truth; our reply is, that the objection does not meet the point of the reasoning. Our argument is not that the martyrdom directly proves the doctrine to be true, but that it proves the sincerity of him who testifies. In regard to the miracles of Christianity, prove the sincerity, and you prove the facts. These facts, it admits of easy proof, are of such a nature, that the reporters could not be deceived. The primitive martyrs had the opportunity of arriving at absolute truth, with regard to the facts alleged ; and their dying for the truth is in the circumstances as strong proof of the miracles as the case admits. Never forget that they could one and all have escaped all their torments, by denying these facts, or by the simplest renunciation of Christianity. Here I will quote another passage from Pliny, in regard to those who were apprehended under the charge of being Christians: "A paper was presented, accusing certain persons therein named of being Christians. These, when, after my example, they invoked the gods, and offered wine and incense to your statue, which for that purpose I caused to be brought, and when, moreover, they had blasphemed the name of Christ (which, it is said, none who are true Christians will ever do), I dismissed." All the tortures of the heathen were intended to bring them to this denial. A single word, a single morsel of incense, an inclination of the head, would have saved their lives. But, no! they died under excruciating pains, rather than renounce. No man, woman, or child suffered for Christianity under any other compulsion than that of conscience. "Every martyr made a voluntary sacrifice of himself to maintain the truth, and to preserve a good conscience." Christianity was not then a religion of imposture.

These men were sincere. No rational mind can doubt it. Multitudes of persons gave the strongest possible testimony to their belief of certain facts, which passed under their own observation, and in which they could not have been deceived. The case of later martyrs, though not so cogent, as to the proof of the original facts, is equally so, as to their own sincerity of belief. These sufferers were true believers. The system under which they suffered was one that commanded the mind's conviction. And the strength of this conviction is measured by the intensity of the sufferings endured, and the terror of the evils threatened. What, therefore, must we say of the sincerity which resists the greatest of mortal apprehensions, namely, that of death! An instance may possibly be found here and there of some fanatical or obstinate villain, who from insane pride may die for what he believes untrue; but here are multitudes of all conditions, and in various ages. If, indeed, this does not prove sincerity of belief, it would be vain to look for any such proof.

(2.) The history of the martyrs is a testimony to *the power of Christianity to support the soul under great sufferings*, and this is the main point in our present discussion. "Persons of all ages, of all conditions in life, and of both sexes, exhibited under protracted and cruel torments, a fortitude, a patience, a meekness, a spirit of charity and forgiveness, a cheerfulness, yea, often a triumphant joy, of which there are no examples to be found in the history of the world. They rejoiced when they were arrested; cheerfully bade adieu to their nearest and dearest relations; gladly embraced the stake; welcomed the wild beasts let loose to devour them; smiled on the horrible apparatus by which their sinews were to be stretched, and their bones dislocated and broken; uttered no complaints; gave no indication of pain, when their bodies were enveloped in flames; and when condemned to die, begged of their friends to interpose no obstacle to their felicity (for such they esteemed martyrdom), not even by prayers for their deliverance." What sustained these sufferers? It was their belief in Christianity. They never pretended that it was aught beside. If any thing may be regarded as established, even by the concessions of adversaries, it is that the Christian system imparted to the humblest and weakest a fortitude and a constancy which were unknown to the schools of philosophy. This was, indeed, the chief mortification of the persecutors. Exhausting their whole resources in vain against aged men, feeble women, and inexperienced children, they were at length driven to wilder means, as discovering that Christianity could not be quenched in blood. These aspects of martyrdom, my brethren, ought by no means to be neglected. That thousands should have died so supported is not an uninteresting fact in the world's history. "Neither," says the noble Arnold, "should we forget those who, by their sufferings, were more than conquerors, not for themselves only, but for us, in securing to us the safe and triumphant existence of Christ's blessed faith—in securing to us the possibility (these are the words of a clergyman of the Church of England), nay, the actual enjoyment, had it not been for the Antichrist of the priesthood, of Christ's holy and glorious church, the congregation and commonwealth of Christ's people.*

O my brethren, we should have higher views of Christ and of his religion, if we could enter more fully into the conflicts of those who have suffered for his sake; if we could trace the growth of Christian martyrdom from its first fainting origin, when the shuddering soul dreaded the hour of coming trial; through the hours, days, weeks, and months of prayer and meditation; up to the critical moment when all was surrendered and all ventured for Christ; if we could comprehend the resignation, the peace, and the victorious confidence of the instant, when the soul reached its highest joy in dissolution, and just hovering between time and eternity forgot its pangs in the visions of God. O what are gibbets, fires, wild beasts, or inquisitorial racks, to one who already feels his union with Christ, and knows that death is swallowed up in victory!

(3.) The martyrdom of God's children is a testimony *that God will be with us in our own coming trials.* The argument is easy: He who was with them will be with us. It is God's presence with the martyr which sustains him, and makes him callous to the knife or the torture, and deaf to the fierce clamours of the multitude. I believe that the soul

---

* Life, p. 498.

may be so raised above suffering of the body as to be as though it knew them not. We have seen it many times in smaller degree, in our common human observation. But the record of early Christians and of those who suffered under popery, shows that grace actually neutralized bodily anguish.

But what we are now to observe is, that this sustaining power is not confined to the dungeon, the arena, or the stake. Martyrs are not the only sufferers; and wherever there are Christian sufferers, there is Christ. In vehement diseases; in long-continued and exhausting pains of body; in paroxysms of anguish; in nervous trepidations, sinkings and horrors; weaknesses more hard to bear than pain; and in the convulsions of death; the bodies of believers often call for the same sustaining power which was granted to the martyrs, and they receive it. There is no affliction which can befall us, that is too great for grace. Let me not confine myself to distresses of the outer man. There are wounds of soul which are greater than all wounds of body. The spirit of a man will sustain his infirmity, but a wounded spirit who can bear! None, my brethren, unless sustained by Him who "healeth the broken in heart, and bindeth up their wounds."

As our Lord told his disciples that persecutions and arrests would surely come upon them, but that this ought not to dishearten, as it should turn to them for a testimony, and thus they should be able more abundantly to show forth the power of God: so he seems to tell us, that trials and adversities will overtake us, but that this shall turn to us for a testimony, and offer new occasions to glorify our supporting God. We cannot tell what our troubles shall be; and we cannot tell what our consolations shall be under them. It is not the plan of our Lord to give us his special grace before it is needed. We are not therefore to be discouraged because we have not at this moment that boldness and resolution which shall be needed in the emergency. God will never be wanting. He has said, "I will never leave thee nor forsake thee." If God be for us, who can be against us! Especially in the inevitable hour of death, when you have passed beyond the reach of physicians and dearest friends, and when those who love you best will be mute and motionless beside your bed; when your limbs have already stretched themselves for the coffin, and your glassy eyes fixed themselves in their last position;—when your soul shall be falling back on its faith (if it has any) and looking forward to its impending judgment; in that hour, the God of the martyrs will be with you! Let every recorded triumph of faith be to you for a testimony. "I tremble," said dying Beza, "lest having come to the end of my voyage, I now make shipwreck, in the very harbour." No, no—Christ will not forsake his people in the hour of their extremity. It is indeed a time, when Satan often rages, because his time is short; but thanks be to God, who giveth us the victory through our Lord Jesus Christ. We ought often to be entertaining thoughts of death, and of our own dying; and among the considerations which help to prepare for this hour, one is the support which God has given in former times to those who were dying violent deaths for his sake. Do not think that this will make death more dreadful. All the contrary.

The writer may be pardoned for making an observation in his own person. Belonging to a profession which often calls me to stand by dying beds, I do here testify, that I have never had the dread of death so much removed, as when I have seen it triumphed over by the true believer, even amidst great pangs of body. O readers (every one of whom is soon to die—though some, perhaps, have little preparation), may God give you the wisdom to be securing that provision for the great hour, which is derived from his gospel! For be assured, the faith of the martyrs is what must be your stay in that tremendous moment.

4. Finally; as it is not forbidden to mingle reproof with consolation, the testimony of martyrs in their pangs is *a testimony against our lukewarmness and unbelief*. It is impossible to reflect on their history and not own this. Theirs was Christianity in earnest. How different from ours! Suppose a mighty persecution to break out in our day; our churches to be closed; our ministry to be imprisoned, or chased away; our Bibles to be burnt. Suppose coming to the communion to be the same as coming to peril or death. Suppose the name of Christ a reproach, and the dominant population armed against us; is it not your belief that many a

Christian church would be thinned, and that many a high professor would be found, like Simon Peter, denying in the outer hall? Of this there were some examples in early times, and some examples even among Christians. They were called *Lapsi*, the lapsed. But O with what bitterness did they lament their weakness, even to the end of life! You remember the recantation of Cranmer, and how soon, how bitterly, and how constantly he repented of it. His dying prayer breathes lowliness for the sin: "O God the Son, thou wast not made man, nor was this great mystery wrought, *for few or small offences*," &c. Then he confessed before the people his inconstancy with great profusion of tears, saying, "the great thing that troubled his conscience was, that for fear of death he had written with his hand contrary to the truth which he thought in his heart. "And *therefore* (cried the old man, in the holy violence of zeal), my hand shall be punished first. If I may come at the fire, it shall be first burnt!" At the stake, accordingly, he stretched out his hand, which was distinctly seen to be burning alive, and cried, "*This hand hath offended!*" Surely he could say, "Like Peter, I have sinned; but by grace, like Peter, I have wept!" God has chosen to let the great and learned sometimes fall, to show us what is in man; and to hold up the timid woman and the feeble child, to show us what is in God. But, fellow-Christians, what preparation have you for trials, losses, fears, pains, bereavements, and death? If you can so ill bear the daily crosses of life, and are so easily affrighted by the sneers or the inconveniences that befall you; if amidst these days of easy and honourable Christianity, ye find it so hard to be Christians, how will it be when you come into the billows of mighty conflict? And the quotation may be repeated: "If thou hast run with the footmen, and they have wearied thee, then how canst thou contend with horses; and if in the land of peace, wherein thou trustedst, they wearied thee, *then how wilt thou do in the swellings of Jordan?*"

Let such things bring us to a most serious consideration of the temper of our religion. Those provisions suit the calm which are utterly insufficient in the tempest. The religion of the martyrs, need I say it, was a religion all in earnest. They died for it, they died by it. It caused them to die; but it caused them to die rejoicing. Christ was their all. When holy Polycarp was summoned to deny Christ, he replied: "Eighty and six years have I served him, and he hath done me no harm: how can I revile my King, who hath saved me?" When Robert Glover, in Queen Mary's reign, was preparing for his death, he prayed all night long for strength and courage, and seemed to find none, till on a sudden he was so replenished with comfort and heavenly joys, that he cried out to his friend Bernher, "Austin, *He is come! he is come!*" and went to the stake with the alacrity of one going to the chief festival of life. Now, these men were in earnest; and theirs was an earnest faith; it was their very life: to them, to live was

Christ; to die was gain. My brethren, how is it with us? I say not, are we ready for martyrdom, for this would be no fair criterion; but are we deeply concerned with the things of God? have they so entered our souls as to be our very life? Are we pressing on, against difficulties and oppositions, with a heart-felt conviction, that union with Christ is every thing? Are we awake to our great necessities, and to the solemn realities which are impending over us? Have we deliberately renounced this world for our rest and portion, as a great bubble, and laid hold on eternal life? Is our faith in any respect "the substance of things hoped for, and the evidence of things not seen?"

Deeply consider, that the visible church has tares among the wheat; and that on the good foundation of gold are built much wood, hay, stubble, which shall not endure the flames. I see no way of arriving at high confidence, but by casting ourselves into religion as the all-absorbing interest. Our halfway Christianity, operative on Sabbaths and in the sanctuary, is not the thing we need. Every suffering of disciples in former days of conflict and confession, ought to rebuke and stimulate us. God has graciously given us prosperity, harvest, peace. But that robe of consistency, which Satan cannot wrest from us by the keen wind of adversity, we sometimes let slip under the sunshine of worldly favour. There are summer as well as winter dangers. It is recorded of a certain man that on reading the New Testament, he exclaimed, "Either this is not Christianity or we are not Christians!" The same might be said of some among us. For what signs do we read concerning primitive believers, and the evidences of their faith? They "had trial of cruel mockings and scourgings, yea, moreover, of bonds and imprisonments; they were stoned, they were sawn asunder; were tempted, were slain with the sword; they wandered about in sheepskins and goatskins; being destitute, afflicted, tormented; they wandered in deserts and mountains, and in dens and caves of the earth." It is remarkable that the most eminent piety has been nurtured under tribulations. Baxter's Saint's Rest, in part, and Bunyan's Pilgrim's Progress, and many of the seraphic letters of Samuel Rutherford, were written in prison. Shall we, therefore, desire prisons, and pray for persecution? I trow not. Let us be thankful for our prosperity; but let us mark its dangers. Sound, unbroken health, honour among men, domestic comforts, great wealth; these are not usually the means of exalted piety. Against the temptations of these we should be vigilantly preparing ourselves. And to aid us, we should be often contemplating the lives and deaths of those who by faith and patience inherit the promises.

The crowning act of the martyrs' Christianity was their despising this mortal life, and deliberately throwing it away for the sake of another. And is this peculiar to martyrdom? What saith our Lord? If any man hate not his own life also, he cannot be my disciple. The martyrs gave up life rather than give up Christ. And can we hope to compound for any thing less? It is of the very essence of all genuine religious experience, that Christ is above all. We are not to count our own lives dear to us. And this state of mind is to be attained only by higher measures of faith, and by keeping the soul's eye intently fixed on the person of the Lord Jesus, until we be ravished with his love, and ready to die that we may be with him for ever. But I must bring these observations to a close, especially when I reflect how many there are who not only have not these eminent traits of piety, but have no faith whatever; and to whom all that can be said on this subject must be matter of weariness, if not of incredulity. Perhaps it may profit even them to reflect, that the way to heaven is not without difficulties; and that many shall seek to enter in, and shall not be able. Among high professors, some shall perish. Among true believers, some shall be saved "as by fire." "And if the righteous scarcely be saved, where shall the ungodly and the sinner appear?"

THE AGED BELIEVER CONSOLED BY

GOD'S PROMISE.

XVI.

HOLY Scripture takes cognizance of the various circumstances and stages of man's life, and we should do the like when we use the pen for the consolation of Christ's suffering people. To the young we often have to address ourselves in cautions fitted to rebuke the sanguine excesses of hope, but to the aged our task is more in the way of cheering, for which the gospel makes ample provision. If their number is small, their demand upon our sympathy and love is not the less imperative. Besides the claim which they make upon us as frequent sufferers, they are repeatedly and earnestly commended to our reverence in the word of God; and any volume of consolation would be strikingly defective from which their case should be left out.

Length of days is a scriptural blessing, and was eminently such under the Hebrew theocracy, where earthly benefits were the perpetual type of spiritual favours. As death was a penalty, so the shortening of man's days was a token of God's anger towards the race; and under every dispensation the hoary head is a crown of glory to the righteous. Longevity, which in the case of the wicked only aggra vates sin, and its awful reckoning, affords to true believers a longer term of useful service and holy example, increased proficiency in gifts and graces, and a corresponding recompense. Old age has its appropriate beauty, no less than youth. To the eye which can wisely discern there is a mature loveliness in the "shock of corn that cometh in its season." Thus we contemplate the kindly decline of the ancient patriarchs with a filial veneration, and in our own circle turn with a healthful complacency from the gayeties of inexperienced youth to the father and the mother "whose ripe experience doth attain to somewhat of prophetic strain;" so that I envy not him who does not often love to draw near the sequestered corner that is honoured by the chair of reverend wisdom and graceful piety, where the wearied ancient or the cherished matron sits enthroned in the affections of an observant filial group. Yet while this period of life has its deserved honours, it has its trials likewise.

First among the ills of old age is infirmity of body. "The days of our years are threescore years and ten, and if by reason of strength they be fourscore years, yet is their strength labour and sorrow." Even if previous life has been exempt from bodily pain and weakness, the season of decline is usually visited with manifold diseases, some of which are peculiar to old age. Burdens which were scarcely felt in the mid-day pilgrimage, are apt to become intolerable torments towards the evening shadows. Scattered over the church and the world, there are thousands of persons in their respective nooks of seclusion, as much lost to society as if they were in dens and caves of the earth. Their place in the house of God has been filled by others, and the church has long ceased to observe the vacancy caused by their absence, except so far as some pastor or pious friend seeks them out, to smooth their rude descent into the grave. But each has his sorrows, and needs his consolation.

The weakness and lassitude of old age are familiar, yet these often take men by surprise. So reluctant are most to admit the mortifying approach of these closing languors, that they need more than the "three warnings" of the poet. The steps by which age advances are often stealthy and imperceptible. Gray hairs are scattered here and there, and they know it not. The beauty of the countenance is consumed, and gives places to wrinkles, sunken features, a stooping frame and tottering limbs. The dainties of the feast invite, but no longer gratify. The senses become obtuse, and the sufferer enters into the experience of Barzillai: "How long have I to live, that I should go up with the king unto Jerusalem? I am this day fourscore years old; and can I discern between good and evil? Can thy servant taste what I eat or what I drink? Can I hear any more the voice of singing men and singing women? Wherefore should thy servant be yet a burden unto my lord the king?" To such a one the grasshopper is a burden, nay he is a burden unto himself. It is a condition in which he manifestly needs support.

The absence of former companions belongs to "the time of old age." Amidst their troops of friends, the young think little of this; but the longer a man lives, the more does he outlive the associates of his early days. And though Dr. Johnson wisely advises men who advance in years to "keep their friendships in repair," it is unquestionably true, that the susceptibility for such attachments grows less with the decline of life. The tree which has outlived the forest stands in mournful solitude, and is lopped of its branches, and exposed to storms. If these pages fall under the notice of an aged reader, he will readily assent to the truth of what is said, being able with ease to number up all that remain of those who shared his early joys. Childhood seems far back in the distance; parents have been long removed; brothers, sisters, friends have gone before; perhaps, we must add poverty, widowhood, and childless desolation.

The solitary condition of aged persons is aggravated by the indisposition of the young to seek their company; so that we often find them constrained to pass days of weariness and evenings of gloom. Except where there is eager expectancy of some wealth to be divided, the old man is left to sit alone, which naturally leads to another trial.

The neglect of society is keenly felt in "the time of old age." We are fond of saying, that old age is honourable; but the writer has lived long enough to observe that in point of fact it receives little honour, except for certain adventitious accompaniments. The famous story of Plutarch concerning the Athenians and the Spartans has its full application here. No man loves to find himself a superfluity. In America we are more Athenian than Spartan in our treatment of the aged. Boys soon become men among us; men soon grow old; old men are soon forgotten. Venerable persons are sometimes honoured for their wealth—such is our trafficking, mammon-serving, ignoble view of things—or for their place or power, but how seldom for their years! The stripling, with his "gold ring and goodly apparel," shall have more to show respect to his "gay clothing," and to say, "sit thou here in a good place," than the poor man of hoary hairs. It is a serious question whether neglect of superiors in general is not a national sin. Carrying to extravagance our notions of equality, we can brook no superior, and will own no master. Hence we have come to hear lads manifesting their spirit by giving to father or mother, whom they should reverence next to God, appellations of jocose familiarity or disrespect. Now he who does not honour his parents will honour no one else, except to eat of his morsel.

The world's neglect is an ingredient in many a cup of old age. The rich may not know it; but the rich are not all the world, nor, taken as a class, the best part of it; and if all their claims to honour are founded on revenue, they are poor indeed. There is many a good man, far gone in the vale of years, who feels the saddening change from the days when all hastened to do him reverence.

Decay of natural spirits belongs to "the time of old age." The outworn traveller says of these days, "I have no pleasure in them." "The daughters of music are brought low." This period of life is proverbially one of caution; and caution easily lapses into timidity. The old man pauses at the leap which twenty years ago he would have taken at a bound. It is the habit of his life to forecast the future, if not to forebode. Experience has taught him to see dangers on every hand. But besides this, weakness of body brings with it depression and sadness. The aged are solitary even in the thronged assembly. They muse and pine. There is much in the past to make them thoughtful: great experience has opened to them many sources of sorrow, all unknown to the gay circle around them; and what can they expect for the morrow? Shut out from active employment, or slow to learn that their competency is lessened, they feel their isolation. If an irritable frame and sensitive temperament superadd to these things irascibility, and peevishness, how greatly are the ills increased! All this makes it the more rare and signal, when we behold a contented and cheerful old age; and, through God's infinite grace, and the influence of his Holy Spirit, we are sometimes called to this edifying and delightful spectacle.

The approach of eternity confers solemnity on "the time of old age." This single consideration is sufficient to overshadow the soul with a solemnity unknown before; and though we sometimes find triflers who are advanced in life, the best and wisest are made serious and considerate. Yet facts do not justify the assertion, that the bare increase of years does any thing towards the conversion of the sinner. The youthful reader should take warning, when he sees the aged dying on every side, and others with hoary hairs standing around their graves unconcerned. Nevertheless some truly lay this to heart, and to these it is a trial. It is the dreadful case of some to be given up to despairing thoughts on the approach of death.

But it is unnecessary to enumerate all the particulars which go to make up the burden of old age: we turn with more alacrity to the consolations which are afforded by the word of God.

There is a sentence of the Psalmist which points out the direction in which he who is laden with years may look for cheering. It is that exclamation in the seventy-first Psalm, "Cast me not off in the time of old age, forsake me not when my strength faileth." Though a prayer, it is also a promise. For when God himself dictates a petition, and so to speak puts it into our mouths, it assures us that what he thus prompts us to ask, he is ready to bestow. These words may therefore be considered as revealing the basis of comfort and support offered to an aged Christian. It is as though he said, Man may cast me off; society may cast me off; friends, helpers, even children may abandon me; but

O my God, cast not Thou me off, in the time of old age! It is a lawful, an urgent, a comprehensive prayer, and may be studied in its several meanings, with edification.

"Leave me not to helpless imbecility!" It is permitted to deprecate extreme poverty. We are taught to pray, 'Give us this day our daily bread." The old disciple is not forbidden to ask under submission to God's holy will, that he may be exempted from wasting languors and decrepitude. But submission has here a large part to perform. As we resign to the decision of our faithful Creator the time and manner of our death, so must we leave ourselves implicitly in his hands, as to the whole colour of our latter days. Competence and poverty are at his disposal. Nevertheless it is thus recorded by one who knew, "I have been young and now am old, yet have I not seen the righteous forsaken, nor his seed begging bread." And if any may appropriate the cheering words, the aged may surely so do: "Be content with such things as ye have, for He hath said, I will never leave thee nor forsake thee;" words which seem written to be a heavenly answer to this very petition of the Psalmist. The whole connection, however, shows, that the servant of God may be sometimes reduced to straits and apprehensions, in which his faith is sorely tried, and in which he can look to none but God. Yet we have reason to encourage every believer, whose old age is encompassed with cares about worldly subsistence, to stay himself on the Lord his Preserver.

The prayer further implies, "Be thou a friend to me under the loss of friends." There is a wide scope of application in those words: "When my father and mother forsake me, then the Lord will take me up." The degree of comfort which this consideration brings to any individual, will be in proportion to the reality of his previous communion with God. He who has made God his friend, and has humbly and lovingly walked with him during a lifetime, is prepared to endure with equanimity the loss of friends. In days of prosperity, when his children were around him, and his table was encircled with guests, he already looked to God as his covenant friend and supporter; how much more when his windows are darkened, and the coals have died out upon his hearth. He has learned before this great trial came, to turn to God as the enlightener of his solitary way, and the portion of his soul. Like Abraham, he has, early in his pilgrimage, heard a voice saying, "Fear not; I am thy shield, and thy exceeding great reward." Now, therefore, when he begins to find himself alone in the world, he is beyond expression thankful that he has not this divine acquaintanceship to seek. He is sure that the Lord has not brought him thus far to make him a laughing-stock to his soul's enemies. God will help him, and that right early. Many are the aged saints who can join in the exultation, "So that we may boldly say, The Lord is my helper, and I will not fear what man shall do unto me."

Suppose the worst case, even that of desolating

bereavement and complete insulation: an aged believer left without partner, child, or relative on earth; if he has made God his friend, he can still say, "My soul, wait thou only upon God, for my expectation is from him." And God is wont to answer the prayer of the desolate by stirring up the tender mercies of man. Friends are raised up for the forlorn and sinking one. This is a consideration which ought to lead pious and charitable persons in our churches to turn their attention to the aged. Very often, it is not so much temporal aid which they require, as the smile of recognition, the light of a friendly countenance, the voice of cheering, the hand that lifts the latch of the solitary chamber, the Christian conference, and the fellowship of prayer. Let the reader ask himself whether this duty has not been neglected, and whether there is not, even within his own communion and neighbourhood, some ancient servant of God to whom he might render the offices of a son or a brother. But by whatever means it may be accomplished, the Lord will not allow his aged servants to sink under their bereavements.

He who prays, "Cast me not off," furthermore asks thus, "Cheer me by thy presence, under the neglects of men." None have greater need than the aged to concentrate their regards on the honour which cometh from God; for the attentions and complimentary tributes of society are usually seen to decrease as age advances. The world casts off its old servants, but God does not cast them off. A man who has set great value on the caresses and adulation of the people during his middle life, is in a fair way to see the matter in its true light when he falls into decay. Then it is that he finds his flatterers vanishing, like birds of passage which seek more sunny climes. In such circumstances it is an invaluable blessing to have the heart fixed on God. His approval and praise have a heavenly quality about them which fills and satisfies the soul.

The prayer of the aged imports, moreover, this, "Sustain my sinking spirits by the hopes of thy gospel and the ministrations of thy grace." This is possible, though it is against nature. We have seen such trophies of grace. Especially could I name an aged disciple, whose latter days were by far his best, even in regard to this point. As years advanced, he became less restless and susceptible under the vexations of life; his temper was more even, his spirits more cheerful, and his benignant smile more abiding. If the reader will give himself the pains to make a survey, he will find numerous instances of this kind among the churches. And such a one is more lovely then in the sight of God than ever amidst the florid exuberance of youthful promise; more wise, more pure, more holy, more tranquil, more benignly humble. Let the young be invited to seek the company of such; the Isaacs, Israels, and Johns of our church. Let them be sought for as hid treasure, though the quest may take us among the humblest of society. Those of us who exercise the ministerial profession have been taught that some of the most instructive and most lovely objects to a Christian eye are concealed in garrets, cellars, and beds of suffering. A poor, frivolous, time-serving, mercenary, contemptible world, judges otherwise; but when their money perishes with them, true holiness and happiness shall survive the shock of death, and go into eternity. The sun shines on nothing more glorious than a truly ripe believer waiting to be gathered into the garner of the Lord. To comprehend the greatness of such proficiency we must know its hinderances. There are many characters which maintain their consistency well during seasons of prosperity, but which would be sadly shaken by the stormy weather of old age.

The aged man's prayer includes, finally, "Cast me not off on the approach of death." Does the reader, peradventure, feel in his members the signs of declining years? Then let him consider that old age is the beginning of death. It is true death may greatly anticipate old age; but he that is old is assuredly on the brink of death. Natural fears hover about the most careless in regard to this impending catastrophe. The relief which most aged sinners have is by the method of diversion, or the turning away of the mind from the revolting object. But this is a miserable resort, and a few spasms or pangs are sufficient to shake a sturdy and impenitent soul out of this refuge of lies. Let the truth be told; there is no real consolation under fears of death but in God. "The peace of God which passeth all understanding" can make an infirm and threatened old man go down firmly into the valley. Suppose God should, after all, cast off his servant in the time of old age! It is a surmise which sometimes darts across the soul. But no, he will not. "Even to old age am I he, and to hoary hairs will I carry you." The dictation of such a prayer is equal to a promise that it shall be answered.

We have looked with wonder and delight on an aged disciple thus waiting till his change come. He is not exempt from the infirmities and pains which beset this season of life; but his mind is drawn away from them to fix itself on the " exceeding and eternal weight of glory." He knows not at what moment his summons may come, but he knows whom he has believed, and is persuaded that he is able to keep the great deposit until that day. Christian hope does not allow him to give way under the disquietudes of life. It is his endeavour to show, by the uniformity of his cheerfulness, that religion can despoil even old age of its terrors. Among younger Christians he sits as a patriarch who has experienced all the diversities of the disciple's lot; has discovered the emptiness of the world, and has made what remains of the present life a meditation of the life to come. His great business, therefore, is to prepare for eternity. But this he does without perturbation or servile dread. Long ago he has cast his burden on the Lord, and ventured his everlasting hopes on the promise of mercy in Christ Jesus; and having been sealed with that blessed Spirit of promise, he looks into the future with a confidence founded on divine authority; having a desire to depart and be with Christ. Such a condition as this is among the happiest on earth; and it throws a radiance of commendation over the gospel which produces it. The Lord does not forsake his people. In those emergencies of life in which their strength is most tried, he may be supposed to regard them with peculiar tenderness. And at length he abolishes death, and admits them to the glories of the eternal state.

Where Christian graces are vigorous, the aged disciple will be much in meditation of that eternal world which he is approaching. Thither the majority of the brethren whom he has known here have entered before him. Every bodily pang and weakness suggests to him by contrast the blessed exemptions and perfect delights of a state where God shall wipe all tears from the eyes. At the resurrection, the soul and body shall be reunited; and the body which shall be raised will have no frailties or susceptibilities of distress. It is comfort for the aged saint, aching with the weariness of a hard pilgrimage, to muse on the day when his body shall be newly fitted for the service of the soul, and when he shall emerge into the balmy springtide of perpetual youth. He knows that he shall exchange the solitude and neglect of a world where he has long felt himself a stranger, for the associations of that communion to which the wise, and holy, and blessed of all nations, churches, and dispensations have been adding themselves for ages. Groaning under the consciousness of imperfection in his best services, he lights up with rapture at the thought of a world where he shall glorify God without weariness, intermission, or defect. Remembering the clouds and darkness of his sad journey, he longs for the perfect light in which he shall see face to face, and know even as also he is known. This hope, which brightens as graces become mature, may be considered the prime consolation of old age. Where it is possessed in large measure, it is a full indemnity for losses and an antidote to the poisonous influences of this mortal condition.

Consolation in old age is much promoted by a thankful review of God's providence as to the past. This appears to be included in that remarkable promise, Isaiah 46 : 4; "I have made and I will bear." He that made us and preserves us, will continue to care for us. God will not suffer those on whom he has expended so much to fail at the last. The fact, that the believer has already passed through so many toils and dangers unhurt, affords good reason to hope that he shall be carried through all, even the last and worst.

The eye of the aged pilgrim takes in, from his eminence of observation and retrospect, a great extent of way which he has traversed. In this he recalls many a spot signalized by its Ebenezer, and testifying to the faithfulness of God. This principle of consolation is the very one which leads the sacred writers to such frequent recapitulations of Israel's way through the wilderness; Moses also recounts the whole, just on the verge of the promised land. This is our assurance that God will not cast off in the time of old age, that he has clung to his people for their help in all preceding times.

If now, as can scarcely be denied, there are professing Christians, advanced in years, and, of course, approaching their eternal abode, who have none of this peace; who feel the burdens of life more keenly with every new step into the last valley, who repine at their lot, indulge the petulance of continual complaint, and shudder at their inevitable and impending change; what shall we say, but that they have failed to take the blessings which are made over in the covenant gift? They have not from the heart uttered that prayer of the Psalmist which we have been considering. From which we learn this momentous lesson, that to be happy in old age, we must regard religion as the one thing needful; not merely as important, but as all-important; that "principal thing," without which all else is vanity and vexation of spirit. For in what other direction can the aged look for comfort? What can this world offer them? They have tasted every cup, and having drunk each to the dregs, have found it first foam and then bitterness. They have but a few days, possibly not a single day, to live. Time is hurrying them with dreadful rapidity into the presence of their Judge. Unless they have sought his kingdom and righteousness first, and above all; unless they have laid up their treasure and their hearts in heaven, they are absolutely cut off from every source of rational enjoyment. The hand upon the awful dial-plate of life points at midnight, and presently comes the fatal stroke. Let none suppose that a mere titular standing in Christ's church, or a name among professing Christians, affords a basis for hope amidst the despondencies of age. Generally, those who possess the serene enjoyments of which we have spoken, are such as began to make God's service their great concern many years ago, and now, in the autumn of their days, are reaping the golden ears, agreeably to the sowing of an earlier experience. And if these lines should meet the eye of any to whom such a preparation is all unknown, he should lay down the book and prepare to meet his God.

One of the greatest consolations of old age is to spend what remains of life in honouring God. David connects this with one of his pathetic prayers: "Now also, when I am old and grey-headed, O God forsake me not, until I have shown thy strength unto this generation, and thy power to every one that is to come." How remarkably this was accomplished in his latter days we know very well. Ecclesiastical history relates of the apostle John, that when for very age he was unable any longer to preach the word, he used to be carried into the Christian assembly, where the most he could utter was, "Little children, love one another!" The modern church affords numerous instances of ancient believers, who "still bring forth fruit in old age." Younger disciples properly look up to them as advisers, and endeavour to profit by their long experience. Their very patience and tranquillity, while they wait for their Lord, is edifying to the church. Their words fall on the ear with peculiar weight from the authority of mature wisdom; and it is an evil day, in church or state, when any for sake "the counsel of the old men."* For these reasons, aged Christians are not lightly to suppose that their work is done, because they are shut out from public service. It may be that God is more glorified by the quiet graces of their eventide, than by their most strenuous exertions while bearing the burden and heat of the day.

In the wonderful ordering of the dispensation of grace, it is observed, that although the susceptibility of new impressions from objects of sense, and the pleasure taken in passing events of a worldly nature, are very much abated by the progress of years, it is not so in regard to spiritual enjoyments; the feeble and departing servant of God is still alive to the things of the kingdom. Memory, imagination, even the perceptive powers may be seriously impaired, but sensibility to the truths of the gospel remains in vigour; the name of Jesus is still delightful, and the coming glory of the kingdom still cheers the soul. For such a blessed experience, however, there must have been a long preparation, by daily communion with God, which affords an inducement at once to early piety, and consistent walking with Christ, throughout the years of

* 1 Kings 12:8.

strength. We cannot err in supposing that the Lord of such a servant looks down upon him with peculiar complacency in these days of bodily weakness but spiritual ripening. He may be likened to the just and devout Simeon, who took the infant Jesus up in his arms, and said, "Lord, now lettest thou thy servant depart in peace." He knows that his salvation is nearer than when he believed. As one long in bondage looks out wistfully for deliverance, so he lifts up his head, because his redemption draweth nigh. Weaned in some good measure from the world, and dead to its appetites and pleasures, he has his conversation, or citizenship, in heaven, from whence also he looks for the Lord Jesus, who will change his vile body, that it may be fashioned like unto his glorious body; hearkening for the footsteps of his beloved Master, who is coming to transport him to himself, he patiently waits till his change come. These are blessed fruits of grace, enjoyed at a period when the world has nothing to offer to its outworn devotees. It is the privilege of aged Christians to expect these comforts, which are the more satisfying, as being altogether independent of all outward circumstances; they may be possessed, nay they have been ten thousand times possessed, by the poor, the infirm, the diseased, the deaf, the blind; the united voice of hope and exultation, which rises from the tabernacles of aged pilgrims is, "For this God is our God for ever and ever, he will be our guide even unto death."[*]

[*] Psalm 48: 14.

CONSOLATION IN REGARD TO THE SAINTS DEPARTED

XVII.

WHEN we inspect a series of ancient Christian monuments, as for example in Rome; or, in default of this, when we examine those collections of antiquaries in which the inscriptions of these monuments are exactly edited, we are struck with a remarkable change of expression which has taken place during the lapse of ages. The later epitaphs, as is well known, frequently contain the words now of established usage among Romanists, "REQUIESCAT IN PACE," (*May he* rest in peace!) But if we trace the series back to a more remote and purer antiquity, we find the primitive expression to be, "REQUIESCIT IN PACE," (*He doth* rest in peace.) A difference which is startling, suggestive, and full of argument. Primitive Christianity believed the departed to be already in repose. And we can, by means of authentic marbles, almost lay the finger on the point of time at which the indicatory and assertory phrase, *He rests*, was transmuted into the corrupt precatory formula, *May he rest!*

We need consolation both when we lay beloved bodies of friends or brethren in the grave, and when we shudder on the brink of our own dissolution. In regard to both, we rest with complete repose of soul on the declaration of the Word, that believers "sleep in Jesus."

Before proceeding to consider this doctrine in its positive meaning, we find it necessary to remove the grounds of two portentous errors; one of which is the familiar tenet of popery, and the other a kindred opinion, that the human spirit lies unconscious from death till resurrection.

There is a communion in glory, which renewed souls have with Christ their head, partly in this world and partly in the next. Death is the point of transition between these two portions of the new life. They are very unequal. The first is troublous, blemished, changeful, and brief; the second is fixed, pure, glorious, and eternal. Yet two strange things are true respecting our judgment of the two. First, we are most taken up, in thought and affection, by that which is inferior, short, and transient; and, secondly, the point at which we pass from one to the other, is that which of all things we most dread. We are about to contemplate this change in one of its aspects, as viewed by the believer, for his encouragement amidst the afflictions of life. That which buoys up his soul amidst toils and privations, is the blessed truth, which causes him to count affliction nothing, in comparison with the " far more exceeding and eternal weight of glory."

The doctrine which we are called to contemplate is, that when the soul leaves the body it passes at once to Christ, to perfection, and to heaven, thus to abide in peace and glory till the resurrection. The body, we admit, is left. The sentence goes into execution: unto dust shalt thou return. After our skin, worms shall destroy this body. It has been the beloved companion and useful instrument; but now it passes to dissolution. The remains of those whom we love are sacred. We have the best authority for confiding them to the faithful tomb, with due solemnity and tenderness. But we are not left to the cheerless dogma, that when corruption has done its work, we shall behold them no more; and that the parent, the sister, or the son, whom we have laid in the earth, shall never again be known in the body, but have shared the lot of beasts. The gospel reveals a blessed hope, which heathenism could not imagine, and which the dreams of enthusiasts and the cavils of atheists cannot take away. The bodies of Christ's brethren do rest in their graves till the resurrection. That union, whereby we are members of his body, of his flesh, and of his bones, still endures. They are still his; and from his heavenly throne he watches over them. They are beautifully said to be asleep in him. "For if we believe that Jesus died and rose again, even so them also which sleep in Jesus will God bring with him." 1 Thes. 4 : 14. It is a reviving hope for those who expect soon to lay aside the flesh, and a consolation for any who have followed their friends to their burial. Though the body is left, it is not forsaken.

But when the soul leaves the body, it passes im

mediately to Christ. Is this a vain speculation? Can it be a thing of indifference, whether at my last breath I enter at once to glory, or plunge into some unknown condition of suspense or pain? Would it not overcloud our dying moment, to have this question unanswered? Your hearts reply, that the investigation is reasonable; and it is answered in the Word. He who is absent from the body is present with the Lord. The teaching of Scripture is so express on this point, that enlargement would be unnecessary, if it had not been for erroneous teachers, who have endeavoured to rob the saints of this part of their inheritance, and to postpone the beginning of their joys. These errors may be reduced to two, which it will be profitable to hold up in contrast with the divine verity.

I. When Christianity began to grow corrupt, and the ministers of Christ assumed to be priests, a dogma was privily brought in, plainly heathen in its source, that souls which are imperfect, instead of entering heaven, enter some intermediate state of further probation, where they are tried with fire, punished for their sins, and rendered fit for heaven. This is known by the invented name of Purgatory. While it has not a single passage of Scripture even speciously in its behalf, it has been a mine of wealth to the hierarchy. It has brought in its train the long retinue of prayers and masses for the dead, indulgences, rich oblations, testamentary gifts, and fresh subjugation to Romish tyranny. In upholding their doctrine, the Papists have gone so far as to affirm,

THE SLEEP OF THE DEAD.

that the patriarchs and other Old Testament saints were not received into heaven at their death, but were retained in what they called the Limbus of the Fathers; the word meaning in Latin the exterior border of a flowing robe or mantle. Though this is distinct in their mythology from Purgatory, the same principles apply to both. How the imaginations of religionists may be inflamed by such teachings, we may learn from the poetic but awful pictures of the great Italian, Dante, who by his potent wand conjures before our horror-stricken fancy blindness, tears, lamentations, blood, and fire. Travellers in Italy are too well acquainted with the horrible paintings and more horrible harangues, whereby an alms is begged from the superstitious, for the poor souls in Purgatory. Turning from these ravings to the truth, we find the Bible teaching that the souls of the patriarchs and other saints who have departed have passed immediately into a state of happiness. This is proved irrefragably by the argument of our Lord against the Sadducees. Moses, says he, calleth the Lord "the God of Abraham, and the God of Isaac, and the God of Jacob. For he is not a God of the dead, but of the living; for all live unto him." Luke 20 : 38. It is proved by the history of the rich man and Lazarus. Luke 16 : 19. You remember the case; it is never said to be a parable; and if a parable, it teaches truth. The beggar died, and was carried by angels—not into purgatory, not into the *limbus patrum*—but into Abraham's bosom, that is, into the joy of Abraham's God. The rich man also died, and was buried, and (not in purgatory, but) in hell he lifted up his eyes, being in torments. This is further proved by the words of our dying Saviour to the thief on the cross: "This day shalt thou be with me in Paradise." I am almost ashamed to rehearse the quibbles by which this passage is evaded. It is said, for example, to mean, "I this day say unto thee, thou shalt;" a violent perversion of the words, which is not favoured by a single ancient version, and which, robbing our Lord's words of all their emphasis, represent him as uttering the most useless declaration. His gracious reply was occasioned by the preceding request of the dying malefactor, "Lord, remember me when thou comest into thy kingdom!" It is said, again, that by Paradise Christ means the intermediate place of the patriarchs. But is it not the uniform method of Scripture, by Paradise, to set forth the highest heaven? When (2 Cor. 12 : 4) Paul tells us of "one caught up to the third heaven,"-he instantly adds, interpreting himself, "How that he was caught up into paradise." In the Apocalyptic message to Ephesus (2 : 7) it is said to the victor: "To him that overcometh will I give to eat of the tree of life, which is in the midst of the paradise of God." Now this is plainly parallel with the promises to the other victors, as (v. 10) "I will give thee a crown of life," (v. 28) "I will give him the morning-star;" (3 : 12) "I will make him a pillar of the temple of my God, and he shall go no more out." This is proved, also, by the hopes which cheered the ancients amidst long journeyings and toils, of a speedy admission to rest, of a city having foundations, and of respite after death. The attempted proof of a purgatorial state from the Scriptures is lamentably defective. The very difficult place in Pet. 3 : 19, concerning Christ's preaching to spirits in prison, is quite as difficult for our adversaries who urge it. To discuss it at length would exhaust modern patience: suffice it to say, "The meaning of the text appears to be, that the Spirit of Christ influenced Noah, who was a 'preacher of righteousness,' to warn the unhappy men, whose spirits were then, and still are, in prison, of the danger which was so near them, while the ark was preparing. Now, to build such a momentous doctrine as that of purgatory on a passage admitting of this construction, and on one or two others, still more violently tortured for the purpose, shows the total want of a solid foundation for the superstructure which is erected. It may also be added, that even the passages which are brought from the apocryphal writings, which are not canonical Scripture, do not warrant this doctrine, as it is held and taught by the Church of Rome." And let us thank God that it is so; and that we have no Christian reason (when we stand beside a dying friend) to suppose that his departing spirit is about to enter penal fires, and the sufferings of his agony to be exchanged for ages, years, or even days, of still heavier torment; no reason (on our own bed of death) to shudder at the prospect of horrible in carceration and fresh conflicts. No, my brethren, "the last enemy that shall be destroyed is death."

II. Leaving this, there is another error, which has prevailed among Romanizing Protestants, a class unhappily increasing day by day. It is equally a denial of our doctrine, for it maintains that the soul sleeps with the body, from death to the resurrection. Such sleep of the soul is an anti-scriptural dream. There is no evidence that the soul ever ceases to think, or that it can so cease, without losing its identity, and ceasing to be a soul. There is no proof, that, the moment after death, the soul shall not exert an unwonted elasticity; or that the body, though an instrument here, is a necessary instrument. That could scarcely be denominated an everlasting life, which should be subject to so direful an interruption. But the Scriptures leave us no doubt. The passages already cited, are here in point. The crucified thief passed into paradise. Abraham, Isaac, and Jacob (not yet risen), are yet alive, and live unto God. Such is the condition of all the blessed, of whom Paul, says (Heb. 12 : 23), "Ye are come," ye are now come, "to the spirits of just men made perfect." Ancient prophecy foresaw the same. "He shall enter into peace; they shall rest in their beds, each one walking in his uprightness." Is. 57 : 2. The body rests: the soul walks in uprightness. When Paul wrote to the Philippians, he felt that to die was gain. He knew not which to choose; and was in a strait betwixt two; which could not have been, if the choice had been between labour and unconsciousness: "having a desire to depart, and to be with Christ;" to be with Christ! an expression, which undoubtedly means more, than rest in sleep, or even joy beyond the resurrection. No, he could say with David (73 : 24), "Thou shalt guide me with thy counsel, and afterwards receive me to glory." And when he felt the frailties of the present state, and was warned of speedy dissolution, he could look beyond the breaking up of the existing fabric, to the escape into an abiding city. "For we know that if our earthly house of this tabernacle were dissolved, we have a building of God, a house not made with hands, eternal in the heavens." He longs "to be clothed with the house from heaven." He exults in the thought (5 : 3) that he "shall not be found naked." More strikingly he tells what shall immediately supervene on death (v. 4) : mortality shall be swallowed up of life! He groans, that "being at home in the body," he is "absent from the Lord." And inasmuch as our whole question with adversaries is concerning the state of the soul when unloosed from the body; and inasmuch as they affirm that this is a state of unconsciousness, we adduce the apostle as a triumphant witness, when he exclaims, "We are confident and willing rather to be absent from the body and present with the Lord." Unless, therefore, these terms can be shown to import an unconscious slumber until the final trump, we may regard the doctrine as established, that when the soul leaves the body it passes to a heaven of enjoyment.

And the doctrine is most reasonable. The term of trial and of suffering is over: it is to be expected that the time of joy should begin. The case of each soul being, as all Protestant Christianity confesses, unchangeably settled, it is proper that the reward should ensue; and that the last pang should be followed, not by the stupor of centuries, but by the garden of pleasures: that Paul, weary of labour, might hope, when absent from the body, not to be happy after four or five thousand years, but to be "present with the Lord." It is consistent with the love, the intercession, and the kingly power of Him who is at the right hand of God, and whose longing is, that those whom the Father hath given him may be with him, to behold his glory. It agrees with the spirit of the holy angels, those loving ones, who are "all ministering spirits, sent forth to minister for them who shall be heirs of salvation," who hover about dying beds with folded hands, and who spread their seraphic wings to carry even a Lazarus into Abraham's bosom. It is beautifully accordant with the doctrine, that the human soul is entirely independent in its actings on its present companion, and may exist without it in an unembodied state.

Contemplate the escape! It is a passing to perfection. In the present life, we acknowledge that sanctification is incomplete. But now the trial is at an end. "Then shall I be satisfied, when I awake with thy likeness." There is no long slumber between the race and the crown. The passage is short. To be dismissed from earth, from temptation, from passion, from the body, and from sin, is to be admitted into that greater but invisible world, upon the verge of which we are continually living. It is to emerge from time into eternity. It is to close the outward eye, as needless, to lose sight of all its objects, and to open the inward eye upon the world or spirits. It is to say farewell to a group of weeping friends, and bid welcome to the multitude of ransomed souls. It is to leave all care, and pain, and uncertainty, and sin for ever behind us.

It is also a passing into glory. God is there! He who is every where present, unseen, is there present to the lively apprehension of the redeemed. Christ is there! And the longing soul finds itself in his embrace. The breaking up of the tabernacle sometimes reveals glimpses of this glory, even here

> The soul's poor cottage, shattered and decayed,
> Lets in new light through chinks that time has made.

The conflict has ended. How else can we explain the words, "Death is swallowed up in victory?" Rest, indeed, there is, but rest in Christ's bosom of love, and on his throne of glory. Heaven is ready for them, and, by grace, they are ready for heaven. Contemplate the change as immediate. God has granted this blessed hope to his dying child. He does not summon him away to a useless inaction of ages, but to the vision of himself, to be with him in paradise, to be present with the Lord. Heartily do we acknowledge that there are many expressions of Scripture which show that the reward of the righteous is not complete until the re-union of soul and body at the general resurrection. But the interval is not only painless, but is conscious, intelligent, and joyful. It is short, when measured on the great scale of heaven. These separate souls are even now beloved; joined to Christ; recipients of his Spirit; bringing forth fruit; sitting down already with Abraham, Isaac, and Jacob, who live unto that God who is the God not of the dead but of the living. And when the trumpet shall sound, and the dead shall be raised, the triumph shall be consummate. We may well consent, my brethren, to leave these perishing bodies in the grave, with such an expectation for the soul. The dust is sacred, being still united to Christ. I am persuaded that not even death (Rom. 8 : 38) "shall be able to separate us from the love of God, which is in Christ Jesus our Lord." The grave is sacred; it is perfumed by the merits of him who lay three days and three nights within its vaults. Those expectant remains are no longer the subjects of disease, weariness, and pain. "The sting of death is sin," and it is no more. The doctrine of the resurrection must be a separate topic; but even here, we must say, that disembodied spirits wait "for the adoption, to wit, the redemption of the body." And if they cast a glance at the ashes of their tomb, they do it in remembrance of Him who has "become the first fruits of them that slept;" and in lively hope of the hour when "that which is sown in dishonour shall be raised in glory."

We cannot follow the departing spirit; the flight

is too rapid, and it is into a world all unseen. Yet as we stand around the breathless, cold, and stiffened corpse, the analogy of faith suggests a shadow of what may be the condition of the ransomed soul. The snare is broken, and it is escaped! The fetters have been stricken off at a blow. How vast the transition! How rapidly is the earth, with all its scenes, left behind! We may justly suppose, that the blessed spirit finds itself surrounded by the instant presence of God; yet (as his unveiled glory would be insufferable) by the presence of God revealed in Christ. Infinite love can and will save the poor, trembling, shrinking soul, newly come into the sublimities of a strange world, from the shock of a surprise, which otherwise would astound or annihilate, and so hold back the face of that throne, and so spread a cloud over it, and so mitigate its splendours, that the frail creature, born into an untried state, shall be able to bear it. There will indeed be the surprise of discovery, and the shock of ecstasy, but he who hid Moses in the cleft of the rock, and spake to Elijah in the still small voice, will doubtless address his ransomed one in the gentlest whisper of redeeming love. Throughout a wearisome lifetime the cry of the church has been, "We would see Jesus!" now the wish is gratified, now the vail is withdrawn, now the separate spirit is present with the Lord. The prayers of a lifetime are answered, and the object of a life-long affection is embraced. And O, what an escape and transition, from dying anguish to a throne! How shall we dare to give utterance to sentiments, which here we can scarcely imagine!

"And is this heav'n? and am I there?
  How short the road! how swift the flight!
I am all life, all eye, all ear;
  Jesus is here—my soul's delight.

Is this the heav'nly friend who hung
  In blood and anguish on the tree?
Whom Paul proclaimed, whom David sung?
  Who died for them, who died for me?

Hail thou fair offspring of my God!
  Thou first-born image of his face!
Thy death procured this blest abode,
  Thy vital beams adorn the place!

Lo! he presents me at the throne,
  All spotless there the Godhead reigns.
Sublime and peaceful through the Son;
  Awake my voice, in heavenly strains!"

"The place of burial," says Chrysostom, "is called a cemetery (that is, a dormitory), a place of slumber, to teach you that they who have departed are not dead, but have lain down to sleep." The ancient Pagans sometimes employed the same figure, but with the adjunct of a terrible epithet; for they take care to call it a "perpetual," or an "everlasting" sleep. Thus, in one of the idyls of Moschus, the Greek poet, after saying that plants cut down by the winter, and seeming to die, yet revive in the spring, subjoins:

"But we, or great, or wise, or brave,
  Once dead and silent in the grave,
Senseless remain; one rest we keep—
  One long, eternal, unawaken'd sleep."

And Catullus,

> "The sun that sets, again will rise,
> And give the day, and gild the skies;
> But when we lose our little light,
> We sleep in everlasting night."*

In agreement with which heathen darkness, the revolutionary philosophers engraved over their famous burying-places, the inhuman blasphemy, "Death is an eternal sleep." It would have been a fit inscription for a field where the carcasses of brutes are cast: but observe, my brethren, it is only of man that the term is used; it is man only who, dying, falls asleep. And the beautiful phrase is too often repeated in the Scriptures to be set aside as a casual metaphor. Hebrew worthies are said to sleep with their fathers. The Psalmist, filled with anticipations of awakening, cries: "Then shall I be satisfied, when I awake with thy likeness." But, as might be expected, the term is most appropriate to the New Testament. It was when Christ died, and the vail of the temple was rent, that "many bodies of the saints which slept arose." "Our friend Lazarus sleepeth," said our benignant Redeemer; "but I go that I may awake him out of sleep." And even amidst the violent agonies of the first martyrdom, the beloved Stephen, already beholding heaven opened, "fell asleep." It seems to have become the usual word among the ancient Christians for departure from this life. For, speaking of the forty days of Christ's tabernacling here, after the resurrection, Paul says, concerning the

---

* Nox est perpetua una dormienda.

five hundred witnesses: "Of whom the greater part remain unto this present; but some are fallen asleep." Nor could human language furnish us a more sweet and tranquillizing emblem. It invests the dying form with a promise of restitution; enlightens the darkened chamber; hangs a garland upon the sepulchre; and draws gentle curtains around the couch of the beloved. Blessed be God for this new aspect of what we thought our enemy!

1. The emblem is natural, and is derived from the obvious resemblance. This is my first observation. In ancient mythology, sleep was the brother of death. The first death was probably thought a sleep; as the first sleep, according to Milton, was mistaken for death. I stand by the side of an infant, and behold it in quiet slumber. What on earth can be more lovely? The eyes are closed; the senses are locked up; the great external world is shut out. All is stillness and repose. We look and wonder, but feel no pain, because we expect a resurrection from this slumber. In like manner, I stand by the couch where a beloved friend has closed his eyes. The doors of sense are shut; the outer world is excluded; but the greater, lovelier, more awful inner world is there. The marble brow; the serene, unmoving features; the settled smile of lips which were late so eloquent; all speak of deep slumber. But Christianity tells me to dismiss my fears; for Jesus comes to awake him out of sleep.

The transition into the two states, under favourable circumstances, is the same. In blessed souls it is "a gentle wafting to eternal life." We make too much of the mere article of dying, and often overrate its pangs. Sometimes, I know, they are dreadful, but even then they are brief. And in a multitude of cases, no doubt, the dying person suffers less than he has endured many times before; while in repeated joyful instances it is only a closing of the eyes for sleep. Let us be thankful when our friends are spared all extreme anguish on their dying beds. The resemblance, therefore, is undeniable; and it is good to contemplate the sacred sleep.

2. Sleep comes at the close of the day To many a soul this is a pregnant consideration; for they are weary of task-work and of working hours. "Is there not an appointed time to man upon earth? are not his days also like the days of a hireling? as a servant earnestly desireth the shadow, and as a hireling looketh for the reward of his labour." When the burden and heat of the day are over, then comes the season of repose. "Man goeth forth unto his work and to his labour until the evening." In that evening God gives him exemption. It is implied in this, that the world's business is over. There is nothing more impressive than to stand amidst a great city at dead of night, when labour rests,

And all that mighty heart is lying still!

Thus is it when life's day is over. Of what pertains to this present time, no more can be done. The season of trial and of labour for our fellows is over; it is the hour of sleep. The time of study, for this life, is over; the time of earthly plans; the time of bold adventure; it is the hour of sleep. "Whatsoever thy hand findeth to do, do it with thy might; for there is no work, nor device, nor knowledge, nor wisdom, in the grave, whither thou goest." And yet that grave is not so much a tomb as a resting-place—a cemetery. How much more lovely and more Christian would our grave-yards be if they had more of heaven and less of earth; more of rest in that blessed sleep, and less of the restless pursuit of human glory; more of our oneness in Christ, and less of our earthly caste and separation!

> "A scene sequestered from the haunts of men;
> The loveliest nook of all that lovely glen,
> Where weary pilgrims found their last repose:
> The little heaps were ranged in comely rows,
> With walks between, by friends and kindred trod,
> Who dressed with duteous hands each hallow'd sod:
> No sculptur'd monument was taught to breathe
> His praises whom the worm devoured beneath:
> The high, the low, the mighty and the fair,
> Equal in death, were undistinguished there,
> To some warm heart, the poorest dust was dear;
> For some kind eye, the meanest claimed a tear.
> 'Twas not a scene for grief to nourish care;
> It breath'd of hope, and moved the heart to prayer."

In that sleep there is an end of human pains to the children of God. "There the wicked cease from troubling, and there the weary be at rest; there the prisoners rest together; they hear not the voice of the oppressor. The small and great are there, and the servant is free from his master." The closing eye loses sight for ever of every annoyance of this life. Perhaps, my brethren, you have never duly considered this important truth, that all the prayers of the believer in regard to himself are answered at once when he falls asleep. The angel of death breaks all chains, delivers from all enemies, repairs all losses, wipes away all sins, and accomplishes all wishes, even of a lifetime—and all this at one moment. These are sweet slumbers, "after life's fitful fever."

3. Sleep is a temporary state; an interval between important periods; it separates day from day. So the repose of death, far from the notion of the atheist, is a season of suspense—a preparation—a momentary hiding, before great events. The departed object of your attachment, who now "draws the sweet infant breath of gentle sleep," is but preparing for a wonderful awaking at the sound of the trumpet. Not that it is unconscious, not that it is inactive, not that the soul is gone; this were to contradict all the analogy; this were proper death, not sleep. "To depart" is "to be with Christ." While we are in this world, "at home in the body, we are absent from the Lord:" but to go into this sleep, is 'to be absent from the body, and to be present with the Lord." Whence I add,

4. The dying believer sleeps in Jesus. How incomparably refreshing the language of the Apostle Paul, 1 Cor. 15 : 18, "they which are fallen asleep in Christ!" What a fragrance exhales from the sacred urn! How does it embalm the very bodies of those whom we have given in charge to Christ! They

sleep in Jesus. It is in his arms they have fainted away, and he holds, sustains, and embraces them. This, which seemed a calamity, is foreseen and contemplated in the covenant. Their very dying has a connection with the blessed Saviour, for it is joined to his dying. The term may have had a primary reference to the martyrs, who laid down their lives for Christ's sake, but was certainly intended to include likewise all who die in union with him. When they close their eyes in holy slumber, they may well be said to fall asleep in Christ; for

(1.) They believe in him. It is of believers that we have been speaking. They are disciples; they have lived as such, and as such they die; if permitted to enjoy any season of tranquil reflection and discourse before they depart, they gather up their powers and declare their confidence in the divine revelation of truth. In this honest moment, they show how sincere has been their conviction. A skeptical frame, or a wavering half-belief, would be but a spider's thread, at such an hour. Now the soul turns to its refuge, now it must hang by its grand support, now it must forget all that is dubious, all that is secondary, all things that are earthly, all things but one—and that is Christ. Now it is, that the greatness of Christianity is revealed, when a man is brought to the great emergency, and must die for it, by it, in it. Let the infidel bring forth his strong reasons; let him show any like confidence in such an hour. Have you known any examples of it? Have you heard any unbeliever on his dying bed send out for his fellow-doubters or fellow-deniers, to listen to his final confession of lies, or to pillow his head in the sinking moment? Have you seen them gathering around their comrade, and trying to pluck the dart from the stricken deer? On the other hand, how often have we stood by the bed of death, when the tranquil believer has said, "See in what peace a Christian can die!" and when, with failing but unwavering lips, he has cried, "I know whom I have believed, and that he is able to keep that which I have committed unto him against that day." Such is faith in these extremities: they believe in Jesus.

(2.) But they also hope in Him. "The wicked is driven away in his wickedness, but the righteous hath hope in his death." From this moment of dying, he looks forward; his blessedness is to come. During all his religious course, this has been his discipline and his habit, and has distinguished him from the men of this world. His "citizenship," his polity, has been in heaven; he has lived perpetually under the impression, that he belonged to another, an unseen state. He has conducted all his mental progress with a direct view to this, and has had his eye fixed on a point, far beyond, at which all his problems shall be solved, and the cup of his knowledge made to run over. He has lived in this world, as not of it, exercising himself to be pure in heart, that so he might see God; a vision in which he has placed his heaven. And his delighted expectation of this has been founded on the intervention of the revealing Mediator, the Word, by whom we draw near to the Father. Conscious that he has joined himself to Christ, he admits the high persuasion of heirship, and such hope at times becomes assurance. Especially in the dying chamber, this hope in Christ, which during the glare of day, and the din of business, has lived apart, with folded wings, a silent unseen dove, having arrived at its proper moment, comes forth, spreads its wings, and soars into the brightest heaven. The eye which is closing on one world, is opening on another, in which its principal object is one, the Lamb slain from the foundation of the world. Thus he hopes in Christ; and

(3.) He triumphs in him.

The term does not imply noise, transport, or outcry. The ocean of thought may be deep while its surface is glassy. The silent language of an eye full of heaven is more than volumes of exclamation. But God does, beyond question, reveal himself in extraordinary supports, at such seasons, and sometimes condescends to open the very windows of heaven, and give light from the inmost sanctuary; so that the child of grace is not merely willing to die, but joyfully prepared to enter into his chief joy, overlooking and overleaping all the intervening pains of dissolution, and the darkness of burial, and exulting in the cry, " O death, where is thy sting! O grave, where is thy victory!"

But whether such graces be vouchsafed or not, and whether the soul departs amidst such visible triumph or not, he who dies a Christian sleeps in Jesus.

5. Sleep is a state from which there is awakening. Here is the glorious point of the analogy. As the mother hushes, and embosoms, and cradles her little one, she awaits the unsealing of the eye, and the unbinding of the fettered limbs, and the resolution of all its features in a wakeful smile of love. And just as truly, when we take our last look of features which we have seen instinct with the varied spirit of a thousand sentiments, and on head, and hands, yea, and heart, which seemed never long asleep here, we close that coffin-lid in sure and certain hope of blessed resurrection. Away with the cold inventions which would summon me to bid an eternal farewell even to the body, which was all allied to soul, and was its chosen exponent; that temple of the Holy Ghost, which he who created it can with infinite ease create anew. Away with the prostituted learning of those who spend all their lucubrations in robbing us of cherished hopes. It is because this night is to have a morning, because this slumber is to be broken, that we are comforted. It is the return of Christ in his glory which is the basis of our expectation. For what says the apostle? "I would not have you ignorant, brethren, concerning them which are asleep, that ye sorrow not, even as others which have no hope. For if we believe that Jesus died and rose again, even so them also which sleep in Jesus will God bring with Him." When Christ the Lord shall appear, then shall they also

appear with him in glory. That will be the day of blessed restitution, "when he shall come to be glorified in his saints, and to be admired in all them that believe." They are now with Christ; they are this moment at home with the Lord. They shall still be with him when he shall come in triumph. Meanwhile his voice is heard among the tombs, saying, "I am the resurrection and the life. He that believeth in me, though he were dead, yet shall he live: And whosoever liveth and believeth in me shall never die."

Faith looks forward to the transcendant glory which, first enveloping in its cloud of light Christ, the head, shall next enclose and transfigure those who are Christ's at his coming; when God the Almighty Father shall bring into the burning focus of universal observation, not the Master only, but all who have loved and followed him; and the beams of that appearance shall be reflected from the central light on all the circle and retinue of attendant saints; for they that are in their graves shall hear the voice of the Son of God; and "them that sleep in Jesus will God bring with him."

Over the grave of those of God's people whom we have loved, a watchful angel seems to stand in silent waiting; his awful hand ready upon the seal of the sepulchre, to enlarge from all bonds, at the appointed moment, those who shall have died in the faith. This may compose our minds amidst the sudden agitations of a violent bereavement; stay the flood of our tears, when those we most loved are carried out of our sight; and kindle hope amidst the darkest sorrow. This may encourage our belief, that when genius, and talent, and learning, and piety, are removed from the church below, they shall reappear in fresh beauty and enlarged capacities, in the church above. This may teach us, when friends and companions are smitten down beside us, in the midst of their labours and researches, to look more at what is yet to come.

If death is a sleep, and if there is an awakening out of this sleep, then we may with confidence commit their bodies to the grave. Let us look back in thought, to the great number whom we have consigned to this sure repose: Few are there among us, who have not some Christian friends over whom to shed the tear. They sleep, but it is to awake again. God hath so promised, and he is faithful. Not only their souls are safe, but their very bodies shall be preserved. How precious is that doctrine of resurrection which Paul spreads forth at length in the fifteenth chapter of the first epistle to the Corinthians! There we learn that the bodies of believers are lost, only in the sense in which seed is lost, which we cast into the ground. It returns to dust; but the day is coming when it shall be raised and glorified. It is the day when our Lord shall bring with him all those who sleep in Jesus. They are as safe as the very angels. Their bodies in the tomb, their souls in paradise. This casts a ray of holy sunshine over the green turf which swells above a father, a brother, or a child. Life and immortality are brought to light by the gospel. Infidelity has no such promises. As to the body, it gives that up to corruption. As to the soul, it can at best only surmise its immortality. The greatest philosopher looks trembling and hesitating into the gulf of futurity: while the humblest, yea (in other things) the most ignorant Christian widow, or Christian child, has an unbroken confidence on the assurance of Him who cannot lie, that there shall be a reunion with blessed spirits gone before, in that world which by a sublime attraction is drawing to itself the pure and the lovely of all ages. So much is a simple faith in the gospel above all philosophy of man.

In the same blessed faith we may prepare for laying our own bodies in the grave. For, beloved brethren, we must soon die. Some avoid the thought, and every thing which leads to it. Some, with a cowardly superstition, dread even the making of a will, lest it should hasten the event. But do what we may, it is hastening on; time, with mighty pinions, is carrying us towards the inevitable doom. There is no discharge in that war; and the true believer has no reason to dread the thought. He would not live here always. This is not his rest; this is not his continuing city; his citizenship is in heaven; his name is registered there. And though on his way thither he must needs pass through the strait of death; it is part of God's teaching to remove his fear of this last enemy. The grave loses its chill, to one who has beheld Christ's sacred body descending into it. And as that sacred body arose, so we know that the bodies of believers shall arise; and them also which sleep in Jesus will God bring with him. God will bring us, with Christ, to meet such as shall be caught up from the earth without dying. In preparing for death (and it is wise to prepare), our thoughts should not dwell long on this transient and comparatively unimportant period of the grave. What is the grave in the scale of eternity? A momentary sleep; and them that sleep Christ will awaken; we shall lie there but a little while. That which is beyond is glorious.

3. That will be a glorious meeting with Jesus and his awakened saints. All earthly things ought to fade in the comparison. It ought to be much in our thoughts. Our contemplations ought to overleap intervening trifles. God has made us susceptible of exquisite social affections, and these are not limited to this world. They will be expanded, satisfied and glorified, in the world to come. There shall be gathered all those holy and redeemed souls whom Christ shall bring with him. New acquaintanceships shall then begin, but, unlike those of this world, shall never end. Ties are often created here only to be sundered: there, there shall be no sunderings. There is no reason known to us why all Christ's people, of all ages, may not learn to know one another during the lapse of a glorious eternity. Why not? Why should we not, as Dr. Watts beautifully represents it in his sermons on Death, be introduced, as a part of our happiness, to all those who have believed and been saved, from Abel down

wards; all patriarchs, psalmists, holy kings, prophets, apostles, martyrs, confessors, reformers, missionaries, philanthropists, sufferers; reading in the history of each the wonderful way in which Divine Sovereign Love works out its problem; and finding new cause to sing loudly to the praise of the glory of that grace, wherein all are accepted in the Beloved? I love not those visionary views of heavenly enjoyment which reduce all to a vapour or a dream. The Scriptures teach otherwise, and lead us to expect a state in which our rational human faculties and propensities shall be sanctified, but not exterminated; and in which we shall still be capable of recognition, of converse, of mutual instruction, mutual love, and resulting peace and joy. And that which shall be so innocent and so rapturous in the possession we may look forward to with hope; distinctly presenting to ourselves the time when Jesus shall gather together in one all the people of God, from among all nations. And their number will be great. For all that I know, the world may stand thousands of years yet; and during that period the conquests of Christianity will probably be unexampled. From the rich harvests of all the continents, God will furnish for himself abundant glory. And in meeting with those who shall be with Christ, we shall meet with the glory of all lands and all ages. It would be narrow and insufficient to confine our views to those only who are of our own kindred. In that day we shall be kindred with the nations of them that are saved, through Him after whom the whole family, both in heaven and earth, is named.

But the doctrine lifts our expectations to a meeting not only with all saints, but with the King of all saints. "God will bring with Him"—with Christ. It is the connection with him that gives the safety and the glory. They died with him; they rose with him; they suffered with him; they shall be glorified with him. The wish of all believers in this world has been: We would see Jesus! Then they shall see him surrounded by all who have loved him. "We know not what we shall be; but we know that when He shall appear, we shall be like him, for we shall see him as he is." This is the apostle John's idea of heaven, "We shall see him as he is." This will be enough. Here we have seen by glimpses, cloudily, in an enigma, "through a glass darkly;" but then, clearly, nearly, fully, "face to face." And the object so seen is of all in the universe the most worthy of being contemplated. God shines in Him. "In him dwelleth all the fulness of the Godhead bodily." To see him, in the fulness of his unveiled excellence, will be a celestial pleasure, well worth dying for.

What serious self-examination ought there to be, to discover whether we are really of the num of those whom God will bring with Christ. Something has already been said as to their character. It remains for us to apply these truths to ourselves. Not all that die shall be so privileged; not all that rise, shall rise to glory, but some to shame and everlasting contempt. Some shall see him, only to hear him say, Depart, accursed! Not all that have sat down at the Lord's table, and enrolled their names among his followers, shall thereby obtain inheritance; for to some who knock he shall say, " I never knew you!" Not all that die, shall sleep in Jesus. Come then, O my reader, with haste, and with deep solemnity, to the inquiry, whether indeed you have any title to indulge this pleasing anticipation. On what is it founded? On your having done no harm—on your innocence—on your having done as well as you could—on your baptism—on your communion? Alas! you have already pronounced judgment against yourself! These pleas will not abide the day of his coming? Have you seen yourself to be a sinful, guilty, helpless, ruined creature? and have you justified the law which condemns you? Have you despaired of all help in yourself? Have you believed the record, that God is in Christ reconciling the world unto himself? And so believing, have you accepted his free and sovereign promise, and cast yourself on his faithful and almighty arm? Do you perceive in yourself any marks of the new creature? Have old things passed away? Have all things become new? Are you striving to live a new life, to the praise and glory of him who hath saved you? Do you war against all sin? Do you endeavour all obedience? Do you pray to God, rejoice in him, and seek converse with him? And have you any witness that you are accepted of him?

If these things, or any goodly number of them, are in you; then you may hope, through infinite mercy, to be among the throng of saved souls.

But if, on the contrary, conscience answers no, to these interrogatories, what shall I say to you? shall I encourage you to indulge pleasing thoughts of death and eternity? I dare not. Fly for your lives! Tarry not in all the plain! Flee from the wrath to come. Dying in your present condition, you will fall into a double death. God gives you warning, he brandishes his sword before he smites. He removes others, when he might as easily have removed you. Some day, he may remove you as a warning to others. Friends and comrades will gather around your coffin, but their words or thoughts about you will have no effect on your destiny. At that moment your soul will be either in heaven or hell. And when Christ shall come, he will not bring you with him. You will indeed have to stand before him, to give an account of the deeds done in the body, to answer for all your Sabbaths, all your light and all your warnings. You will then see these things in their true light; but it will be too late. It is still your day of grace, Christ's very warnings tell you so. I beseech you, lay a good foundation for time to come. Believe in this Saviour of sinners, that you may be safe in that day of alarm, when the elements shall melt with fervent heat. Resolve, with God's aid, that you will be of that company, who shall have washed their robes and made them white in the blood of the

Lamb. I am conscious of the reiteration of these entreaties and exhortations; but, till you heed them, what can I do but reiterate them? O be persuaded to be happy. O consent to be safe. O resist no longer the gracious arm that would lift you up to heaven.

ALL CONSOLATION TRACED UP TO ITS DIVINE SOURCE.

XVIII.

AS we have pursued the various topics of consolation which reside in the attributes, the covenant, and the promises of God, in their application to different conditions of humanity, we have been perpetually led to observe that these means of comfort have no efficiency of themselves, but need to be impressed upon the sufferer's soul by an omnipotent hand. If in treating our subject we had observed the order of nature, and begun with the cause, we should have opened our subject with the Fountain of all grace, even God himself. We have, however, arrived at the same point by an inverse method, and singling out some of the numerous streams, have traced them up to the divine excellency from which they flow. But this deserves our more particular consideration.

In much of the foregoing remarks we have found occasion to make reference to the Apostle Paul. There is scarcely a single writing of his preserved to the church in which this subject is not touched. But there is one of his epistles, namely, the second to the Corinthians, in which he more fully opens the stores of Christian consolation. It was penned after emerging from a great and severe trial, in which he was pressed out of measure above strength, insomuch that he despaired even of life, and had the sentence of death in himself. (2 Cor. 1 : 8, 9.) These extraordinary afflictions, as he informs us, were intended to fit him for the delightful work of consoling others. "And whether we be afflicted," says he, "it is for your consolation and salvation, which is wrought in the enduring of the same sufferings which we also suffer: or whether we be comforted, it is for your consolation and salvation." (1 : 6, *margin.*) And in recollection of what he had graciously received, he breaks forth into a doxology, which contains a very remarkable expression: "Blessed be the God and Father of our Lord Jesus Christ, the Father of mercies, and the GOD OF ALL COMFORT!" Although this is introduced by us only as introductory to the chief subject, it certainly merits a moment's regard. When God is here spoken of as the source of all consolation, it is to be observed that he is so exhibited, not in his essential or his rectoral glory, but in his covenant relation; that is, as the "God and Father of our Lord Jesus Christ;" justifying what we have had repeated occasion to say in these pages, that all God's mercies, and all his comforts, come to us only through the channel provided by the plan of grace in Christ Jesus.

That God is the great Consoler is abundantly testified by the Old Testament, which in all its parts is a consistent prelude and anticipation of the New

To establish this assertion, we might cite a large portion of the book of Psalms. Every parental heart comprehends and feels the tender figure, when David sings, "Like as a father pitieth his children, so the Lord pitieth them that fear him. For he knoweth our frame; he remembereth that we are dust." (Ps. 103 : 13, 14.) And the same assurance is presented even more touchingly, where the Lord thus addresses his people: "As one whom his mother comforteth, so will I comfort you, and ye shall be comforted in Jerusalem." (Is. 66 : 13.) This special work of fatherly kindness is largely set forth in the prophecies. "For the Lord shall comfort Zion, he shall comfort all her waste places; and he will make her wilderness like Eden, and her desert like the garden of the Lord; joy and gladness shall be found therein, thanksgiving and the voice of melody." (Is. 51 : 3.) Without resorting, however, to textual proof, we cannot fail to observe, from the patriarchal days downward through all the tracts of the Hebrew annals, how benignant a regard the Almighty bestows upon his suffering servants, and how ready his hand is to wipe away their tears. Yet it must be acknowledged, that during all this preparatory discipline of the ancient church, their eye is directed to a period yet future, in which divine consolations should have larger scope. And the blessed agencies thus indicated are seen to centre themselves in Him who is "the desire of all nations." It has frequently been remarked by commentators, that the hope of the coming Messias is thrown in, upon many occasions, precisely where the prospects of the chosen seed were most enveloped in darkness. The Messias of prophecy characterizes himself as a Consoler. "The Spirit of the Lord God is upon me; because the Lord hath anointed me to preach glad tidings unto the meek; he hath sent me to bind up the broken-hearted, to proclaim liberty to the captives, and the opening of the prison to them that are bound; to proclaim the acceptable year of the Lord, and the day of vengeance of our God; *to comfort all that mourn;* to appoint unto them that mourn in Zion, to give unto them beauty for ashes, the oil of joy for mourning, the garment of praise for the spirit of heaviness; that they might be called trees of righteousness, the planting of the Lord, that he might be glorified." (Is. 61 : 1, 2, 3.) Accordingly, when the Lord Jesus Christ, in the fulness of time made a public demonstration of his Messiahship in the synagogue of Nazareth, he unrolled the sacred scroll, and read aloud this very prediction. (Luke 4 : 16.) And the whole series of his words and his benefactions were in the spirit of this prophetic word.

But we approach more touching manifestations of this spirit of consolation in those days when the cloud of his mediatorial sufferings was growing more dark, and he was about to be separated from his disciples. We shall here find a new aspect of the doctrine which may properly occupy our thoughts in conclusion.

After the institution of the Lord's Supper, and

in that discourse which preceded his arrest in the garden, our blessed Saviour uttered some of his most remarkable words of grace. Among these one great promise stands pre-eminent; it is in these terms: "And I will pray the Father, and he shall give you another comforter, that he may abide with you for ever; even the Spirit of Truth, whom the world cannot receive, because it seeth him not, neither knoweth him; but ye know him, for he dwelleth with you and shall be in you. I will not leave you comfortless (orphans), I will come to you. These things have I spoken unto you, being yet present with you. But the Comforter, which is the Holy Ghost, whom the Father will send in my name, he shall teach you all things, and bring all things to your remembrance, whatsoever I have said unto you." (John 14 : 16, 17, 18, 25, 26.)

For the satisfactory understanding of this delightful passage, it is necessary for us to give especial attention to its principal term. Expressive as is the word Comforter, it does not reach the full comprehension of the original, *Paraclete*, which signifies also a monitor and an advocate.* The first.

* The verb from which it is derived means to call upon, to admonish, and to exhort in the way of consolation. The derivative here used, Παράκλητος, is therefore an advocate, an intercessor, who pleads the cause of any one before a judge, and then a consoler or comforter. See Robinson's Lexicon. The word Paraclete has been freely introduced into the elevated language of all Christian churches. It early appeared in the Latin hymns: for instance,

> Beata nobis gaudia
> Anni reduxit orbita,
> Cum Spiritus Paraclitus
> Illapsus est apostolis.

observation which suggests itself is that this promised visitant was to come in Christ's stead. "These things have I spoken unto you, being yet present with you; but the Comforter, which is the Holy Ghost, shall teach," &c. That is, He shall come in my name and place. And there are unspeakable grace and fulness in this, which we shall not duly estimate unless we consider what the actual presence of Jesus conferred on the disciples. They were "the children of the bride-chamber," and could not mourn, because the Bridegroom was with them. He was to them an ever-present spring of consolation. Imperfect as were some of their views, before the resurrection and Pentecost, they were nevertheless with Christ. They saw his countenance. They witnessed his mighty works. They heard him speak as never man spake. They had communication with him. They enjoyed his love. They were overshadowed by his continual protection. If sorrow sometimes broke forth, there was a hand always near to wipe away their tears. He was himself their personal monitor, advocate, and comforter. The promise is one which intimates a gracious substitution, and was suited to that moment of sorrow. How much they were confounded by the tidings of his approaching departure, is sufficiently manifest from the words, "What is this that he saith unto us, A little while and ye shall not see me: and again, A little while and ye shall see me; and, Because I go to the Father?" (16: 17.) And it is to console them under this expected removal, that the Comforter is promised, just at this juncture.

The Holy Spirit is here unquestionably proposed, as able and willing to do for disciples all that they would seek from the personal presence of Christ. Our Lord expresses this most strongly, when he represents the mission of the Comforter as a great reason why he was about to ascend into the heavenly places. "It is expedient for you that I go away; for if I go not away the Comforter will not come unto you; but if I depart, I will send him unto you." (16: 7.) They should not lose, but gain, by such a departure of our Lord to the completion of his mediatorial work. The Spirit, as we shall presently see more fully, was eminently able to supply these wants, for he is the Spirit of Christ, by whom, as man, Jesus himself was anointed above measure, and endowed for his work; by whom also, in their measure, each believer is endowed and anointed, receiving from his fulness, "and grace for grace." We are therefore authorized to believe, that the divine Paraclete fully, gloriously, and increasingly, supplies to disciples the place of a present Jesus.

Another observation, by no means to be omitted, is that the promised Comforter is to come from the Father. God himself is the author of this consolation; as he is the eternal fount of all excellency. But it is not as Creator, Preserver, Sovereign, or Lawgiver that he now acts, but as the God of grace and redemption. And hence we are led anew to admire the harmony of the Divine Persons. The

Holy Spirit is not a creature, however exalted, nor a power, nor an effluence, nor an agency, but a co-equal and co-eternal Person in the Divine essence. In every moment of the mediatorial work the Three, who are One, are equally and gloriously operative towards the end in view; but according to a mysterious economy, in which the office and acts of each are distinguished. The Comforter is the Spirit of the Father and the Son. He proceedeth eternally from the Father and the Son. And in the dispensation of time, he is sent by the Father, in those influences which are needed to complete the work of grace in believers. The adorable Father himself, "our Father which is in heaven," loves us. He is especially and primarily the fountain of redeeming mercy; the deviser of the covenant, the giver of the Surety. He moreover loves his people, in the carrying on of this very work; and it is in the exercise of an eternal and ineffable love that he sends the Holy Spirit; for he is "the God of all comfort." This should dispose us, especially in times of trial, to look up to God the Father with unwavering filial confidence. Yet these manifestations of favour observe a due order, and are connected with the merit and intercession of Him, who is more strictly our Redeemer.

This will be more apparent, when we add the observation, that the promised Comforter is to come in Christ's name. All spiritual blessings so come; and we may regard the Holy Ghost as the all-comprehensive blessing. He who has this gift has all

Now, this gift is bestowed with a direct reference to the Lord Jesus Christ. "Whom," said he, "the Father will send in my name." We have already seen that he comes in Christ's place. It remains to be said, that he comes at Christ's request. The Lord assured them that he would pray the Father for this gift. For our blessed Redeemer, though ascended to heaven in his human nature, is not indifferent to the interests of his people; "seeing he ever liveth to make intercession for us." Every benefit of the covenant which we receive during our whole existence is the result of Christ's prevalent agency for us in the court of heaven. No application of the righteousness procured by his suffering and obedience would ever be made but for the perfect carrying on of this work in the Holy of Holies, beyond the vail of the visible heavens. And when, as High Priest, he bears the stones of the breastplate graven with the names of the holy tribes, he forgets no one of his chosen, but looks down with an individual regard on each of his people, with a wise and merciful reference to every particular case of want or affliction. Nor can I think of a doctrine more fraught with consolation, if properly considered, than that the Lord Jesus Christ makes each of us the subject of his prayers in heaven; unless it be this further limitation of the same truth, that what he so prays for is nothing less than the gift of the Holy Ghost.

When it is said that the Comforter shall be sent in Christ's name, the meaning unquestionably is that he shall be sent in consideration of Christ's **merits**. We are not to look on this august communication as among those bounties which come to us in the ordinary routine of common providential dispensations. There would have been no sending of the Holy Ghost but for the covenant work, the righteous deserving, the federal subjugation, and the atoning death of the Son of God. This death placed the crown of glory on his work of humiliation. When, at a certain time, preaching in the temple, he promised this blessing under the beautiful image of rivers of living water, it is added by the evangelist: "But this spake he of the Spirit, which they that believe on him should receive: for the Holy Ghost was not yet given; because that Jesus was not yet glorified." (John 7 : 39.) Some communications in this kind had doubtless been made, even under the Old Testament dispensation; but the moment was not fully come "for the ministration of the Spirit;" nor could it come until the day of his ascension in triumph unto glory. Let it then be fixed in our minds, that the gift of the Comforter is a purchased gift. It is the desert of our Lord's mediatorial obedience unto death. The work of Gethsemane and of the cross must precede this effusion. So felt the apostles on the day of Pentecost, when, after visible and audible tokens of this presence, Peter, speaking in their name, said, "Therefore being by the right hand of God exalted, and having received of the Father *the promise of the Holy Ghost,* he hath shed forth this, which ye now see and hear." (Acts 2 : 33.) Indeed the communication of the Holy Spirit is but a carrying forward in heaven of the work which Christ began on earth. It is Christ himself working by the Spirit in the hearts of his people.

An equally important observation is, that, even in his consoling work, the promised Spirit comes as a teacher and monitor. Not only "is all truth, in order to goodness;" but it may be added, all truth is in order to consolation. Hence we read concerning "patience and comfort of the Scriptures;" the solace of divine truth. This connection is very obvious in the promise, "He shall teach you all things, and bring all things to your remambrance, whatsoever I have said unto you."

No careful reader will fail to observe, that this is one of the most important senses in which the Holy Spirit, as the Paraclete, was to supply the place of Christ. The Lord Jesus, in his prophetic office, was the teacher of his disciples. These his personal and direct instructions were valuable and delightful beyond expression. Grace was poured into his lips. The loss in this respect must have seemed irreparable, and all human instructors must have been despicable in comparison. Remembering how he spake, we may be almost forgiven if we sometimes regret that we had not seen one of these days of the Son of Man. But that which the Lord Jesus once did with his own lips, he now and henceforth accomplishes by the Holy Spirit. "He shall teach you all things." The apostle John, in speaking of false and seducing teachers, contrasts with them this teaching of the Holy Ghost, as enjoyed by believers. "But ye have an unction from the Holy One, and ye know all things. But the anointing which ye have received of him abideth in you, and ye need not that any man teach you; but as the same anointing teacheth you of all things, and is truth and is no lie, and even as it hath taught you, ye shall abide in him." (1 John 2 : 20, 27.) Thus we are enabled to perceive more clearly and fully how the adorable Spirit comes in Christ's name. He teaches what Christ taught. He takes of the things of Christ, and shows them unto us. From the infinite fund of wisdom and knowledge, of which he is the inspirer, and which is no less Christ's, he draws and dispenses, according to the diversified necessities of the church. It is scarcely a change of teacher. The Spirit gives the same lesson. He repeats and revives it; brings out afresh in the chambers of memory the characters which had faded on the walls; and touches the sluggish heart to awaken it to new impressions. All this we believe to be by a direct influence on the soul; opening the receptive faculty, pouring in light, causing knowledge, belief, emotion, and will, no less than providing an objective revelation in the Scriptures. There is a condescension even to the weakness of human memory. It need scarcely be said that truth derives much of its value from being seasonable. Experience testifies that a doctrine or promise of the word, long neglected or forgotten, may be so applied in a moment of emergency, by the Holy

Spirit, as to diffuse a sudden and unspeakable joy over the soul. It is this which accounts for the difference between reader and reader, between hearer and hearer, and between different states of the same individual. In order that truth be efficacious, especially to consolation, something more is necessary than that it should be revealed; something more than that it should be apprehended by the natural understanding; it must be brought home to the spiritual perception and the faith. And to do this is the especial province of the Holy Spirit. In the preceding discourses our minds have been brought into the presence of many divine truths which are suited to lift up the heart that is cast down; but this effect will not be produced, except so far as the Holy Spirit takes, shows, and impresses them. And this he graciously does to many a broken-hearted Christian.

But why should we be detained from that which after all is the great import of these divine communications? The promised Spirit is sent to believers, as a Comforter, in the common acceptation of the word. This it is which brings the subject more particularly within the scope of the present investigation. It is the "God of all comfort," in the person of the adorable Spirit, pouring his consolations over the sorrowing heart. For the words of Jesus had failed of their application if this had not been included. The disciples were in unexampled grief; sorrow had filled their hearts; they were expecting orphanage and desolation. That which the benignant Redeemer promises them is a Comforter; and this it is which we all need. It is into a world of sighs and tears, from manifold and multiform calamity, and into a church which through much tribulation presses on towards the kingdom, that this divine Visitant deigns to come.

The primary mode of communicating consolation has been already pointed out. It is by the instrumentality of truth. This truth, as to the matter of it, is not a new revelation; but the Spirit takes of the things of Christ and shows them to us. This truth is summed up in the canon of Scripture; and, therefore, the word of God is beyond all other volumes the Book of Consolation. Though neglected in days of prosperity, and seasons of religious decline, it is sure to be open on the tables and in the hands of sorrowing disciples. The disposition to fly to the Bible in hours of trouble is so strong and constant, that it may be denominated an instinct of the new nature. Not more naturally does the new-born babe turn to the fount of infant nutrition. And the testimony of all Christian mourners is, that at these wells of salvation they have found refreshment and solace. It would be next to death to remove the Scriptures from a burdened saint. But though persecution has often removed the letter of the external volume, the Holy Spirit, even in dungeons, has awakened the inward ear of the sufferer, and brought to remembrance the words of this life.

The truth which we have been last considering,

is clearly taught in those words of the Apostle Paul, in which he says, "Now the God of hope fill you with all peace and joy in believing, that ye may abound in hope through the power of the Holy Ghost." (Rom. 13 : 3.) Here the consolation is very distinctly ascribed to belief of the truth. This truth, as containing the plan of salvation for lost sinners, is denominated the Gospel, or good tidings; and as such it is made to rejoice the believer's heart from the very beginning of the Christian life. To a soul properly exercised, all its truths are consolatory, and more and more so as progress is made in divine things. As the views of divine truth become more clear and comprehensive, the comforts of the Spirit become more abiding, agreeably to what we attempted to lay down in treating of Hope and Joy in the Lord.

It is of great importance to remember, that direct and large and believing views of precious Christian doctrines, concerning God, Christ, salvation, and heaven, are the principal means which the Holy Spirit uses for the support of the soul, even under heavy afflictions. On this head serious errors are prevalent. First, the thoroughly worldly man, having treasure and heart in the present life, neither desires nor seeks any portion but that which is carnal; and if this is taken away, he is like Micah of old when bereft of his gods. Remaining in this condition, he is utterly insusceptible of any spiritual relief from the chosen means of the great Consoler. He lacks all taste and relish for those divine realities which are angels' food. Under sudden and alarming strokes of providential judgment, he is sometimes stupefied and sometimes frantic; and when the storm of rebellious passions lulls itself to rest, he murmurs awhile, like the tempest-tossed ocean, and then subsides into the calm of unbelieving security. In all this there is no operation of comforting truth. Secondly; the partially enlightened believer, as yet inexperienced in these lessons of the heavenly Monitor, is at first greatly surprised by the access of severe chastening. The mode in which divine comforts are communicated is as yet unknown to him. He looks for removal of the rod as the only relief which can suffice; and for a time his earnest supplications go out in this direction. If, for example, he has been impoverished, he expects some indemnity in kind. If some grievous burden is laid upon him, he hopes that it may be removed; and it is only after repeated trials that he learns the method of grace. But thirdly, the ripe Christian, long tried in the school of sorrows, is made to know that the soul may be comforted amidst the very billows. In some unexpected moment divine illumination reveals to him the great abiding truths of the spiritual world; truths which are as precious and as satisfying, in adverse as in prosperous days. By a process of holy attraction, his thoughts are drawn away from self and all its interests and losses, to be fixed and absorbed by the character of God, by his mighty works, by the person of the Redeemer, by the work of redemption.

by the progress of the kingdom, and by the glory yet to be revealed. Filled and animated and tranquillized by these, he is led to forget his private griefs; and thus the Comforter performs his office by means of the truth. "The things of Christ," applied to the inner sense, direct the mind from its earthly pangs, and to a certain extent afford a prelibation of the celestial joy.

From what has been said it might readily be anticipated, that the processes by which the Holy Spirit forms the soul to holiness, do, at the same time, conduce to its consolation. Here the work of the Sanctifier and the work of the Comforter really coalesce. Sin is a disorder of the human powers, in which their harmony is destroyed, and the result is the turbulence of wretched passions. If this discord were not limited, it would become absolutely hellish; and such is in part the penal woe of the eternal torment. "There is no peace, saith my God, to the wicked." But every step in sanctification is a restitution in measure to the primitive harmony and peace of man. And this work cannot go on without a proportionate augmentation of happiness. To arrive at consolation we must be made more holy.

Nothing is more evident than that those graces which are denominated the fruits of the Spirit, are in their very nature modes of happiness. No man can possess them without a diminution of suffering. Some of them are directly consolatory, because they strike at the very root of our inward disquietudes

"The fruit of the Spirit is love, joy, peace, long-suffering, gentleness, goodness, faith, meekness, temperance." (Gal. 5 : 22, 23.) "For the fruit of the Spirit is in all goodness, and righteousness, and truth." (Eph. 5 : 9.) For instance, Faith, by realizing to the soul the divine truths which we have been considering, carries it away above its sufferings, and so consoles; while we look not at the things which are seen, which are temporal, but at the things which are not seen, which are eternal. Goodness, or evangelical benevolence, is delightful in its very acts; and we never so forget our own sorrows as when we are endeavouring to increase the happiness of our neighbour. Gentleness diffuses a blessed calm over the nature. Love is the atmosphere of heaven. Long-suffering and Meekness counteract all those distresses—and they are innumerable—which arise from pride, anger, and revenge. Joy, as we have already seen, drives out the soul's pains by the expulsive power of a new dominant affection. And Peace is but the scriptural name for the entire result of combined holy satisfactions in the heart. When the promised Spirit enters into a soul, and produces these its fruits, it does, in the same degree, tend to dispel troubles, and is the efficient cause of consolation amidst the greatest fight of afflictions.

We might here enlarge upon the comforting effects produced by the witness of the Spirit, and the assurance of God's love; but this has already been made the subject of a separate discourse. Let us rather bestow a few thoughts upon the enduring nature of this spiritual influence. It is found in these clauses of the promise: "For he dwelleth with you, and shall be in you;" "And he shall give you another Comforter, that he may abide with you for ever." Their Lord was about to be removed from them, in respect to his personal presence, and they were filled with sorrow. He promises them a Consoler who should never be removed. It is one of the most precious truths of our holy religion, that the Spirit of grace is not merely a guest or visitor, but a perpetual inhabitant. This is true in regard both to the collective body of saints, who are a temple of the Lord, and to the individual believer. Both were prefigured by the constant residence of Jehovah, with the manifested Shekinah, in the tabernacle and the temple. "I will dwell among the children of Israel," said the Lord, "and will be their God." (Exod. 29 : 45.) He is, therefore, addressed as dwelling between the cherubim, that is, in the Holy of Holies, above the golden propitiatory of the ark. The temple was typical of the New Testament church, "built upon the foundation of the apostles and prophets, Jesus Christ himself being the chief corner stone; in whom all the building fitly framed together, groweth unto a holy temple in the Lord; in whom ye also," says Paul to the Ephesians, "are builded together, for a habitation of God through the Spirit." (2 : 20, 21, 22.) And to other Christians of primitive days, "Ye are the temple of the living God; as God hath said, I will dwell in them, and walk in them; and I will be their God, and they shall be my people." (2 Cor. 6 : 16.) Nor is this inhabitation confined to Christians as a collective church; for the same apostle says, with individual application, "What! know ye not that your body is the temple of the Holy Ghost which is in you, which ye have of God, and ye are not your own?" (1 Cor. 6 : 19.)

There is something at once dreadful and delightful in this indwelling of the Holy One in houses of clay. It is dreadful to be so near that divine glory, before which the Seraphim veil their faces. The argument hence derived against the abuse of the body to purposes of sin, is natural and cogent. It is on the other hand delightful to consider, that the source of all holiness and comfort is within us, if we belong to Christ. The promised Comforter has made his shrine in our very bodies, and possesses our souls with his presence. He cannot be ignorant of our condition, and no trial can befall us without his permission, as there is also no sorrow which he cannot assuage. This is felt with unutterable peace when the Divine witness testifies within the soul. "And hereby we know that he abideth in us, by the Spirit which he hath given us." (1 John 3 : 24.)

While, as we have seen, there is a perpetual indwelling of the Holy Spirit in the soul of the true believer, it by no means follows that the manifestations of his consoling attributes are equal at all times. On the contrary, as he keeps his throne in this palace of his choice, so he exercises his sovereignty in regard to the time and the degree of his joy-giving disclosures. There are various stages of advancing comfort, and sometimes there are decays and eclipses of the beatific light. Nevertheless, the Spirit of grace, by whom we are sealed unto the day of redemption, is never absent, and never inaccessible. It is sometimes his pleasure to shine forth with splendour from amidst the tempestuous cloud; and his chief triumphs of consolation often gleam from the falling ruins of his frail sanctuary, in the hour of dissolution. Happy would it be for us, if we could always maintain an unwavering persuasion as to the reality and the greatness of this inhabitation of God through the Spirit. It would confer a dignity of which we now know too little upon the whole tenor of a Christian life. Temptation would be disarmed by the sense of such a presence, and we should tremble at the thought of grieving one so great and yet so near. The current philosophy of this world disallows the existence of all these spiritual facts, which are matters of pure revelation, and loves to dwell in the realm of bare phenomena, seemings, or appearances. Yet to one whose mental eye has been purged of its film, and who is raised "above the stir and smoke of this dim spot, which men call earth," there is nothing more substantially true than the reality and presence of this divine and blessed Paraclete. And when by long habits of holy contemplation the human spirit has acquired the sacred art of turning inward, resorting to the most holy place, and consulting the

Urim and Thummim of divine communications, these truths begin to establish themselves as articles of faith, sources of peace, and principles of action. Can we then too earnestly crave the presence of the Comforter in our souls? Or can we any longer be indifferent to the means whereby we may receive more of his consoling suggestions?

When we spoke of Divine Truth, as an instrument in the hand of the Spirit, for the accomplishment of his work, we really indicated one of the principal ways in which to seek this great blessing. If we would be comforted, we must seek it by the truth. The Comforter is the Spirit of Truth. The consoling process is carried on by the application of truth. In all which we find a very strong argument for making ourselves early familiar with the Scriptures. Afflictions come with so little warning, that it is a part of our Christian forecast to have knowledge in store, against the time of need. Our very acquaintance with the Divine Consoler himself, is derived solely from the revealed word; and there also we learn the methods of Providence and the grounds of consolation.

If, as has been already observed, the Holy Spirit works our comfort by means of our sanctification, then holiness must be reckoned among the means of Christian enjoyment, and we should seek our solace in conformity to God's will. Excluding every self-righteous or pharisaic assumption on this subject, we may nevertheless say in a safe sense, that God will not pour so rich a balsam into an impure vessel. It is no part of his gracious plan to comfort us in our sins. The very pains and fears into which his good providence casts us are occasioned by our delinquencies, and are chastisements for our faults. The way of return is, therefore, by the thorny path of contrition and repentance. Nor do backsliding disciples usually find themselves restored to favour, until they have done their " first works," and passed afresh through exercises like those which first brought them to Christ. We may state the truth therefore with some generality, that genuine consolation is not to be looked for independently of increased holiness.

The conclusion which ought to be drawn is, that he who leads a worldly life under a Christian profession is in a most unfit state to grapple with great trials. To him they will be sore surprises, "as snow in summer and as rain in harvest." They will arouse him at midnight, as when besiegers suddenly break upon a city without gates or walls. We have been called to witness such experiences, when some poor carnal professor has been driven up from his resting-place, and cast into utter discomfiture. It is well for such, if the rod in God's hand is made the means of bringing them back to holy living. For as it is altogether uncertain in what hour or instant the dart may pierce us in the most sensitive spot, it is the part of wisdom to be always in a condition suited to receive divine communications, and in a posture in which it shall be easy to roll our burden on the Lord. And in the very height of afflictive visitations, when all God's waves and billows go over the soul, the method of seeking relief is the same; we return to peace only by returning to God.

Before leaving the means of attaining religious consolation, we must name the most important of all. It is indicated in those words of our blessed Lord: "If ye then, being evil, know how to give good gifts unto your children; how much more shall your heavenly Father give his Holy Spirit to them that ask him?" (Luke 11 : 13.) It is difficult to conceive of greater encouragement to pray for this gift than is afforded by this promise of our Lord Jesus Christ. The comparison which he uses goes home at once to the parental heart. The benefit which he offers is plainly exhibited as the greatest; for, indeed, if God gives us his Holy Spirit, he gives us all that is requisite to our comfort here and our salvation for ever. " Blessed be the God and Father of our Lord Jesus Christ, which according to his abundant mercy hath begotten us again unto a lively hope by the resurrection of Jesus Christ from the dead, to an inheritance incorruptible and undefiled, and that fadeth not away, reserved in heaven for you who are kept by the power of God through faith unto salvation, ready to be revealed in the last time, wherein ye greatly rejoice, though now for a season, if need be, ye are in heaviness through manifold temptations."

THE END.

www.ingramcontent.com/pod-product-compliance
Lightning Source LLC
Chambersburg PA
CBHW052137300426
44115CB00011B/1418

9781556357060